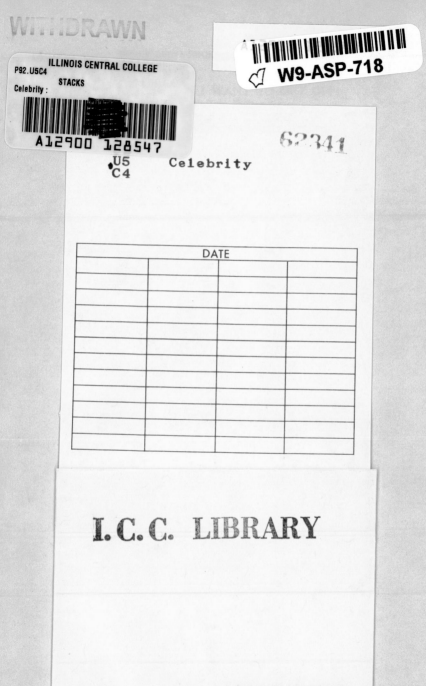

DATE			

Celebrity

The Media as Image Makers

JAMES MONACO

and, in order of their celebrity, Ingmar Bergman, Norman Mailer, Donald Barthelme, Nora Ephron, John Leonard, Joan Didion, Morley Safer, Richard Schickel, Wilfrid Sheed, Ron Rosenbaum, Lois Gould, Haskell Wexler, Alexander Cockburn, Roland Barthes, Peter Schrag, David Thomson, Roger Rosenblatt, Roy Blount, Jr., Bill Davidson, Saul Braun, Rees Behrendt, Lew Grossberger, Garrison Keillor, and Mary McGeachy.

A Delta Book

"Porter Goes to the Convention: A Fable" by Nora Ephron: Reprinted by
permission of International Creative Management. Copyright © 1976 by
Esquire Magazine. First published in *Esquire*.

"Who's Who in International Chaos" by Rees Behrendt: Reprinted by permission of Esquire Magazine. © 1973 by Esquire, Inc.

"Getting the Vegas Willies" by Joan Didion: Reprinted by permission of
Wallace & Sheil Agency, Inc. Copyright © 1977 by Joan Didion. First published in Esquire Magazine.

From "Medium Cool" by Haskell Wexler: Excerpt from the motion picture
screenplay, MEDIUM COOL, by Haskell Wexler, reprinted by permission of
Paramount Pictures Corporation and Haskell Wexler. Copyright © 1969 by
Paramount Pictures Corporation and H & J Pictures, Inc. All Rights
Reserved.

"Until Joey Bishop, Merv Griffin, and Johnny Carson Do Us Part" by Saul
Braun: Reprinted by permission of the author.

"Heeere's Johnny" by Peter Schrag: Reprinted from MORE—The Media
Magazine by permission of Namequoit, Inc.

"Docudrama: Fact or Fiction?" by Bill Davidson: Reprinted with permission
from *TV Guide*® Magazine. Copyright © 1976 by Triangle Publications,
Inc., Radnor, Pennsylvania.

"The Mythologizing of Citizen Patty" by James Monaco: Reprinted from
MORE—The Media Magazine by permission of Namequoit, Inc.

"The Kent State Girl: An American Tragedy": From 60 MINUTES. © 1977
CBS, Inc. All rights reserved. Used by permission.

"The Casualties of 'Revolver Journalism'" by James Monaco: Reprinted
from MORE—The Media Magazine by permission of Namequoit, Inc.

For my sister
Judith

CONTENTS

x *Contents*

PREFACE

"A man should control his life," Rudolph Valentino once complained, shortly before his early death. "Mine is controlling me. I don't like it." Like most celebrities of years past, the great romantic star of the twenties exists for us now more as legend than as fact. Valentino is the very model of celebrity sacrificed upon the altar of fame and public adulation. It's a rather melodramatic and perhaps supercilious image, no doubt, but no less true for all that. And that quietly plaintive description of his own increasingly untenable situation is an apt summary of the condition of celebrityhood: the root of the phenomenon is a matter of control. Increasingly, our lives are acted out in a social sea of celebrityhood; we are submerged in such images—based to some extent on fact, but also pervasively fictional: more the creation of our own collective fantasies than the result of measurable historical conditions. We control them; they control us.

We celebrate ("proclaim," "praise") them. They celebrate ("observe," "perform") for us. Some of them control the personas we observe (the Farrahs of the media world); some of them do not (the Pattys). Some thrive on the power celebrityhood bestows; others are destroyed by it. But whichever way the energy flows, we seem to be suffering more and more from an overload of this sort of collective "celebration"—both by them and by us. We don't control our own lives; we let these public figures act them out for us in movies, television, radio, newspapers, books, and magazines. The fictions they perform (even when they are politicians, say, rather than actors) increasingly become more valid than our own unpublicized existences.

What follows is a cooperative attempt to redress the balance between life and fiction—to regain some control—by investigating some of the basic factors that make up the phenomenon we call "celebrity."

We begin with a few general comments on the "State of the Art," then move on to a description of "The Medium Connection"—the function of media celebrity in the real world. The section on "Victims" discusses three of the most recent sacrifices in the mode that stretches back to Valentino and Charles Lindbergh. "For Farrah, With Lust and Artifice" is the rhinestone centerpiece of *Celebrity*. "Personas" suggests a number of approaches to the job and function of celebrityhood, while "The Self As Art" describes the contemporary fascination with the do-it-yourself persona. We conclude with a number of pieces—a couple serious, a couple not so serious—on the commodity value celebrity has for others as "Gossip." Garrison Keillor's "Oya Life These Days," is the envoi to the book.

Throughout, no distinction has been made between supposedly non-fictional journalism and presumably fictional works: they present different kinds of truths, but truths nevertheless. Nor is this printed collection purely a collection of print: movies and television are represented, too. *Celebrity* began as a straightforward anthology of pieces that I like and consider significant, but as the work on the book progressed, I found myself increasingly in the position of the host of a talk show in conversation with the writers represented here. The headnotes to each selection and, for the most part, the photos and captions that accompany them are my own contributions to this reconstructed colloquy. I want to thank everyone who has contributed to the book (and not necessarily in the order of their celebrity) for participating, and for describing (or exhibiting) aspects of this strange phenomenon much better than I could have myself.

A number of people whose names do not appear in the table of contents contributed to the book. I want especially to thank Martha Kinney, editor in chief of Delta Books, who gave the project the necessary encouragement, and Jeri Cummins, Rachel Klein, Giorgetta McRee, Kathy Simmons, Carole Stoddard, and Ann Watson of the Delta staff who dealt with the numerous little problems always involved in book production with unfailing good humor and efficiency.

David Lindroth designed the cover and contributed advice and counsel. I also want to thank Maureen Lambray and Sylvia Plachy for allowing me to reproduce their photographs, which appear on pp. 146, 151, and 152.

As always, I'm grateful to my wife, Susan Schenker, for her help, wit, and support.

Celebrity is set in Times Roman linotype, 9 point on 10 point slugs. Commissioned by *The Times* of London in 1931, the design of Times Roman was supervised by Stanley Morison, and since its introduction it has become one of the most widely used and admired text faces. It is known for its clarity, simplicity, and readability. The headnotes in *Celebrity* are set in Permanent linotype. Permanent was designed in 1962 by Karlgeorg Hoefer and fits the basic pattern of the clean sans serif typefaces that became popular in the 1960's. It is a slightly heavier, perhaps less elegant face than the famous Helvetica. The display type used in *Celebrity* (for chapter titles and part titles) is Helvetica (designed by M. Miedinger in 1957), perhaps the most influential typeface of the last twenty years. (For more information on the significance of this face, see Leslie Savan's "This Typeface Is Changing Your Life," in *Media Culture,* the companion volume in this series.) The text for *Celebrity* was set by Maryland Linotype. The book was printed by Vail-Ballou.

JAMES MONACO
New York City
December 1977

STATE OF THE ART

1. CELEBRATION
by James Monaco

The commercial opens on a close-up of a pleasant, middle-aged woman in her kitchen, talking to the camera:

> I'm Doctor Joyce Brothers' mother. Even when Joyce was little, I knew she was going to be a psychologist. I'd say, "Joyce, come to dinner." She'd say, "What do you mean by that?"

We cut to a close-up shot of a plate of Mueller's Tuna and Noodle Casserole and Mueller's package. The narration continues:

> Then I'd say, "But Joyce, I made your favorite! Mueller's egg noodles with tuna!"

Cut back to mother.

> She said, "Fine. Very often a good, hot meal establishes a feeling of security in a growing child."

The announcer delivers the tagline:

> Egg noodles and tuna are one reason mothers say . . .
> Nothing goes with everything like Mueller's.

Very nice ad. The Needham, Harper & Steers agency did a little research. They'd say, "Mueller's macaroni." People replied more often than not, "Oh, yeah, my mother used to use that." To capitalize on the traditional connotations of the product, they developed a series of thirty-second spots featuring mothers of celebrities—Pat Boone's Mother, Julius Erving's Mother, Joyce Brothers' Mother. All the spots are cute, probably effective. But Joyce Brothers' Mother is more than that: an historical event.

Not because Mrs. Estelle Bauer, Joyce's mother and a New York lawyer, is important in her own right, but because she's Joyce's mother,

Dr. Joyce Brothers' Mother

Mrs. Estelle Bauer, "Joyce Brothers' Mother," as envisioned by the Needham, Harper & Steers agency. The commerical created a secondary career for Mrs. Bauer, who practices her profession in New York. Within months, she was the subject of a two-page fashion spread in Good Housekeeping, *along with her daughter, and her daughter's daughter, Lisa Arbisser, a medical student. Other offers followed.*

and Joyce Brothers is, arguably, one of the great self-made celebrities of our age. The Mueller's commercial now admits her family to the pantheon. As I write, Estelle Bauer has not yet hit the talk-show circuit, but it's only a matter of time. She is a member of that rare breed, the "paracelebrity." Daniel Boorstin's classic definition of celebrities has them "well-known for their well-known-ness." Well, paracelebrities are well-known for being known by people who are well-known for their well-known-ness. We've had examples before: Nixon's pals, Bebe Rebozo and Bob Abplanalp . . . a covey of Hollywood hairdressers (Jon Peters probably the most successful of the bunch) . . . Steven Weed (Patty Hearst's ex). But those people never did ads. They were good for a short paragraph here and there in stories whose subjects were the stars they revolved around, but they've seldom been considered of real interest in themselves. Joyce Brothers' Mother has changed all that: paracelebrity is now a valid, established category.

What's so perfect about this is that Estelle Bauer's daughter herself is such a classic, pure celebrity. You remember, I hope, her appearance on the *$64,000 Question* as the psychologist whose specialty was boxing. You know how she parlayed her win there into a major career as a media advisor: books, lectures, television shows, radio spots, a syndicated column—the works. What you may not know is that this superb career has been carefully designed from the start. Joyce knew nothing about boxing when she and her husband, Milton, conceived their plan to get her on the ill-fated quiz show in 1955. Six weeks later, she had memorized the book. It wasn't quite a sham, but it wasn't entirely straight either. Hal March didn't introduce her as "a lady psychologist who knew nothing about the manly art of boxing when she first decided to appear on this show and win the jackpot but who has, in the space of two short months, completely mastered the statistics of this relatively limited field." No, he didn't. She was put forth—like the shoemaker opera buff—as an incongruous expert.

Moreover, in the twenty-year career that followed, Joyce carefully husbanded her celebrity resources. She kept a low profile in order to channel her admittedly limited energy as a celebrity into work more useful than sheer publicity. "I've tried to keep people from knowing about me," she told *People* magazine in a rare interview (a two-page spread). "I've tried to sidetrack things into articles *by* me rather than *about* me." So Joyce is the very model of the modern celebrity: self-made, and focusing the energy of her notoriety into a productive career.

The most absorbing question is, where does that energy come from? It has been a source of unique power throughout most of this century. By the thirties, it had become a favorite topic for movies. In *The Gilded Lily* (1935), a perplexed Claudette Colbert has to choose between two suitors: aristocratic Ray Milland, and down-to-earth Fred MacMurray. MacMurray is a newspaper reporter. It is his secret edge in the courtship dance. In the end it turns out to be more valuable than Milland's title. MacMurray threatens to turn the confused Colbert into a celebrity: "One of those peculiar people made strangely important by ordinary newspaper print," as he defines it. Like all good heroines of thirties newspaper movies (*The Front Page, It Happened One Night, The Philadelphia Story*), Claudette has a proper fear of celebrity. She eventually gives in to Fred.

The word has been defined more elegantly since then perhaps, but never with more precision. In the first place, celebrities are, of course, well-known. But people have been well-known, more or less, for centuries. Celebrities, as Fred points out succinctly, are "peculiar," their importance strange, and how they got that way a puzzle.

Before we had celebrities we had heroes. In the last century essayists like Carlyle and Emerson delivered themselves of regular discursive treatises on the subject. It was easy to define the special qualities that set heroes apart. Carlyle found six classic types that fit neatly into historical periods: the hero as divinity, the hero as prophet, as poet, as priest, as man of letters, as king. Now, what these hero types all share, of course, are admirable qualities—qualities that somehow set them apart from the rest of us. They have *done* things, acted in the world: written, thought, understood, led.

Celebrities, on the other hand, needn't have done—needn't do—anything special. Their function isn't to act—just to be. "Peculiar people," indeed. To a large extent, celebrity has entirely superseded heroism. Not that we don't have heroes—we do, of course—but the qualities of our admiration are distinctly different, and the actions of heroes are often lost in a haze of fictional celebrity unrelated to the nonfictional heroism. Often the pure glow of celebrity comes first; action follows. Celebrity makes the accomplishment possible. Ask Joyce Brothers. Ask any politician of the last thirty years.

Celebrities, as Fred explained to Claudette, are passive objects of the media—created whole out of "ordinary newspaper print," or film, or broadcast airwaves. It doesn't matter what material you start with—lilies or dandelions, 24-carat or dross—celebrity is ultimately a result of gilt by association. The record—history—exists only in the media, and the people who make the media, make history. The people they make it up *about* really have less and less to say about how it eventually shapes up. Presidents know this. Truman Capote and Norman Mailer know this. Farrah Fawcett-Majors and Patty Hearst know it too. It used to be, many years ago, that you knew really well only the people in your village. You lived with them, you watched and listened to them daily, you drew your own conclusions. You did hear about other people—kings, thinkers, warriors—but since you'd never seen them, they had no immediate presence, and anyway, you had only the broadest of caricatures of these strangers.

All this changed with the rise of the mass media. Marshall McLuhan's term "global village" is particularly apt. First gradually, with the development of newspapers and magazines in the late nineteenth century, then explosively with the birth of film and broadcasting, the village of knowledge expanded.

The growth and development of the history of celebrity is closely tied to the development of media technology, although it is not specifically dependent on it. In the mid-nineteenth century, rotary printing presses made possible the cheap dissemination of printed matter for the newly literate middle classes. Periodical magazines, much less expensive than books and rapidly distributed to all parts of the country by railroad, were the main means of mass communication in the rapidly condensing media community. Magazines permitted writers like Charles Dickens and Mark Twain to reach much wider audiences than their predecessors had, and this in turn led to celebrityhood. The author became a focus of public interest rivaling and at times surpassing the work itself. Dickens' phenomenally successful (and profitable) lecture tours in America provided salient evidence that the community of literacy had multiplied exponentially since the beginning of the nineteenth century, and that the curiosity about the people who make art (and history) was an extraordinarily powerful force.

The other great media invention of the nineteenth century, photography, had a minimal effect on the phenomenon of celebrity at first. While the daguerreotype and its successors allowed the inexpensive production of personal icons, replication of the image and, consequently, mass distribution remained limited until the invention of the halftone process which permits photographs to be reproduced by printing. In the 1890's, the newspaper halftone provided the striking visual image to go with the narrative story. Soon afterward, moving pictures allowed performers (of both fact and fiction) to be seen by thousands of audiences at once. Stars were born. By the time of the First World War, actors like Pickford, Fairbanks, and Chaplin were such enormous box-office draws that film producers literally could not afford to hire them. The stars had to form their own producing company, United Artists.

As the banks and other power centers of capital moved into the entertainment industry in the twenties and thirties, producers reexerted control over stars. By the mid-thirties, a streamlined and rigid system of production created artificial images of ideal personalities into which fairly interchangeable actors were then plugged. There was an occasional maverick, but for the most part the Hollywood moguls exercised strict control over the role models projected by the media. The advent of sound also worked to constrict celebrityhood as truly international stars became less common.

At the same time professional celebrities were rolling off the Hollywood assembly lines, newspapers, magazines, and radio were creating celebrities out of "real life" material. Personalities like Father Coughlin, the famous radio commentator of the thirties, exerted powerful influence on the political life of the nation, and ordinary people were "made strangely important by newspaper print." It became clear that the substance of action was not a necessary ingredient in the celebrity mix. It was enough to be known for being well-known. Radio and, later, television were important in this respect since they could project relatively pure personality. Neither the acted fictions of the movies nor the fictional history of newspapers and magazines was a necessary adjunct to the broadcast personality. People tune in, not to hear the news or the stories, especially, but simply to spend time with the personalities. Hence the rise of the talk show, true home of the celebrity.

In the sixties, it became perfectly clear once and for all that the main life of the nation was inextricably cross-woven with media. Demonstrations became powerful political tools and it was clearly understood that these symbolic actions had effect only when they were covered by the media. By the early seventies simple "manifestations" (as the French call them) of political points of view were not sufficient to draw the attention of an increasingly jaded national audience. High drama was more effective. Hence the rise of the hijacking and kidnapping: dramatic events that rivet attention through their theatricality and demand coverage implicitly because of their narrative structure—an unfolding story must be seen through to its conclusion. These "real-life dramas," highly charged with pity and fear and the exciting threat of violence, were natural and predictable outgrowths of the development of videoculture. Surrounded as they are by violent fiction, television newscasts are increasingly forced to match that level of excitement. Why stage a sedate march or demonstration to call attention to, say, the problem of hunger in America, when you can stage a kidnapping instead? Which will get higher ratings?

At the same time as celebrity has become the most important political tool, it has also served manifestly as the main arena in which a person can achieve some sort of personal and private historical attention quickly and easily. From *Guinness Book of World Record*-holders on the one hand to mass murderers and assassins on the other, the media serve as relatively controllable channels into history and a type at least of immortality. The pull of such celebrity has proved irresistible.

Since the sixties, the balance of power between star actors and producers has shifted perceptibly back toward the stars as the media industries concentrate more on distribution and less on production. But the media industries in general—stars and producers, writers and celebrities; television, radio, film, books, newspapers, and magazines—find it increasingly necessary to depend on nonprofessional celebrities to provide their raw materials. As people have learned to manipulate media celebrity for personal and political ends audiences apparently have developed an unquenchable interest in what used to be called "real life"—at least as it is recycled by the media. Hence the recent popularity of docudramas and other such quasi-fictional products which have the undeniable advantage from a business point of view of having been presold in the news.

What of the future? There's an old sci-fi story from the fifties that opens in the streets of New York. Grass is growing through cracks in the pavement. The buildings are more or less well-maintained, but there are only occasional people on the streets. As it turns out, all the people over the age of twenty-five have made enough money to retire to their basements and plug themselves into their television sets. They no longer have to live out their lives: TV does it for them—this week John Wayne in a Western, next week a gangster Jimmy Cagney or a sardonic Humphrey Bogart. Be what you want to be, so long as someone has written the script already. Every day, the man in white from *Catch-22:* one tube going in, another coming out, the drip bottles switched periodically.

It's the logical extrapolation of the global village. "In the future," Andy Warhol once predicted, "everybody will be famous. For fifteen minutes." That's the truth of the near future. In the distant future, nobody will need to be famous. We all may be plugged in directly to the fiction machine.

Already it's clear that the once essential differentiation between fact and fiction no longer operates usefully. Truthfulness—verism—is an adolescent affectation. No one presents himself directly, even among friends. Everyone is more or less fictional, made up, constructed. The larger the audience, the greater the fictional quotient. Patty Hearst/ Tania is as many distinct personalities as there are media versions of the elements of the story. Cher and Farrah Fawcett are corporate constructions. Nixon was a superbly complicated (some would say tricky) and entirely self-made character who surpassed the talents of any novelist this country has yet produced. Norman Mailer is his own best creation; his own persona puts his literary characters to shame. Likewise, we care more about "Marlon Brando" than about any of the imaginary people he halfheartedly tries to mimic. Reporters and novelists both have discovered that we care more about the teller than about the tale (unless—best of both worlds—the tale is about the teller). Mailer has introduced the concept of the "factoid"—like a humanoid, almost indistinguishable from the real thing but definitely artificial. Alex Haley, who is ipso facto the most influential American writer of all time, talks about "faction"—it's true, but . . .

So what? Not to worry. The error was in thinking that there was a clear line of demarcation between fact and fiction in the first place.

Writer Jeremy Larner, director Michael Ritchie, and producer/star Robert Redford created Bill McKay for their 1972 film The Candidate. *Warner Brothers, pursuing the obvious publicity course, produced these campaign buttons with Redford/McKay's portrait. One now rests in the Smithsonian Institution's campaign button collection, alongside the relatively more real memorabilia of such politicians as John Lindsay (now a television commentator, actor, and novelist), who served as a model for McKay. Uncannily, the film now looks like a documentary of Governor Jerry Brown's campaign which took place in the same state as the film, only years later.*

There wasn't. There has always been a continuum. Once we realize this, we're much better able to judge the relative facticity or fiction of an observed personality or event. We've become much more healthily critical. We no longer accept at face value the pretty global village the media deliver. Large numbers of people in a recent survey admitted that they didn't really believe the Apollo moonshots took place (whatever that still means): it must have been done in the Nevada desert someplace; maybe that guy who did the special effects for *Earthquake* had a hand in it. Nobody believes the Warren Commission report, but few people really care. That's one version of the story. Okay, there are others. That rather naive belief in the absolute separateness of truth and falsehood was a Victorian characteristic, no longer useful and connected with the now outmoded creed of the efficacy of science. If physics now operates comfortably with the Indeterminacy Principle, why can't reporting? In fact, we have a much finer sense of reality and fantasy now that we admit they are always inextricably entwined.

If celebrities have taken over a large part of our personal universes formerly occupied by family and friends, that may not necessarily be so bad. We've let them into our lives for good reasons. I've never actually met George Segal, for example, but I consider him a good friend (that's George Segal the actor, not George Segal the sculptor). I've enjoyed our conversations over the years—even if they've been one-way—and I go to see him mug through his parts in the movies for the same reasons I'd go to see my brother: let's see what ol' George is up to now. On the other hand, I personally don't particularly like Johnny Carson running my conversations for me. There's often a better quality of talk in our house when the set is off. Nevertheless, there are millions who listen to Johnny's friends not simply out of habit but because they find them more stimulating than Uncle Ed and Aunt Mary. Yes, it would be nice if they went out and tried to hold their own conversations with new people. But maybe the celebrity model actually suggests a more active social role. If John Davidson can actually hold a conversation, are there any of us who can't?

We've been talking about celebrities as if they all fit the same mold, and of course they don't. There is a calculus of celebrityhood, even if there isn't yet a very good vocabulary to talk about it. There are—essentially—three categories: heroes, stars, and what we might call "quasars." Heroes gain their celebrityhood for what they do, stars for what they are, and quasars for what we *think* or surmise they are. (Likewise, astronomical quasars—"quasi-stellar objects"—appear to be much larger and moving much faster than the laws of physics allow and in consequence are clearly different from what we think they are even if we'll never be able to observe them in such a way as to be sure.)

There are very few real heroes around these days. That's not so much a comment on the darkening horizons of the modern mood as it is a sign that other types of celebrity are so powerful that they outshine figures who might, in other times, have been heroes. Ralph Nader is perhaps a good example of a modern hero. For the most part, he is admired for what he has done rather than for what he is or appears to be, but even Ralph suffers from celebrityhood. His lifestyle has probably gained him ten times the coverage in the media that his work has, and even Ralph is not averse to playing at self-mockery on *Saturday Night Live*. Astronauts, on the other hand, are definitely pseudo-heroes: personalities elected to fill certain personas designed by others. They're halfway to being stars; admittedly the trips to the moon were difficult jobs of acting, but the roles were clearly defined and the scripts written out in greater detail than Hollywood ever dreamed. If it hadn't been Armstrong and Aldrin, it would have been some other astro-actors who exhibited the right qualities for the parts.

Stars, paradoxically, are not necessarily actors (nor are actors always potentially stars). Actors play roles, stars play themselves. There's a continuum here, too. Olivier is clearly an actor, but Brando—although he is famous in part for his "acting ability"—is 90 percent star. No matter what the role, he's Brando first, character second. People didn't go to see *Last Tango in Paris* because they were interested in a character named Paul. They paid five dollars because they were irresistibly drawn to the spectacle of Marlon Brando—*the* Marlon Brando— talking dirty and simulating sex. Meanwhile, someone like Paul Newman (or the aforementioned irrepressible George Segal) plays only the persona. Nothing wrong with this. Famous nineteenth-century actors generally stuck to two or three popular roles. The development of the celebrity persona as it was expressed in movies, then radio and television, is in fact a quantum advance over particular written roles. Watch Humphrey Bogart find himself, grow, work variations on the theme, then decline into self-parody over the course of his seventy-five movies. What single role could match that performance spread over a period of twenty-five years?

Then, too, there are plenty of stars who aren't even nominally actors. That is, they don't usually take fictional roles in movies, stage, or television productions. Most of the working politicians you can think of are stars and, in fact, we haven't had a president who wasn't a celebrity first and a politician second since before Teddy "Rough Rider" Roosevelt. This is the wide, gray area of "personalities"—celebrities who are well-known for what they are but who also have careers of sorts outside the theatrical professions.

Quasars are no doubt the most interesting celebrity phenomena. Unlike stars and heroes, they almost never have any real control over the image they project. Often they're victims of media. Patty Hearst is perhaps the pre-eminent quasar of our day, but there are many other examples. These are the "peculiar people made strangely important by ordinary newspaper print." Here, the focus is clearly on the function of the media in transmitting the image to us. It's not what they are or what they do, but what we *think* they are that fascinates us. This is the fictional crux of celebrityhood. Making our own fiction is something we all do, more or less, but having fiction made out of us, without our control, is a psychotic experience. Garbo has to be the patron saint of unwilling quasars, Nixon the everyman. "You won't have Dick Nixon to kick around anymore," he told the artists of the press in 1962, and in a sense he was right—for a while. When he returned to the public arena in 1968 he was in perfect control of the media image, even using the residual fifties persona of tricky Dick to his own best advantage as a kind of dummy sparring partner off whom he could score easy points. "Sock it to *me*?!" he declared on *Laugh-In* in 1968, and we all laughed, even when it hurt. With exquisite and tragicomic irony, it was his own obsession with control of the media that finally did him in. There hasn't been a character of such dimensions since Faust.

Control is obviously a major determinant in the celebrity formula. Stars have a great deal of it—it comes with the territory; heroes don't need it. But quasars have considerable trouble with it. One thinks of all the famous rock star deaths of the sixties, for example. Or of Citizen Patty, the Kent State Girl, and Katharina Blum, discussed in detail later in this volume.

Often, when the media people are sharpest, quasar celebrity is crystalized in iconic images. Fairbanks and Pickford, the first of the monumental film celebrities, may both have had a proper hand in the construction of their relatively constricting personas, but they each reacted differently to them. Doug was relatively complacent; Mary, in middle age, fought to escape the stereotype of America's sausage-curled Sweetheart in gingham. Like so many tragically affected women after her, she failed. She retreated to her bed and bottle where, physically, she seems to live forever, well out of her time. Whether or not Garbo was successful in her own negation of celebrity we'll never know—a fact which in itself suggests success.

Even in politics the iconic image often seems to obviate thought and action. The Kennedys, of course. Che Guevara was probably more influential as a poster than as a leader. It killed him. Fidel without his beard, fatigues, and cigar is, very bluntly, not Fidel. The list of iconic examples is endless.

There have been conscious artists of the icon, as well. Warhol celebrated Monroe and numerous others in repetitive silkscreen prints in the sixties, then hired an actor, Alan Midgette, to go on a lecture tour in his place. Why? "Because he was better at it than I was," Warhol explains. "They never really did discover that he wasn't me. I can't remember how it finally came out." Chris Burden, the conceptual artist, tried to pry open the back door to the iconic pantheon with a television commercial for himself a few years ago. Late at night, amid the "Johnny Ray's Greatest Hits" ads and the sewer service commercials, the screen all of a sudden went blank. In clean orange letters on a bright blue background the following names zoomed out at us: "Leonardo da Vinci Michelangelo Rembrandt Pablo Picasso Chris Burden," with audio to underline them. It didn't work. Burden is no Warhol. Now, if he got himself shot by a crazed radical feminist. . . . You just can't

It has been important for popular critics to be celebrities ever since
Alexander Woollcott developed the vituperous insult as a critical form.
Woollcott was immortalized as a character first in Edna Ferber's Show-
boat, then even more memorably in George S. Kaufman and Moss
Hart's The Man Who Came to Dinner as the title character, Sheridan
Whiteside. Woollcott admired the irascible mirror-image of himself
enough to play the role on tour, as did Hart, but the image of Woollcott that has come down to us is the actor Monty Woolley's, who took
the role in the film version. Woollcott? Woolley? What's the difference?

Of contemporary critics, John Simon is by far the most acutely
conscious of the function of personality in the craft. He has spent more
than fifteen years perfecting his latter-day Woollcott image as "the
critic you love to hate." This celebrityhood sui generis reached a peak
in the early seventies when a New York novelty manufacturer thought
to produce rolls of bathroom tissue with Simon's smiling face on each
sheet. There is no record that Simon protested.

sneak your way into celebrity. At least not without help. Ask Cher or Farrah.

In a play that deals with many of these issues—*The Balcony*—Jean Genet speaks of "being admitted to the nomenclature." It is probably the primal urge of those who really want celebrity. It's being the biggest kid on your block. But it's much more than that. It's not enough to be known; you must be well-known. The first test of celebrityhood is passed when there is a significant number of people who know your name and face even though you don't know theirs. This is protocelebrityhood. A little notoriety in your profession will get you to this stage. Real celebrityhood, however, doesn't come until you realize that there are other images of you being propagated that don't quite jibe with what you know about yourself. To be quoted in *People* magazine is to be a protocelebrity; to be misquoted is to be a true celebrity. When *The New York Times* runs a story about the *People* story, that verges perilously close to stardom.

No matter what the category, celebrity permits a public voice; it shifts opinions, acts, decisions, feelings from the private stage to the public. It is a different order of existence. And, until the time comes when everyone is famous forever, it happens that the public life is the only one recorded. The media are history; history is media, distorted though it may be. The present movement for each of us to discover a personal history—private rather than public—is hopeful. Roots provide an interior celebrity, a religious condition that brings us back to the first stage of herohood in divinity. As one of the more colorful celebrities of the last century put it:

> I celebrate myself, and sing myself,
> And what I assume you shall assume,
> For every atom belonging to me as good belongs to you.

2. PORTER GOES TO THE CONVENTION: A FABLE

by Nora Ephron

Watergate remains a major milestone in the history of contemporary media. Not only did it mark the downfall of one of the great self-conscious personalities of our day, it also shifted attention to the image-makers: reporters became celebrities in their own right. Nora Ephron fantasized on this new phenomenon in her monthly column in *Esquire* late in 1976. (The reader is humbly requested to remember that Ephron had recently married Carl Bernstein. She insists he won't tell even her who Deep Throat is.)

Porter checked into his hotel on Sunday night and went to Madison Square Garden to pick up his credentials. He wasn't sure what he was going to need them for, since his story had fallen through. Porter was a reporter for the Tulark *Morning Herald* of Tulark, Idaho, and his editor had sent him to the Democratic convention to cover the mayor of Tulark, J. Neal Dudley, who was a delegate. "Just follow him around," said the editor. Porter had had big plans. He would follow Dudley to the Empire State Building and the Statue of Liberty. He would follow him into a taxi and they would have a funny experience with a New York cabdriver. He would follow him to Eighth Avenue, where J. Neal Dudley would be mugged while Porter looked on helplessly, taking notes. He would follow him to dinner at Windows on the World, where with any luck Dudley would be thrown out for wearing a leisure suit.

Porter had begun by following Dudley to the Boise airport and onto the plane to New York. After a couple of drinks, he asked Dudley what he planned to do at the convention.

"Fuck my eyes out," said Dudley, "and if I catch you within twenty feet of my room I'll kill you."

"I'm supposed to follow you around," said Porter.

"Make it up," said J. Neal Dudley.

Dudley got into a cab at Kennedy airport and vanished. Porter got onto the bus and rode to his hotel. It occurred to him that if he could just find J. Neal Dudley fucking his eyes out, he could bring down the administration of Tulark, Idaho, such as it was.

On the other hand, Porter had read enough articles in journalism reviews to realize that he would have to find J. Neal Dudley *in flagrante* with a secretary who could not take shorthand and who had been flown into town on a ticket paid for with the proceeds from a secret sale of Tulark municipal bonds. Otherwise, his editor would refuse to print the story on the grounds that it was an invasion of J. Neal Dudley's privacy and a surefire way for the paper to lose the advertising from J. Neal Dudley's appliance dealership.

Porter decided to forget it. He would make the story up. He could always talk to enough delegates to put something together about what J. Neal Dudley would have done at the convention had he actually attended it.

So after getting his credentials, Porter set out to find a delegate. He went to the Statler Hilton lobby and spotted a large man wearing a ridiculous hat. Porter approached him.

"Porter of the Tulark *Morning Herald*," he said.

"Ken Franklin of *Newsday*," said the man in the hat. "Can I interview you?"

"I beg your pardon?" said Porter.

Franklin explained that he was the media reporter for *Newsday* and he just wanted to ask Porter the questions he'd been asking other reporters.

"Sure," said Porter. "Shoot."

"What are you planning to write about?" asked Franklin.

"I don't know," said Porter.

"That's what they all say," said Franklin. "There are twice as many media people here as delegates, and there's no story."

"There's no story?" said Porter.

"That's what they all say," said Franklin.

"What else do they all say?" said Porter.

"They all say that because there's no news story, there are no feature stories either."

"What about the hookers?" said Porter.

"All the hookers are taken," said Franklin. "The *New York Post* signed them all to exclusive contracts last week."

Porter bought himself a beer in the bar and looked around. He spotted a man wearing delegate's credentials and went over to him.

"Porter of the Tulark *Morning Herald*," he said.

"Suzanne Cox of the *Chicago Tribune*," said the woman sitting next to the delegate. "Get lost. This one's mine for the week."

"Could I ask *you* a question?" Porter said to Suzanne Cox.

"No you can't," said a small boy next to Miss Cox.

"Who are you?" asked Porter.

"Brian Finley," said the boy. "I'm a reporter from *Children's Express,* and *I'm* covering *her.*"

"Who's covering you?" asked Porter.

"Scotty Reston," said Brian Finley, "but he's gone to the men's room."

"I see," said Porter and went back to the bar.

"Jarvis of *Time* magazine," said a voice behind him. He turned around. Jarvis of *Time* magazine was very pretty. She was also a media reporter.

"Porter of the Tulark *Morning Herald*," Porter said. "I don't know what I'm writing about. There's no story. Because there's no news story, there are no feature stories either."

"What about the hookers?" said Jarvis.

"The hookers are taken," said Porter.

"Oh God," said Jarvis, "I wonder if my writer knows that."

"Your writer?" said Porter, but Jarvis had rushed out of the bar.

Monday night Porter got a floor pass and watched Sally Quinn and Ben Bradlee being photographed. Then he joined a large crowd that was watching in disbelief as Evans and Novak had a conversation with each other. In the distance, Porter could hear Barbara Jordan speaking, but just barely. He wished he had stayed in his room and watched the convention on television. When the session ended, he bumped into Ken Franklin from *Newsday*.

"What are you writing about?" asked Franklin.

"I don't know," said Porter.

"Nobody's saying that today," said Franklin. "Today people have figured out what they're doing."

"Not me," said Porter.

Franklin took Porter to the *Rolling Stone* party that night. When they arrived, several hundred people on the street were pushing up against the door to the party, and several dozen police were trying to hold them back.

"Who's that with Seymour Hersh?" someone asked.

"Paul Newman," someone answered.

Porter managed to push his way up to the front door, but it was locked. Every so often, a man would appear at the door and point out someone in the crowd and the police would scoop up the someone and get him through the door. Porter squeezed in with Walter Cronkite's entourage, but once inside he found that the only topic of conversation was what was going on outside. A large group of people upstairs were watching a television monitor showing pictures of the scene on the street, and another large group of people were watching themselves on a public-access television channel.

"Porter of the Tulark *Morning Herald*!" a voice shouted.

Porter looked around. It was Jarvis of *Time* magazine.

"What are you doing?" she said.

"Leaving," he said. "Do you want to come?"

"Yes," said Jarvis.

Later, in Porter's hotel room, Jarvis began to undress. "I hope this is off the record," she said.

"Likewise," said Porter.

At that moment, the phone rang.

"Porter of the Tulark *Morning Herald*," said Porter.

"This is the New York City police," said a man on the phone. "We picked up a naked man dancing on Thirty-sixth Street. He says he's the mayor of Tulark, Idaho. Your name was in his pocket."

"Is he with his secretary?" asked Porter.

"Yes," said the policeman.

"Was she flown here on city money?" asked Porter.

"Yes," said the policeman.

"Can she take shorthand?"

"No," said the policeman.

"I'll be right there," said Porter. He put down the phone and started to dress. "I'm sorry, Jarvis," he said. "I have to go out to become a media star."

"That's all right," said Jarvis. "I can wait."

3. WHO'S WHO IN INTERNATIONAL CHAOS
by Rees Behrendt

If, on one hand, the reporters are covering themselves covering themselves (like a Moebius blanket), on the other, we suffer from a plethora of fuzzy-imaged minicelebrities (well-known for being confused with others who are even less well-known). Rees Behrendt devised this test for *Esquire* several years ago. See how you score. Extra points for identifying Rees's brother.

We were at a party the other day and a friend said: "Yes, well, Uta Hagen is a terrific actress. I mean, Ulu Grosbart is. A producer, I mean. It's Ulu Gros*bard* that's the . . . No, that's Una *Mer*kel that's the pro*du*cer, and it's Oona O'*Neill* that's the . . . Hold it, did I say *Hagen*? I meant *Jacobs*son. I meant *Ulla* Jacobsson! That's the actress, and it's *Ull*man . . . *Ull*mann . . . *Liv* Ullmann. I beg your pardon, it's Ursula *Thiess* that's . . ."

Anyhow, we took careful notes, and what follows is a carefully edited list of the kind of people that are giving everybody so much trouble nowadays. We think the best thing to do with this list is to read it aloud. Then when you get to the end you could mentally complete it with whoever pops into your mind, and then—only then—carefully fold it up very small and try to put it where you won't remember it ever again.

Robert Crichton, Michael Crichton
    Peter De Vries, Peter Viertel, Peter Viereck

Mike Wallace, Mike Douglas
    Mildred Natwick, Mildred Dunnock

Anne Bancroft, Anne Baxter
    Christopher George, Jordan Christopher

Jaye P. Morgan, Jane Morgan, Morgana King
    King Hussein, King Hassan

Kim Hunter, Kim Stanley
    Alan Alda, Alan Arkin

Patrice Munsel, Mimi Benzell
    Pierre Boulle, Pierre Boulez

Schuyler Chapin, Dwight Chapin
    Sandy Dennis, Sandy Duncan, Sandy Wilson, Duncan Sandys

George Peppard, George Grizzard
    Mike Frankovich, Peter Bogdanovich, William Jovanovich

Carlo Gambino, Joseph Colombo, Joe Bonanno
    Barbara Cook, Barbara Harris

Julia Child, Julia Meade
    William Rehnquist, Roy Newquist

Claes Oldenburg, Robert Rauschenberg
    Eileen Farrell, Suzanne Farrell

James Farentino, Joseph Campanella
    Sergio Franchi, Enzo Stuarti

Bobby Darin, James Darren
    Roger Kahn, Roger Angell

Red Barber, Red Smith
    Lance Rentzel, Lance Alworth, Lance Reventlow

Hayley Mills, Patty Duke
    Lana Cantrell, Lainie Kazan

Cannon, Gannon, Banyon
    Dr. DeBakey, Dr. Leakey, Dr. Cooley

Sax Rohmer, Eric Rohmer
    H. R. Haldeman, John Erlichman

Mark Lester, Lester Markel
    Justice Blackmun, Honor Blackman

Jack Newfield, Jeff Greenfield, Josh Greenfeld
    Ernest Dichter, Midge Decter

NBC's Saturday Night Live *crew of satirists picked up Behrendt's shtik for a spring 1977 skit in which Ricardo Montalban, Fernando Lamas, and Cesar Romero (pictured here from left to right, or vice versa) meet their dates Elke Sommer, Britt Ekland, and Mai Britt. They themselves can't quite tell the difference. One thing they're sure of: they are* not *Ricky Ricardo. They finally decide that "the only way to tell is to run out to the parking lot and see which one's keys fit the Cordoba." The skit gets more complicated when George Chakiris/George Maharis/ George Hamilton show up, and are followed hard upon by Sergio Franchi/Rossano Brazzi/Enzo Stuarti. "Let's see your keys, boys! Whose fit the Volare?" (Photo: Edie Baskin)*

Elke Sommer, Anita Ekberg, Ursula Andress,
Ursula Thiess, Ulla Jacobsson, Gunilla Knutson,
Liv Ullmann, Mai Britt, Mai Zetterling, Britt Ekland
    John Huston, John Ford

Clint Walker, Clint Eastwood, Lee Van Cleef
    John Denver, Bob Denver, Denver Pyle

Rita Moreno, Chita Rivera
    Bernardo Bertolucci, Paolo Bortoluzzi

Milton Caniff, Ray Conniff
    Chuck Berry, Ken Berry

Allen Ludden, Bill Cullen
    Coral Browne, Pamela Brown

George Shultz, Charles Schulz
    Carroll Baker, Carol Lynley

Eleanor Parker, Jean Parker, Parker Tyler
    Billy De Wolfe, Iggie Wolfington

Chris Welles, Chris Chase
    Dore Schary, Dory Previn, Dorothy Provine

Skitch Henderson, Mitch Miller
    Patti Page, Janis Paige, Ann Page

François Mauriac, André Malraux
    Jules Romains, Romain Rolland, Roland Petit

Wladyslaw Gomulka, Oscar Homolka, Oskar Kokoschka
    Shari Lewis, Shani Wallis, Shana Alexander

Harry Morgan, Henry Morgan
    Lisa Kirk, Phyllis Kirk, Grayson Kirk

Peter Hall, Peter Brook, Peter Glenville
    Irving Wallace, Irving Stone

Gene Hackman, Gene Wilder
    Gerald Freedman, William Friedkin

Ina Claire, Clare Luce, Clare Booth Luce
    Rod Serling, Robert Sterling

William Wyler, Billy Wilder
    Vera Miles, Sylvia Miles, Sarah Miles

Jerry Lee Lewis, Joe E. Lewis
    Ron O'Neal, Ryan O'Neal, Patrick O'Neal

Anthony Dowell, Malcolm McDowell
    Ionesco, Enesco, UNESCO, GENESCO

Nathan's Famous, International Famous
    Connie Francis, Connie Stevens, Stella Stevens, K. T. Stevens

France Nuyen, Nancy Kwan, Pat Suzuki
    The Everly Brothers, The Eberle Brothers

Vincent Sheean, Martin Sheen, Fulton Sheen
Will Geer, Michael Greer, Rosey Grier, Germaine Greer

Steve Forrest, Forrest Tucker
Preston Foster, Robert Preston

Allan Sherman, Shelley Berman, Max Shulman,
Herman Shumlin, Harold Clurman
Calvin Trillin, Calvin Tomkins

John Berryman, John Betjeman, Wendell Berry, John Berry
Paul Douglas, Broderick Crawford

Joni Mitchell, Joni James
Robert Conrad, William Conrad

Mike Connors, Chuck Connors
Carlos Santana, Lola Falana, Chiquita Banana

Morton Gould, Glenn Gould, Chester Gould
James Gould Cozzens, Norman Cousins

Judy Klemesrud, Jill Krementz
Kaz Garas, Alex Karras, Andrew Sarris, Lucas Samaras

Walter Hinckle, Walter Hickel
Sidney Skolsky, George Solkosky

Sylvia Ashton-Warner, Sylvia Townsend Warner,
Mollie Panter-Downes
Anthony Howard, Anthony Lewis, J. Anthony Lukas

Alicia Markova, Natalia Makarova, Alicia Alonso, Alicia Bay Laurel
William H. Whyte, E. B. White, T. H. White, Theodore White

Alvin Epstein, Jason Epstein
Dorothy Collins, Judy Collins

Stanley Ellin, Stanley Elkin, Stanley Elkins, Hilly Elkins
Guy Madison, Guy Mitchell, Cameron Mitchell

Joey Faye, Joey Adams, Joey Bishop
Jim Brown, James Brown, Johnny Brown

James Cain, James Caan
Calder Willingham, Alexander Calder

Arrabal, Marisol
    Abbe Lane, Chiquita Banana

Evelyn Keyes, Evelyn Ankers, Evelyn and Her Magic Violin
    Maureen O'Hara, Maureen O'Sullivan

John Barth, Karl Barth, Donald Barthelme . . .

                . . . and the hell with it

4. GETTING THE VEGAS WILLIES
by Joan Didion

Vegas, of course, is the Valhalla of show business celebrity. Joan Didion's nerves are always exquisitely tuned to the harmonics of emptiness and absurdity. She spins magnificent meditations out of West Coast silliness. This is one of her best.

Of course, Didion is working metaphorically here. The medical genesis of the Vegas willies disease may be considerably simpler to explain. It has long been rumored that the casinos pump an extra dose of oxygen through their air-conditioning systems. So it's no wonder that visitors remain bright-eyed and feverishly interested in the action at the tables throughout the dreamless night.

Las Vegas hotels all smell alike. The Sands smells like the Flamingo and the Flamingo smells like the Riviera and the Riviera smells like the Dunes and the Dunes smells like the Stardust and also like the Thunderbird, the Frontier, the Desert Inn, Caesars, the Hilton and the MGM Grand. I had never set foot in the MGM Grand before last night but I should have known how it would smell. This smell is sharp and thin and chemical, not exactly the smell of air conditioning but acrid and a little stale and specific to Vegas: I have never smelled it in the hotels of other cities, nor can I duplicate it. The nearest I came was once when I threw a perfume box on a fire that would not catch, but that smell went away, and the Vegas smell does not. The Vegas smell permeates hair follicles and locked suitcases and sealed packets of Kleenex and even the baggage carrousels at LAX after a flight comes in from Vegas. The Vegas smell sticks.

The Vegas smell is with me today, and so is the Vegas fright, which is what I am talking about here. This is a fright as particular and specific to Las Vegas as the smell is particular and specific to Las Vegas, and I have never gotten through a night there without catching it, like a cold. Last night I thought I might. Last night I went to Las Vegas, for the first time in six years, under the most benign and protected conditions possible: a friend, Helen Reddy, was opening at the MGM Grand, and she and her husband, Jeffrey Wald, had invited seventy or so people to fly in for the midnight show. Actually this kind of thing is called a celebrity opening (CELEB OP is how the code reads on the envelope with the room keys) and is a relatively fixed feature of life among big-room Vegas headliners, but since Helen Reddy Wald is the only friend I have who happens also to be a big-room Vegas headliner, the details of the evening seemed to me entirely novel, and exotic, and to leave no time for the fright.

In the first place there was, for the hour's flight over, a chartered Boeing 737. In the second place there were, when this Boeing 737 touched down at McCarran Field in Las Vegas, thirty limousines waiting on the tarmac, thirty Cadillac and Lincoln engines idling at wing tip, thirty drivers standing around in a light rain opening doors and holding umbrellas and waiting for the police escort to move the convoy out. The name HELEN REDDY blazed from a lighted marquee just off the tarmac. The name HELEN REDDY blazed from billboards every twenty yards on the drive from McCarran to the Grand. The police stopped traffic. Walkie-talkies crackled. The limos proceeded in formation through green lights and red. In front of the Grand there were crowds, cordoned off, and a red carpet and banks of blinding theatrical lights and, on top of every taxi, on every marquee, everywhere the eye rested, the name HELEN REDDY, and her face. So hallucinatory was the power of all this celebrity and all these arrangements that it was three in the morning, in a vast CELEB OP suite with a mirrored walk-in bathtub in the middle of the bedroom, before I caught the Vegas smell, the Vegas fright, the craven apprehension that I had to get out. On less benign nights in Vegas the fright has found me before I checked in. On this particular night, this three a.m., last night, this morning, it found me when I called room service, and was put on hold for fifty-eight minutes.

I suppose the fright comes because I do not understand. I did not understand, for example, what the guests at a Strip hotel did ordinarily that gave them the psychic will and physical stamina to tie up room service for fifty-eight minutes at three a.m. I did not understand why so many men I had seen downstairs appeared to have nineteen-inch necks. I did not understand why anyone would arrive with his wife in Vegas for the weekend and rent a pink Cadillac Coupe De Ville, but I had watched such a rental arranged. I did not quite see why a woman visiting the Grand might decide to get some cosmetic breast surgery done and charge it to her room, but it was possible to do this, at the office of a Dr. Tippit, on the arcade level. I thought I knew why all the hookers in all the bars seemed gotten up for a Princeton weekend in 1956—their sweaters and skirts and little black dresses appeared, *in situ*, theatrical and seductive and slightly outrageous—but in that case I did not entirely understand the market for rhinestone brassieres in the hotel shops. Nor did I understand, in the hotel shops, a certain rage for large objects made entirely of spun glass: spun-glass whaling ships, spun-glass caravans, spun-glass Washington monuments and spun-glass dogs.

Q: *How do you get a three-foot spun-glass dog home from Vegas?*

A. *Rent it a pink Cadillac Coupe De Ville.*

There is a great deal I never understand, out there on the Mojave with the spun-glass dogs. I have never understood the ability of large numbers of solid citizens to land at McCarran and enter cheerfully into the spirit of a Genet brothel. I have never understood why the point of the exercise is believed to be money, when the place is in fact profoundly immaterial, all symbol, all light and shadow and metaphor, a *tableau vivant* of lust and greed. I know Las Vegas to be a theater dedicated to the immediate gratification of every impulse, but I also know it to be a theater designed to numb those very impulses it promises to gratify. Nobody in this theater rushes the stage. Nobody handles the actual money. I know Las Vegas to be The Entertainment Capital of the World, but I also know it to be a capital of the willies, a place where the promise is everything and the payoff elusive, a place where the level of frustration and nervous boredom is so pronounced that a crowd will form around the search for a dropped dime. I recall once drawing a crowd in the lobby of the Stardust simply by asking to see the assistant manager. Certain tables will attract crowds and then, with no perceptible change in the play, lose them. Lights flash and no one blinks.

A glaze of overstimulation hangs over these crowds that form and dissolve. A kind of electrical charging and recharging replaces all one's notions of cause and effect. The name "Carl Cohen" on a Vegas paging system will always draw a crowd. All I know about Carl Cohen is that he used to manage the Sands casino and that he once hit Frank Sinatra and that, on the evidence, watching him take a telephone call is considered something to do. Those crowds cordoned off in front of the Grand last night appeared to have gathered and to disperse with no particular rise and fall in expectations: watching a couple of William Morris agents get out of a limousine and watching Olivia Newton-John get out of a limousine seemed equally to satisfy the watchers, resolve the moment, discharge the electricity and fill the time. Time is a great presence in Vegas, since the only obligation is to fill it. People filling time move around the Strip in waves, flowing from casino to casino, swirling through a keno lounge here, eddying around a showroom door there, flooding on out to wait a moment under the bright cold cross-walk lights and then, as if programmed to some lunar pull, surging on to fill another keno lounge, watch Carl Cohen take another call. The place is a hydraulic model of human tedium.

Vegas notes. (1) At a party in Beverly Hills I was once seated next to a stranger who played the Riviera several times a year. I asked him how he filled the day in Vegas. He looked at me as if I were demented. He said filling the day was "no problem at the Riv." He said he got up, ordered breakfast, played nine holes, took some steam and did the

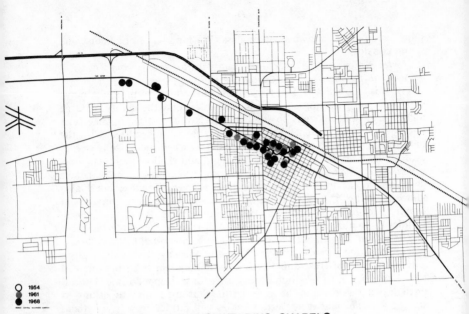

O 1954
● 1961
● 1968

COMPARATIVE ACTIVITY PATTERNS: WEDDING CHAPELS

In their highly influential book Learning From Las Vegas, *architects Robert Venturi, Denise Scott Brown, and Steven Izenour discuss the structure of "theater dedicated to the immediate gratification of every impulse . . . all symbol, all light and shadow and metaphor." They reprinted a series of "activity pattern maps," of which this is an example. Vegas is an automotive experience. "The system of the highway gives order to the sensitive functions of exits and entrance, as well as to the image of the Strip as a sequential whole." Wedding Chapels, for example, make a few tentative appearances early along the Strip, then crescendo to a conglomerate climax just before Fremont Street. (Source: Central Telephone Company)*

dinner show. He did not understand me any better than I understand Vegas. (2) When my mother first saw the Las Vegas Strip she was surprised and disappointed. She had been hearing for years about these hotels, she said, and she had imagined places more along the lines of the Broadmoor or the Greenbrier. "Caesars Palace has no lawn," my mother said. My mother does not understand Vegas any better than I do. (3) My husband wrote a book in Vegas and for a year and a half maintained a furnished duplex apartment just off the Strip. I bought dishes and wastebaskets and three changes of king-size sheets for this apartment but saw it only once, the day he vacated it. I say "vacated" rather than "moved out" because he never exactly lived in this apartment: during the eighteen months of his tenancy he slept in the king-size bed only two or three times. Sometimes he would take a look at the apartment and then check into a motel. Later on he began skipping the look. He says that he does not understand Vegas any better than I do but I believe he does: anyone who could keep an empty duplex apartment off the Las Vegas Strip and sleep in a motel a few blocks away has some instinct for the radical immateriality of the place, and also for the willies.

Fly out of Vegas and the lights go off. The hallucination vanishes. I recall a night in 1968 when my husband happened to be in New York and I happened to be in Las Vegas, reporting a piece and having a bad time. To be a woman alone in Vegas is usually to have a bad time, to be made immediately aware of one's class position. We are all "sweetie" and "sweetheart" and "dear" to the Vegas management. We are all out for something: a comped meal, an angle. They have seen us before.

Nighttime is purely an outdoor phenomenon in Vegas, the city of signifier without signifieds. Indoors, where the action is, it's always cool—and the air is abnormally fresh. (Photo: Charlotte Rosenberg)

They have our number. On this particular night in 1968 I had checked into the Sands and ordered a sandwich and the room-service waiter had advised me that there was no need for me to be alone: there were a lot of lonely people around, and he knew where. I recognize now that this was on the part of the waiter no more than a reflex, a Vegas tic, but at the time it unnerved me, and I called my husband for solace. Never mind that, he said when I finally got him in New York: he had just visited a circle of New York hell. He had just come from the Oak Room of The Plaza, where he had seen, having dinner together at the table next to his, Clay Felker, Gloria Steinem, Arthur Schlesinger, Jr., and Leonard Lyons.

I said what about me.

He said what about you?

I said quite frankly I would rather be having dinner at The Plaza with Clay Felker, Gloria Steinem, Arthur Schlesinger, Jr., and Leonard Lyons than having a sandwich alone at the Sands with the room-service waiter trying to fix me up.

"That's just Vegas, it doesn't figure," my husband said, and of course he was right. Vegas figures only in the minds of those who are there. I know for a fact that Ann-Margret is playing the Hilton tonight. I know that Bobbie Gentry is playing the Frontier. I know that Helen Reddy is sold out at the Grand and I know that someone is paging Carl Cohen and I know that outside the blackout curtains in the vast CELEB OP suite where I slept last night there is still this view: the roof of the jai alai palace and an empty lot where the sand is blowing. I know that at the airport the taped voices of Liberace and Joan Rivers and Jan Murray are even now advising travelers to take it easy on the moving sidewalk, stand to the right and pass to the left "and come see my show." I know the place is out there, but all that sticks now is the smell.

THE MEDIUM
CONNECTION

5. *MEDIUM COOL:*
THE BLACK MILITANT SCENE
by Haskell Wexler

Haskell Wexler's *Medium Cool* is, I think, the best film about media since *Citizen Kane* and also one of the two or three most important American films of the sixties. Filmed on location in Chicago just before and during the Democratic convention of 1968, it merges fiction and fact perfectly. John Ketsalis is a television news cameraman who is more fascinated by the medium than by the people and events he films. In the course of the film, however, as he discovers both the power the media wield and the subversive relationship between his station and the FBI, he changes radically.

This scene is the apex of the film. Ketsalis and his soundman, Gus, have covered a "human interest" story. A black cabdriver named Frank has turned in $10,000 he found in his cab. The action has been met with public reactions ranging from contempt to surprise. Ketsails wants to follow up on the story. . . .

INTERIOR: TV STATION OFFICE—DAY
[*The News Director, Karlin, starts to punch a new number.*]

KARLIN [*into phone*]: Mrs. Harris?

[*The other party has hung up. Karlin stops, turns.*]

KARLIN: Well?

JOHN: Remember the story about the cabdriver who turned in the money?

KARLIN: Forget it.

JOHN: There's a story there, Karlin. It's worth following up. I think it'll go on the Sunday night report show.

KARLIN: No. I got a convention coming up. Plus I got a war. Plus I got baseball. Plus I got a nervous city. Plus I got chickenshit cameramen who are afraid to go into the ghetto without police protection. No. N-O. You stay out of those neighborhoods until I send you in there.

JOHN: I want film and lab.

[*Karlin indicates our camera.*]

KARLIN: Look: *they* got film.

JOHN: Film and lab.

SECRETARY [*off-screen*]: Mrs. Evans' office on the phone, Mr. Karlin.

KARLIN [*reaches for phone—turns to John*]: Write up a voucher. [*Picks up the phone.*] Yes, sir. Good morning, sir.

CUT TO:
EXTERIOR: GHETTO STREET—DAY
[*A group of black kids precede camera down the street ahead of us.*]

KIDS AD LIB: Hey, TV man! What you doin' round here? What's doin', TV man?

[*They wave and shout and dance in front of the car.*]

INTERIOR: THE CAR
[*John and Gus look for a place to park.*]
THEIR POV
[*An alleyway. Beyond it, a paddy wagon cruises across frame.*]
ANGLE AT SIDEWALK
[*As the TV8 wagon pulls over, stops. John and Gus get out, lock their doors. Immediately a kid looks inside.
John and Gus start down the sidewalk.*]

JOHN: You know you're two blocks away, don't you?

GUS: Well, they had some trouble in there last night. I thought I'd at least keep the equipment safe.

[*John gives him a look. Camera trucks as they start down the street.*]

CUT AWAY TO:
INTERIOR: FRANK BAKER'S APARTMENT—DAY
[*Black militants sit or stand around the kitchen table. It is cluttered with food, fruit juice, liquor, etc.*]

ONE BLACK: *White* bread is not too cool, man [*drops it in trash can*]. It's out of it. Out of it. O-U-T: out.

FRANK: I don't think we have any other kind, but I'll take a look-see.

THE GUY: I read your name in the paper. What's happening? You're somewhat of a celebrity now. You going to fill me in?

FRANK: Yeah, well . . . you know. Not really a celebrity, but . . . I . . . I found the bread and I turned it in.

THE GUY: You turned it in.

FRANK: Yeah.

THE GUY: Were you acting as a black man or as a Negro? How do you feel? I'm concerned about this.

FRANK: What do you mean was I acting as a Negro or as a black man?

THE GUY: Because I feel that if you were acting as a black man, you would have *kept* the money. If you were acting as a Negro, you turned it in. [*A beat.*] You're my man. You're my man and everything.

ANOTHER BLACK: How much money was there?

Frank Baker's apartment, friends, white bread (on the coffee table), and television.

FRANK: Ten thousand dollars.
ANOTHER FRIEND: Hey, dig . . . now look. You know how much ammunition and guns ten thousand dollars would have bought?
FRANK: Well, I . . . I'm not quite there yet, you know?
THE FRIEND: Well, I'm talking about . . . you got to be *alive* to be honest!

CUT AWAY TO:
EXTERIOR: A STREET CORNER
[*Gus stands at the corner. Behind him, a small store. John is not in view. A black youth has confronted Gus.*]

YOUTH: What you doin' around here, man?
GUS: Buying some cigarettes.
YOUTH: You know you ain't got no right to come around here and buy cigarettes.
GUS: . . . Well . . .
YOUTH: Guys like you get shot all up, you know?

[*John comes into view from the store, moves to join Gus.*]

GUS: . . . Yeah . . .

Levels of the Medium. *A shot from the film. Gus (Peter Bonerz), soundman, and John (Robert Forster), cameraman, interview a group of young Kennedy workers.*

Levels of the Medium. *Forster and Bonerz on the set with writer/ director/cameraman Haskell Wexler.*

Levels of the Medium. *Forster punches a mirror, and fractures the image of himself, symbolically, as Wexler (seen in reflection to the right) photographs.*

YOUTH: Yeah, so don't come around here no more for no cigarettes. You know what I mean?

[Camera pans as John and Gus move across the street.]
VARIOUS SHOTS
[Ghetto kids, people sitting in doorways.]
LONG SHOT
[John and Gus approach Frank's apartment building.]
CLOSER ANGLE AT BUILDING
[The curtains in an upstairs window are seen to be pushed aside as someone looks out.]
INTERIOR: FRANK'S LIVING ROOM
[As one of the militants turns away from the window . . . goes to whisper in the ear of a "brother."]
INTERIOR: APARTMENT BUILDING STAIRWELL
[John and Gus come up the stairs toward camera.]
INTERIOR: THE APARTMENT—AT DOOR
[A knock is heard . . . A tall, bearded militant, Jeff, comes into frame near the door. He pauses to put on his dark glasses. He waits. Again, a knock. Jeff turns.]

JEFF [*to the others, off-screen*]: We have a visitor.

[*He opens the door, revealing John and Gus.*]

JOHN: Frank Baker live here?
JEFF [*mimics*]: Frank Baker live here?
JOHN: Frank Baker, cabdriver?
JEFF: Frank Baker—cabdriver?
JOHN: Yeah, does he live here?
JEFF [*turns—addresses the others, off-screen*]: Does he live here?
VOICE OFF-SCREEN (VAL): There's no Frank cabdriver here.

[*Jeff turns back to John.*]

JOHN: You don't know him? He's a cabdriver. I did a story on him.
I'm a reporter.
JEFF: What's his name again?
JOHN: Frank Baker.
JEFF [*turns around—announces*]: Frank . . . Baker.

[*Frank comes into frame.*]

FRANK: Come on, Jeff—you're putting the cat on. This is the cat who
put me on television in living color, man. How are you?

[*He shakes John's hand. They exchange ad-libbed hellos as Jeff turns,
shrugs, goes out of frame.*]

JOHN: I didn't want to bust in on you. I just wondered if you've got five
minutes to talk.
FRANK: Let's do it over a drink.
JOHN: Good.

[*They go off. Gus is left standing at the door. He closes it behind him
. . . looks around.*]
NEW ANGLE
[*To include Jeff, standing nearby, watching him.*]

JEFF: You know . . . Chicago cops are getting funnier looking every
day.
GUS: I'm not a cop, I'm a soundman.
JEFF: I'll bet you got credentials, too. The FBI supplies the best cre-
dentials. We know, you know, that one of the best ways to spy on
black people is to impersonate a TV man.
GUS: I'm up here with John. We're talking about Frank . . .
JEFF: Well—what's *that*?

INSERT
[*Jeff reveals Gus's Pageboy clipped to his belt.*]
BACK TO SCENE

GUS: That's my Pageboy.

JEFF: Your . . . "Pageboy" . . . ?
GUS: . . . Yeah.

[Jeff laughs, turns.]

JEFF *[off]*: Hey, Richie? Come dig this cat's . . . "Pageboy."

[Gus stands uneasily by the door as Richie approaches.]

JEFF *[to Gus]*: Now, what do you *do* with . . . "my Pageboy" . . . ?
GUS: Well, I don't do anything. It just hangs there. The station—if they want me to go someplace or do something, they call me over this.

[Jeff takes it.]

JEFF: —Oh. You mean—they give you orders on this.
GUS: Yeah.

[Jeff examines it. Gus reaches for it. Jeff slips it to Richie.]

RICHIE: You mean to tell me . . . they talk to you and you can't even talk back?
JEFF: That means he's a receiver and not a sender.
RICHIE *[listens to it—puts it to Jeff's ear]*: You hear somebody talking? *[to Gus]* Looks like they calling you now.

[Gus takes the Pageboy back—moves away.]

RICHIE *[after him]*: What you: a white flunky or something?

INTERIOR: THE KITCHEN
[Frank talking with John.]

JOHN: . . . Wrong, you've gotten a bad idea of . . .

[Coming into frame.]

GUS *[interrupts]*: I forgot something downstairs. I'll meet you in the car.
JOHN: All right.

[Gus goes off, back to:]
INTERIOR: LIVING ROOM AT FRONT DOOR

JEFF: He's coming back! He's coming back! *[as Gus opens the door]* There he goes! There he goes!

[Gus is gone.]

RICHIE: A honky flunky . . . !

[He shuts the door.]
INTERIOR: THE KITCHEN

FRANK: . . . Look, man. I've been on television. I've been in the newspapers. And it's made my life total confusion. What did I do? I find ten thousand dollars in the back of the cab, I'm boob enough to turn it in, and I get my butt kicked by everybody in the world. No, man.
JOHN: Well, that's just it, Frank—it's a human interest story.

FRANK [*shakes his head*]: No, man.

JOHN: People *identify*. [*a beat*] I'll give you a call, we'll have another talk about it. Thank you very much.

NEW ANGLE
[*Pan with John as he goes to the front door—finds himself confronted by Val, who blocks his way.*]

VAL: Excuse me, TV man—but you wanted somebody for an interview, right?

JOHN: Yeah—I haven't got time now, dear. I got to run.

VAL: Yeah, but I wanted to talk to you about it. You see, I'm a black actress, and—

JOHN: Listen, honey, I haven't got time.

VAL: Don't "honey" me. I'm a black actress. I demand respect. I—

JOHN: All right, now. Listen—

VAL: No. You said you wanted to talk to somebody. You wanted to find out what's going on, what black people are doing.

[*A younger militant has come into frame.*]

JOHN [*to Val*]: Listen, honey, I'm not—

YOUNGER MILITANT: Now listen. No. No—you got to start respecting our women.

JOHN: Look, I had no disrespect in mind—[*indicates his watch*]. I don't have time!

VAL [*insistent*]: I want to talk about what *I* want to talk about! You see, you people are always busy—

JOHN: Listen—dear—!

YOUNGER MILITANT: We *told* you about that "dear" . . . !

VAL: We demand—

JOHN: *You demand what? ? ?*

VAL: *Don't scream at me!*

INTERIOR: THE LIVING ROOM
[*Sensing trouble, Jeff turns to a black brother.*]

JEFF: Oh, no. Oh, dear. Take care of this, will you . . .

[*The Brother gets up, goes toward the front door, off-screen.*]
AT THE DOOR
[*Even as the Younger Militant grabs John.*]

FRANK: Now wait a minute—wait a minute! This is the guy that came by the house to put me on TV—

[*Frank and the Soul Brother break up the argument—Frank leading Val and the Younger Militant back into the living room. As he is finally going through the door, John is stopped by the Brother, who restrains him by the arm.*]

BROTHER: Now wait a minute. Come in. Come in.

JOHN [*glances at the black hand holding his arm*]: Let me ask you something. Are you being friendly? Or are you being tough?

BROTHER: Am *I* being friendly? Listen, I just saved your life. You understand that, don't you?

JOHN: If I got to be afraid in order for your argument to work, then you got no argument.

BROTHER: Oh, no. No. What I want you to understand is that I saved your life. See? Now. You came down here to do some sort of jive interview. You did that. You came down here with fifteen minutes of a black sensibility. And, see—you don't understand that. You came down here to shoot fifteen minutes of what it's taken three hundred years to develop. Grief. You know.

JOHN: Look, I'm not interested in—

BROTHER: And all I want to explain to you is that *you* don't understand.

JOHN: I do something. See? I do it well. That's my job.

BROTHER: Yeah. But you don't do it black enough. You can't understand because you're not black. *We* are.

MEDIUM CLOSE SHOT—A MILITANT
[*He speaks directly to camera.*]

MILITANT: When you come in here . . . you come to do something of human interest. It makes a person wonder. Whether you're going to do something of interest to other humans . . . or whether you consider the person human in whom you're interested. And you got to understand that. Because when you walk in here out of your arrogance, you brought the establishment with you. And you got to understand that too. You brought La Salle Street. City Hall. And all the mass communications media. And you are the ones who distort. You are the ones who exploit us. You are the ones who emasculate us. And that ain't cool.

MEDIUM SHOT—FELTON
[*A younger militant, Felton, speaks directly to camera.*]

FELTON: You people don't know. You don't want to know. You don't know the people. You don't *show* the people. Sometime when some poor cat who's nobody—some cat who wakes up and says I'm nobody, I'm going to die and nobody but my old lady will even know that I ever lived . . . when this cat throws a brick through Charlie's window . . . [*uses his finger like a gun at camera*] . . . and *shoots* . . . then he lives. He lives on the tube. A hundred million people know that the former invisible man *lives*. The whole world knows where he went to school. Even the kids know about his wife and mother. The tube is life, man—life. And you make him the TV star, the Emmy man of the hour. On the six, the ten, and the twelve o'clock news. Cause the tube is life, man—Life. ·What he's sayin', man, is the truth. Why don't you find out what really is. Why do you wait till somebody gets killed, man? Cause somebody is *going* to get killed.

6. UNTIL JOEY BISHOP, MERV GRIFFIN, AND JOHNNY CARSON DO US PART

by Saul Braun

Nobody has captured the feel of the intimate global talk-show village better than Saul Braun in this piece written for *Esquire* in 1968. Some of the names have changed—Joey is no longer with us, Dick Cavett has come and gone—but the game's the same.

January 22: So far this year, have written three letters to Editor, *New York Times,* on downright rudeness of subway guards, fecal excesses of dogs in our society, and need for stricter guidelines on young people. None have been published. Intend to write to Editor, *New York Times,* about this.

Visited with Johnny last night. He was in real fine form. Tony Curtis was on. Tony wouldn't last long at Beldon, Frick & Peabody if he showed up in that Cossack shirt with Cossack boots and that chain around his neck made of charms. I have to disagree with him when he says, "I think the kids of today are more courageous. They wear what they want and I think it's exemplatory." I don't think it's so exemplatory when you can't even tell the boys from the girls anymore. Tony's a fine American actor (going to play The Boston Strangler no less!), but what does he know about raising kids?

I'm happy to say I was powerfully proud of Joey tonight. He performed a real public service in that he had Senator Birch Bayh on. The Senator discussed the truly important job we are doing in Vietnam, that is, the job of nation building. Joey said, "This is the first time I realize we are actually building a country." I know exactly how he feels. I can't get over it either. "Do you see a way out?" Joey asked, in that thoughtful, puzzled way he has. "Do you see a negotiating table?" Well, of course, Senator Bayh doesn't have all the answers (even the President doesn't have *all* the answers), but he really thrilled me, looking directly at the camera, urging our allies out there to "get the job done." As Senator Bayh indicated, we have the inspiration of Indonesia to look at: "You have to say the Indonesians did a very good job of rooting out communism, although not in a way we would perhaps recommend. Our presence, however, gave the Indonesians the courage to do this."

I think this is true. So much so that, frankly, I'm surprised the same thing hasn't happened in China.

January 30: My three favorite frozen dinners are Temple's Chicken Chow Mein without noodles, with Shrimp Egg Roll and Fried Rice, Patio Beef Enchilada Dinner, including two enchiladas with beef chili gravy, re-fried beans and three beef tacos, and Swanson's three-course Turkey Dinner, including Campbell's cream of tomato soup, turkey with gravy, Pepperidge Farm dressing, whipped potato, peas in butter sauce and, for dessert, apple crisp. I used to eat dinner early to be finished for Merv. This year I started eating late *with* Merv, and it's much better, it's not like eating alone. Ann Miller, remember her? The dancer in the movies of the forties? She has some gams. She's auditioning for Auntie Mame. You could have knocked me over with a feather. Stars *audition*? I asked myself. "Stars audition?" Merv asked. "Oh sure," Ann replied. I was glad the question didn't bother her, because it implies that she's not really such a big star anymore. But Merv is such a nice fellow he can get away with it.

Some other old-timers were on. Gabe Dell and Huntz Hall did an old routine that Huntz used to do with Leo Gorcey when they were Dead End Kids. *Trance? Oh, I thought you said dance.* Gabe, Huntz and Jack Carter got to cutting up, and finally Merv had to shout, "Shut up! It's my show!," just to get a word in. Frankly, I think Merv lets his guests go too far sometimes. Guests are just like kids, you have to let them know where the limits are. Merv is too permissive.

Joey was very serious tonight, with an edifying discussion of capital punishment. Sammy Davis, Jr., and Ben Gazzara were with him. Ben is against it. Joey handled the topic with typical thoughtfulness and puzzlement. "Now what do you do with someone, a cold-blooded killer? What becomes then the deterrent? Now, mind you, I am not for capital punishment, but by taking the other side we can have a discussion." Ben said he thought we should turn our prisons into hospitals, and Sammy said, "Most of the psychopathic murders, when you check back into their case history, there has been a need for psychiatric help." Then they talked about the conditions in the prisons. Ben said, "The homosexuality, the cruelty, it's incredible." "It's frightening," Joey said, "it really is." At least with capital punishment, I felt like saying, you don't have any of that, but there was a commercial then. After it, Sammy explained the reason for capital punishment. "It's all part of our society's emotional—now please don't think I'm being frivolous when I say this—*hang-up.*" Ben agreed. "They never lay on 'turn the other cheek.'" That's really true. How Christian is our society when you come down to it? But you can't just coddle criminals nevertheless. Joey represented this other view: "What I'm talking about is, should they be analyzed, right? Do you honestly think we could reach a point where we could categorize the people. . . . Well, I must say, in all honesty, that I can agree . . . but somehow, you know. . . ." Frankly, I still haven't made up my own mind.

January 31: I live in a single room with a kitchenette. The bathroom is down the hall. I watch Merv on the portable set in the kitchenette and I watch Joey and Johnny on the big set in the living room. I'm saving up for a color set. When the ads come, I switch back and forth. Sometimes they both have ads at the same time. Usually I try Les Crane at that point, or Joe Pyne. But they have such creeps and oddballs I get mad as hell. Dope addicts, topless go-go dancers. American Civil Liberties Union, people of that type.

Tonight Merv introduced Arthur Treacher this way: "You all know Westminster Crabby . . . uh, Abbey." Cute. I've also heard him say, "The Leaning Tower of Sardi's," "The Geritol Guru." Arthur takes it all in good fun. He's quiet, he doesn't say too much. After all, he's seventy-three, almost seventy-four, he's been around, not like Joey's sidekick Regis Philbin. Regis is just a kid, always hopping around and kidding, sometimes he's downright disrespectful to Joey, sometimes I feel like giving him a slap and telling him to sit down and behave. Ed McMahon's all right, he's a straight guy. Johnny always kids him about his drinking. Merv does that with Arthur, too. I'm surprised they talk about it in public so easily.

Merv played a game tonight, getting people in the audience to portray different emotions. They're pretty lousy at it. But having to turn on emotions like that, that could be very difficult. It gives you an insight into how hard acting is.

Merv played the piano. He sings too. I guess of the three he's the most talented. The others are only comics. But that takes talent too. Hermione Gingold was on, wearing a frilly blouse that she called a shirtwaist, and Merv said, "You have a short waist?" She didn't answer that. Hermione read from an item in the *Washington Post* that got me annoyed. It seems the Army has a plan for an elephant drop over Vietnam, to parachute four three-ton elephants into South Vietnamese villages after being injected with an experimental drug M-99. It seems that under the influence of this drug the elephants expel flatulent gases. The code name of the operation is Baroom. Frankly, I'm all for supporting our boys, but this seems like it won't do too much good at all, a total waste of tax money.

February 1: Johnny brought his car in tonight and boy, was that a mistake. He had to park it on East Forty-eighth Street. In Passaic. Johnny had a wrestling match with his first guest, a former professional wrestler. George Burns was on with Joey. George grew up in the Lower East Side of New York. He lived on Rivington Street and had a sister named Goldie. I didn't know he was Jewish. He doesn't look Jewish.

February 5: I'm very proud and happy to announce that Merv won an award as a Starmaker by the TV writers and critics, and Johnny was nominated for an award. I had a lump in my throat. A man brought Merv the award in a paper bag. That was a cheap touch. It should have been in a wrapped box. And what about Joey, for that matter?

Tonight I noticed that Arthur wears suspenders. Aliza Kashi was on. Merv calls her "the darling of the desert." She reminds me of Yvonne Constant. They're both pretty, both from foreign countries, and both have funny ideas. Eva Gabor is like that, too. All the shows like to have that kind of guest. They usually have a singer, a girl, a couple of entertainers and maybe a serious guest, like an author. I like the serious guests best, they give you good insights.

Merv got Aliza a little mad, I think, when he mentioned she has blue veins in her legs. She was about to sing, and she got up from the stool and went to his desk and said, "Even if it's true you shouldn't say it." Well, he means it in a nice way, but I think she's right. He got out of it graciously though. "Yours are nice," he told her, "they spell out Aliza." Charlie Manna was on. Ultra Violet was on. She's a kook, what they call an Undergraduate Film Star. Aliza didn't like her at all. "What are you doing now that you can tell us about?" Aliza inquired oh so sweetly. Boy, women sure are something. Merv was joshing Ultra, too. If he thinks the audience doesn't like someone, he'll do that. He got her to stand up and scream at the top of her voice. Then he looked at the audience with a straight face, you know, and said, "Boy, aren't we having fun." Listen, if somebody's a kook and wants to make a fool of himself in public, that's his business. Merv doesn't *make* them come on, does he? Roy Cohn was on. He was Senator Joe McCarthy's sidekick that looks like a bloodhound. Merv recalled the Army-McCarthy hearings. "Was it that Senator McCarthy wanted to prove the Army was riddled with Communists? I don't think I missed a day of it, Roy. *Were* Communists found in the Army?" You bet there were. Roy mentioned one or two.

Roy also put his finger on the important fact of the cold war that few people realize: "They're not willing to fight us fairly." Amazingly, Roy was only twenty-six when he was chief counsel. That's young for chief counsel, and yet events have borne out his beliefs. "Since the fall of Cuba, Vietnam, North Vietnam, and of course the Philby case, it seems Senator McCarthy had something after all." Roy explained that Joseph Welch, the Army lawyer, "was just a great actor," and in crying "was going for the jugular. McCarthy had a poor television personality and that's a poor way to judge a public figure." I would agree with that. I would certainly never judge Roy by the way he appears on television, that wouldn't be fair. I recently noticed in the papers that he's been having legal difficulties. I wonder if the government is just being vindictive. Roy says that in retrospect he would do it over again. "But I only hope that with the added years I would do it better."

Johnny was on vacation tonight. Harry Belafonte is subbing for him.

Joey gave us a chance to see what the prompter cards look like. He does that a lot, shows us the "backstage" picture of the studio. He even talks to the stagehands. The floor manager's name is Mr. Bernhardi. Paul is one of the propmen who often appears. Joey tells him, "You stay over there, Paul, because if you go on camera you got to be paid." Joey is very nice to his associates. Even when he teases Regis he does it with a laugh, as if to say he doesn't mean it. "I want to tell you how nice it is being on the Regis Philbin Show," he'll say, or, "How would you like to be the announcer on *Death Valley Days?*" Joey doesn't even like to cut off a guest who stinks. "Gee," he'll say, "I want to be fair to my next guest." Joey has come a very long way from a poor boyhood in South Philadelphia, which can account for his humbleness.

February 6: I see Merv is trying out the turtleneck-sweater style. He wouldn't last long wearing that at Beldon, Frick & Peabody. Jack Carter told some good jokes. He's an old friend, of course. He was born in Brighton Beach, Coney Island, and his parents used to hit him over the head. Jack went into the audience and gave Miss Miller a kiss. She's the lady who's such a dedicated fan. "Isn't she cute?" Jack expostulated. "Look how she gave up Jack Paar for you?" There's a name out of the past. I used to watch Jack all the time. According to my records, his last *Tonight Show* was March 30, 1962. Here's some more interesting data and facts from my records. Johnny's first show was October 1, 1962. Other hosts of *The Tonight Show* between Jack and Johnny include—guess who? Merv and Joey. Miss Miller has a pale appearance. She wears big thick glasses. She is a real faithful person. I would like to meet her someday.

Jack Carter was quite active today. He went into the audience to kiss Miss Miller, he took off his snap-brimmed hat and squashed it on Merv's head, he played with the boom mike, calling it a Hebrew National bologna, and finally leaped at Merv and pinched his cheek. "Oh, I adore you," he shouted. "Let me see if there's a real person under there." He was only joking, of course.

February 13: Johnny's back! Of course, the show is originating in California, so it isn't exactly like it usually is. The set is different. At first it bothered me. I really felt like I was in a strange house. I kept wanting to get up and say, "Excuse me, but is this Johnny Carson's?" But after a while I got used to it. There's a lot of greenery. Behind Johnny there's a real California vista, a row of open windows and a view of Los Angeles at night. In front of the guest couch there are two coffee tables, a nice homey touch. I think I'll try that with my couch. Johnny's desk is really grand, with ornate Spanish carving. Joey's desk takes second place now.

A rodeo rider named Larry Mahan was on. He had a rig with him to simulate bronc riding. It was a barrel with a saddle tied onto it, and it was slung up by four ropes. Behind it was a typical Western street, like in movies. Johnny tried it and fell right off. Ed tried it and he fell off. Well, sir, it was a ball. Ray Bolger was on. You wouldn't believe that man is sixty-four years old. Shari Lewis was on. She's a ventriloquist who wears a boa around her neck, with a face of Eva Gabor at one end and Phyllis Diller at the other. Her dress was slit almost to the waist on both sides. The front of the dress went between her legs and attached right onto the back of the dress, just like those continual roll towels they have in men's rooms. Andrew McLaglen was on, he's Victor McLaglen's son and a Hollywood director in his own right. He's six feet seven inches tall, three inches taller than Ed McMahon. Andrew staged a typical Hollywood Western-saloon fight starring Johnny. It was a real brawl and only afterward they admitted a stunt man took Johnny's place halfway through. Listen, they have to be careful, he's a big star. Suppose he got hurt? He's always doing things, handling snakes, going up in a hot-air balloon, they have to be careful.

Joey doesn't participate like that, much. But he goes into the audience and kisses old ladies. Sometimes Regis goes with him and they both kiss old ladies. The old ladies often bake cakes for Joey. Johnny also has comedy routines like The Great Karnak, in which he gives the questions after Ed McMahon tells him the answers, and The Mighty Carson Art Players, which performs funny skits. He goes into the audience and asks people to give song titles for the band to guess. Merv has a few games, like enacting emotions, or finishing the sentences. He'll go into the audience and say to a man, "I wish my wife would . . ." Once the man said, ". . . go home." The wife wished her husband would "give me more money." It's all in good fun, but maybe Merv shouldn't have said to Arthur, "Now we know what this marriage is all about." But he's so nice, he can get away with things like that.

February 21: This was old friends' night all the way around. Merv had Hermione on and she went into the audience to talk to Miss Miller. She wanted to write a book based on Miss Miller's life. Hermione said, "We'll cook up something that will make *Valley of the Dolls* look sick." "Oh," said Miss Miller, "I've had a drab life." And she said, "Men are the cause of all women's problems." I would certainly have to disagree with that one. In my view, women are the cause of all men's problems. Who gave who the apple? Who tempted who? Remember what Tertullian wrote: "Do you not know that you are each an Eve? . . . You are the Devil's gateway." Miss Miller sees a show every night. She lives at the Hotel Holland. Maybe I'll drop her a note and introduce myself. Maybe we could go together to some of the shows.

So that was one old friend. Joey had another, the great, the one and only Sammy Davis, Jr. Uncle Miltie was hosting the opening night of the movie *Half a Sixpence*. It was a glamorous Hollywood opening night. Joey was his usual modest self. "You know what bothers me?" he told Regis. "We're not worthy of it. It's such a big show." He had Sammy, Carol Channing, Uncle Miltie, Carol Burnett, Robert Merrill, and others. Walter Matthau on with his lovely family. Uncle Miltie taught Walter's five-year-old son to talk. He would say, "Kid you're reading that paper upside down," and the boy would reply, "You think it's easy?" Kids like a dad to do that. I never could.

February 22: Saw Mrs. McIlhenny on Broadway. She wanted to stop and talk but I hurried on. Don't want her getting ideas. A woman like that, divorced, with kids, you say a kind word and right away she wants to have a relationship. Joan Crawford was on with Merv. She is very careful about cleanliness. Merv calls her Mrs. Clean, and Van Johnson calls her Mrs. Ajax. When she goes to a hotel room she scrubs the bathroom on her hands and knees. I wonder why anybody would be *that* worried about dirt? I have a little headache. Roger Ray has played Atlantic City twenty-one years in succession. There's a University of Southern Nevada in Las Vegas. Merv asked Miss Crawford about her youthful experiences. There was a long pause. Finally she said, "All I wanted to do was dance." She was very poor. Joey was very poor. George Burns was very poor. Miss Crawford said she'd talk about anything but religion and politics. That really took me back to the days when Hollywood stars had glamour. Mickey Rooney is starring in a movie which I believe he said is called "The Extraordinary Semen." That shows what movies are coming to. Jackie Mason always wants to be serious. Joey told him, "On my show you're serious, then you'll go on Ed Sullivan and be funny." Johnny used to do magic. His mother used to give away the punch line. She'd say, "Do the trick where you bring the card out of your pocket." Hermione wears harlequin glasses for reading purposes. Peg Leg Moffit is a Negro who dances on a peg leg. There's a law against raising peacocks in Beverly Hills because they shriek. Took a couple aspirin. Headache a little better. Merv called his final guest "one of the most famous women in her field in the world." Dr. Rose Franzblau. Never heard of her, but she was very penetrating. "Adolescents have had problems through the ages," she said. That was certainly true of my son Jimmy. I haven't heard from him since he got married and moved to California. His kid must be in high school by now. He must be real big. "Physiology means the onset of puberty," Dr. Franzblau explained. That was certainly true of Jimmy.

In Hollywood you can stage a big fistfight in a saloon in three or four days. Because of State Department regulations many eligible Jews were not allowed in during World War II, and many of them perished. They are planting trees in the John F. Kennedy Memorial Forest in Israel in Joey's name. He's a great humanitarian. I knew *he* was Jewish. He *looks* Jewish. When Henry Cabot Lodge was a young reporter, President Coolidge had a pretty secretary. "You're very comely, very personable," President Coolidge told her. "I tell you this to put you in a good humor so that you'll be more careful about your spelling in the future." There was a price on Henry Cabot Lodge's head in Vietnam. It was just part of the risk of being Ambassador. But he can say this, we've accomplished a great deal there. Eva Gabor went up in a parachute in a bikini. Six little Mexican boys grabbed her. She was never so happy in her life. President Johnson is having Duke Ellington over to play for the President of Liberia. Dr. Franzblau feels that man has seven chances to correct his errors. I don't know. I just don't know. My head hurts.

February 26: Have resigned from Beldon, Frick & Peabody. What an outrage! Those people don't know how to talk to their most trusted and

A. A young Johnny in 1968.   B. The more mature Johnny of today.

loyal employees. The hell with them. I have some money tucked away. The hell with the rude subway guards too. I have to say that Joey is probably one of the most kindly men in show business. But Johnny's collar is the widest. Also, his plants seem healthiest. Merv doesn't pick the newcomers on the show. Bob Shanks and a very able staff do. Charlie Manna is one of our cleverest young friends. The third guest sits to the left of Johnny in a chair all his own. Merv's third guest is the first one on the couch, the one who makes Arthur get up and move. James D. Watson was only twenty-five when he discovered DNA. That's very young to discover DNA. You can't judge him by his television personality. DNA is just like an electron, it isn't worth anything. It's just science. Molecules are tall and thin. James D. Watson is tall and thin. Anne Heywood was sitting next to a writer at a party. He turned to her and said, "You're my March." So she got the role in *The Fox.* She flipped over the role. Clair and McMahon are an attractive young comedy team who accepted a job writing a funny toilet-paper commercial. Carol Channing saw Joey at The Factory the other night. He was dancing the Funky Broadway. Bill Holden knows a couple of tribal chiefs.

Andrew Pollock does Merv's wardrobe. Diahann Carroll opened at The Plaza and her straps broke. Her top came down. Her bra showed. Some critics thought she did it on purpose. Gypsy Rose Lee wears a Ranger Rick ring that whistles when you blow it. Gypsy Rose has forty birds in her dining room. Kay Starr is an Indian. Arthur is not. He's not going to tell analysts when he last wet his bed to make *them* happy. Estimates of bomb deaths at Hiroshima range from 60,000 to 250,000. Officials of Hiroshima itself estimate 240,000. Official U.S. and Japanese estimates are 78,000. Jack Douglas' Japanese wife Reiko is so cute, she doesn't understand English too well. She doesn't know what means keeping up with the Joneses. I have Excedrin Headache Number

Seventy-two. Eh, Buitoni, we got more marinara. Watju mean, more marinara?

March 4: New show on at ten-thirty with Dick Cavett as host. Gave it a try. Dick's a nice lad, the sort you'd want your daughter to come home with for a son-in-law. Jackie Leonard, that big, fat, loudmouthed comedian, tried to outwit him but he got back as good as he gave. Bravo, Dick! Tonight Joey gave Sammy the ultimate accolade. Called him the world's greatest entertainer. The February 24th issue of *TV Guide*, with Joey on the cover, hit an all-time circulation high of 14,620,940. Bravo, Joey! My headaches have gone away. I'm fit as a fiddle now. Don Rickles' dad, rest his soul, used to tell Don that to be a success he should be different. His goal is never to hurt somebody but to laugh at ourselves. Joey thinks that every once in a while it is a delight to see the serious side of Don Rickles. I agree. Bravo, Don! Leo De Lyon is able simultaneously to whistle *Blue Skies* and hum *My Funny Valentine*. Bravo, Leo! Abbe Lane just had an eight-pound, four-ounce baby. Congratulations, Abbe. Bobby Rydell is an old pal of Joey's from South Philadelphia. He calls everybody sir. Good lad.

My days are so full now. And to think I used to fear retirement. Nonsense. Sometimes I lean back and close my eyes, and the voices, the voices, the beautiful voices. They sound so close by. So real.

7. HEEERE'S JOHNNY!
by Peter Schrag

Peter Schrag has a more objective, if just as jaundiced, view of the talk-show syndrome. This analysis appears in *MORE* in 1975.

There are still a lot of people in this country who have never participated in a radio or television talk show—either as host, guest, or as one of those muffle-voiced telephone callers ("Hello, Sunny Hills, you're on the air")—but their number must be dwindling rapidly. Seasons come and go, but Talk runs on forever: Heeere's Johnny, Merv, Mike, Tom, Kup, Steve, David, Pat, Nat, Regis, Dorothy, Nancy, Barbara, Bea, Bill, Bob, Betty, and maybe a thousand others, gobbling up guests, pinning a mike on them, and spitting them out during the commercials. In a typical recent week in San Francisco, I could have treated my calloused ears to Jason Robards, Florence Henderson, Paul Williams, Kaye Ballard, Freddy Fender, Percy Knauth, Sally Quinn (twice), Midge MacKenzie, Roberta Flack, Robert Moses, Anthony Sampson, John Rubino, Marilyn Patel, Shelley Winters, Maya Angelou, Orson Bean, Sonny Griffith, Alex Comfort, Truman Capote, Dick Van Dyke, Perla Meyers, Cleveland Amory, Martin Brown, Maharishi Mahesh Yogi, Burt Reynolds, and maybe fifty others. I still don't know who some of these people are, and never will, but somewhere along the way I learned that Meyers is a chef who wrote a book called *The Peasant Kitchen* and that Rubino is a pumpkin sculptor.

For all that apparent variety, media talk emits a sort of constant hum in which all things are more or less equal: diets, dogs, rape, flower arrangements, the financial problems of New York City, the comeback of a half-forgotten pop singer, the marriages of a Hollywood actor, Don Rickles' last week in Vegas (on the talk shows, people are perpetually flying in from Vegas), the new production of the local dance company, the book on Jerry Ford, the book on biofeedback, the book on money. There are, of course, the different styles and tones of the hosts—their different levels of indifference: Kup isn't Carson, and Merv isn't Mike, and none of them bears much resemblance to serious interviewers like Studs Terkel in Chicago or Mike Beeson in San Fran-

cisco or Harrison Salisbury when he served as moderator of the now-
defunct "Behind the Lines" or (on the other hand) to those dreary
people who smother the foreign press on public television. Sycophancy
still reigns here and there on local outlets, fawning over last year's
primal screamer and this week's diet doctor, while, in Carson's studio
in Burbank, the cosmetic cynicism of the three-million-dollar man
transforms all the world's agonies into a disposable string of one-liners.
Earl Butz jokes aren't funny to those who can't afford the food, and
welfare jokes don't generate a lot of laughs among the poor. It is not
(as in more primitive days) *our* problems we are laughing away, the
cynicism of the victim about the exploiter, it is *their* problems, comfort
cutting misery down to size. The message seems clear: no need to feel
guilty, everybody is ripping somebody off.

In the end, the sycophant and the cynic are the same person anyway,
and the collective effect is to raise or reduce everything to the level of
that hum. Even the best—the most probing, the most honorable, the
most committed—are somehow contaminated by the calculated indifference of the rest. "Mr. Carson alone presides over our consciousness,"
wrote John Leonard a few weeks ago in *The New York Times.* "Whereas
Ed Sullivan (by way of comparison with the variety shows of the fifties)
sought excuses to celebrate, Johnny Carson is crystallized cynicism."
On the night after Leonard's piece appeared, Carson and his announcer,
Ed McMahon, began their program with allusions to what the audience
could only assume was a highly flattering article in that morning's
Times, and Carson modestly acknowledged the applause.

No need to argue that Leonard was right about Carson; Carson himself slapped him with the confirmation. Dick Cavett, the last serious
challenger for the crown, was dropped by ABC because he managed
too often to commit himself to his guests and subject, to value things
for what they were, and thus not only to take attention from himself
but to block the trivializing escapes through which Carson leads his
audience. Cavett played the country boy awestruck by the new world
around him; Carson is the post-industrial slicker who has the goods on
everything, and who knows that the only thing that matters is appearances. TV talk now exists in his chilling shadow.

What seems most notable about that chilling effect, however, is
neither its cynicism nor its casual vulgarity (which, as in a recent Merv
Griffin conversation about diets, tends to sink ever deeper into its own
excremental innuendos) but the underlying emptiness which gives them
rise. The big newspaper gossip columnists have nearly all been replaced
by the talk shows—the most recent casualty was Joyce Haber's Hollywood column in *The Los Angeles Times*; after mediatalk gets through
with the celebrities there isn't much for the writers. Yet the electronic
replacements are not merely substitutes for people like Haber or Hedda
Hopper or Louella Parsons; in embracing what purport to be serious
matters in their vitiating grasp—pollution, welfare, inflation—they corrupt subjects, which the print media usually restrict to the book page
or to news columns or to other sections of (more or less) serious

treatment. In print, society and celebrity gossip tend to remain distinct from the more pressing matters; on the talk shows they are all part of the same idiom.

There are, of course, exceptions, particularly on radio, where the word rather than the personality still tends to dominate; on television, even in the presence of the most soberly respectful host, the guest is usually an ornament for the star's crown. The show goes on: if you don't want to hear this palaver about the famine in Africa, just wait a few minutes and we'll bring on the contortionist. When Ralph Nader appears on *The Tonight Show*, the real beneficiary isn't the cause of consumerism, it's Carson. Because everything is of equal worth nothing is worth anything.

I've been on that circuit myself, pushing a couple of books in which I deeply believed, basking in the hot light of borrowed fame, yet coming away with the feeling that my own work was worth no more than that of the contortionist. A few years ago I appeared on *Kup's Show* in Chicago with (among others) Leonard Woodcock of the United Auto Workers, a director and choreographer from the Joffrey Ballet, an Irish revolutionary, and Evel Knievel. Host Irv Kupcinet interviewed each of us in turn, then expected us to sit politely while the next guest did his thing. We were permitted a few conversational intrusions, but the guest who interjected anything beyond his quota was stared down by Kup's forbidding look: equal time, equal time. On other shows we operated by the End Chair Principle: the guests who didn't vanish during the commercials were moved over to make room for the new arrival, trophies to be displayed in an occasional pan shot of the set. "Would you welcome please . . ." Move down, move down.

Along the way you meet the talk-show junkies, an old acquaintance who assures you that his book and yours don't compete, and that therefore it's all right for both of you to be on the same show (I'll say something nice about you if you say something nice about me); the feminist writer with the big book who has just taken a TV make-up course and who expects to be on the circuit for four months carrying sixty dollars' worth of TV make-up in her suitcase; the old hand who reminds you to talk to the red lights on the camera, not to the host, to take the act away from him. You learn how to respond to irrelevant telephone calls on midnight radio shows and use them to turn attention to the Book (yet wondering all the time how someone sitting up at this hour to listen to this could ever be expected to read any book, let alone yours), and you begin to suspect that your contempt for the host and his shallow questions is matched only by his contempt for a string of writers, actors, and politicians willing to run to some station in the boondocks and sit up half the night trying to get a little public attention. Yet you also persuade yourself that somehow, somewhere, the message is getting through, that all this promiscuous talking has some effect.

This is the emptiness: a service is performed—some instruction in baking or cosmetics or child care, some moral edification, some opinions on Watergate or the oil companies, a few good morsels to replace village gossip, for some a whole universe of chatter for the Laundromat, perhaps even someone to call in the night with an opinion—yet the essence of the service is to fill the awful void with the sound of the human voice and the reflected glow of even the most tarnished glamour. We all meet in those studios the people on the way up, the people on the way down, the people going nowhere. But the audience isn't supposed to know that, isn't told about the differences and isn't encouraged to distinguish between the genuine and the phony. Quite the contrary. Because we are on we are all celebrities.

A few months ago, Eric Sevareid of CBS made a speech in which he took a swipe at critics who suggest that television is damaging conversation. "Nonsense," said Sevareid, "TV programs have stimulated billions of conversations that otherwise would not have occurred." It seems almost inevitable, however, that talk shows which deny or accept all things with the same indifference can teach only one thing, and that is the value and legitimacy of the form itself. Those people are something—the actors, writers, gymnasts, singers—because they are there in that studio, are on the air, and have thus been certified as people of accomplishment, influence, or talent. This is what makes junkies—the need for that fix. But how are we certified? What the show celebrates isn't the accomplishment or the talent or the intelligence, despite all pretense to the contrary; what it celebrates is the star and the certifying medium. It celebrates itself. The very informality of TV talk (though often more feigned than real) tends to emphasize the medium rather than the content. Drama, news, and sports, however trivial, violent, or silly, generally focus on some substance (though people like Cosell and the happy talkers are beginning to intrude even there); that Chancellor and Cronkite are also "personalities" created by media research and puffed by network promotion seems to me an evil incidental. But in TV talk the personality—and the medium—are the essence. I don't know what people do to get studio tickets for Carson or Douglas, but in Cincinnati the housewives wait for a year and a half to be admitted to Bob Braun's daily *50-50 Club*. His station, WLWT-TV, says it could get enough requests to fill the 250 studio seats for the next six years. They don't come to hear the visiting guest, perhaps not even to be near the star, but to touch the medium, to have their faces on the screen in that instant when the camera pans the audience, to be on. This may be the ultimate end of those billions of conversations. TV talk teaches that everything outside the view of the camera is worthless. The camera is everything. The problem isn't unique to Squeaky Fromme or Sara Jane Moore, nor does the fault lie in our stars.

8. DOCUDRAMA: FACT OR FICTION?

by Bill Davidson

Probably the most significant development in television styles in the 1970's has been the rise of docudrama. There are good economic reasons, as Bill Davidson, a veteran, explains in this *TV Guide* analysis; but ultimately the appeal of docudramas rests in their confusion of fact and fiction. They give us real life—which has a significant commodity value—in the more comfortable language of melodrama. You can have your cake and eat it too, but at what cost to our sense of the difference between reality and fiction?

I have long since reformed, but I began my career in journalism as a writer of lies for a sportscaster named Bill Stern, who, in renown at least, was the Howard Cosell of his day. Every week, another writer and I—on Stern's direction—would unabashedly make up so-called "true sports stories," mostly about historical characters who were dead and could not protest. One of my classics was about Abraham Lincoln, who, having been assassinated at Ford's Theater in Washington, regained consciousness just long enough to say to Secretary of War Stanton, "Tell General Abner Doubleday not to let baseball die." After that whopper, NBC ordered Stern to label his dramatizations "sports *legends*," but his weekly radio show continued to prosper.

Now, with the age of docudrama, "actuality drama," or whatever it may be called, the broadcasting industry seems to have come full cycle. There it was again, the word "legend," as in *The Legend of Valentino* on ABC-TV. Rudolph Valentino was introduced as a starving house-burglar (actually he began as a fairly successful hustler and movie bit player); his benefactress, June Mathis, was portrayed as a beautiful minor writer who went back to obscurity in Brooklyn to suffer her unrequited love for Valentino (actually she was fat and ugly, one of the most powerful screenwriters in the history of the movies, and much more influential than Valentino); etc., etc., etc.

But ABC at least had the good grace and honesty to label its Valentino picture "a romantic fiction." The problem is that too many other

THREE VERSIONS OF VALENTINO.

Valentino's.

Franco Nero's.

Rudolf Nureyev's.

blockbuster network docudramas *also* are tainted with romantic fiction, but, just as with Bill Stern's tall tales, they are presented to the public as essentially true stories.

In 1975, for example, NBC gave us *Eric,* about a real-life young man who died after a courageous struggle against leukemia. The two-hour film began with a flat-out statement that "this is a true story," yet the boy's name was changed, the locale of his battle for life was transposed from Connecticut and New York to the state of Washington, chronology was altered, the unpleasant but most inspiring facts of Eric's ordeal were excised, his athletic prowess as a soccer player was blatantly exaggerated in a scene just before his death, and—most inexcusable of all—there was a tender love story between Eric and a nurse named Mary Lou, which according to the boy's mother, Doris Lund, didn't happen as it was portrayed.

Earlier came *I Will Fight No More Forever* on ABC, which at first viewing seemed to be a noble, historically accurate look at the persecution of Chief Joseph and the Nez Perce Indians by the U.S. Army in the late 1870's. The show's sponsor, the Xerox Corporation, even sent out printed classroom guides for use by school children throughout the country. But then the historians were heard from. They complained that not only were there incorrect juxtapositions of time and place in the docudrama, but that even attitudes and recorded events had been distorted. For one thing, Chief Joseph's pursuer, General Oliver O. Howard, was shown as a liberal in his thinking toward Indians; but actually, at the time of the events depicted, he was one of the Army's hardliners, dedicated to the use of all means to defeat the Nez Perce. Another typical historian's complaint: the show opened with the murder of an Indian by a white settler, who later was killed in an act of vengeance by the Indian's son. Historically, a Nez Perce Indian *was* murdered, but his son's revenge was exacted not on the actual malefactor but on nineteen other innocent settlers in the area.

How about *Babe* on CBS, the "true story" of the great woman athlete Babe Didrikson and her valiant losing fight against cancer with the help of her wrestler-husband, George Zaharias? As CBS vice president Steve Mills told me, "We frankly set out to make this a warm, idyllic, unusual love story, from the facts as supplied by Zaharias himself. I guess he can't be blamed for remembering only the good things of the marriage." Unfortunately, too many sportswriters were witness to the frequent storminess of the Didrikson-Zaharias relationship and they complained, in effect, that Hollywood had made a sugarcoated Disneyized version of what essentially was an *All in the Family* conflict, with tragic overtones.

Similar accusations of truth-bending have been leveled against nearly all of the 1976 docudramas, among them *The Silence, Fear on Trial, Foster and Laurie, The Deadly Tower, Collision Course* and *Guilty or Innocent: The Sam Sheppard Murder Case.* Swipes were taken in advance at *Helter Skelter* (the dramatization of Vincent Bugliosi's book about the Charles Manson murders), *Return to Earth* (the story of astronaut Buzz Aldrin's emotional breakdown after walking on the moon) and *Farewell to Manzanar* (a personal reminiscence of our controversial concentration camps for Japanese-American citizens during World War II).

Does this mean that the docudrama is more drama than docu? Probably yes.

Are facts sometimes distorted to make a better story? Probably yes.

Is the American public deliberately being misled by representations that these films are in fact true stories? Probably yes.

My answers to all three questions are qualified because there are some extenuating circumstances in what is an ages-old conflict between hard fact and dramatic license in all forms of theater, dating back to William Shakespeare and beyond. There are no better illustrations of this problem than the two most challenged docudramas of the 1976 season: *Fear on Trial* and *Guilty or Innocent: The Sam Sheppard Murder Case,* which, incidentally, had one of the highest Nielsen ratings of any TV-movie of the season.

Fear on Trial, you will recall, was CBS's *mea culpa* about how it contributed to the anticommunist blacklisting of radio-TV personality John Henry Faulk in 1956, and his long court fight for vindication. The show, though generally praised, has been accused of selective condensation to the point where important CBS witnesses against Faulk (and on the side of the blacklisters) were eliminated. Also, there has been considerable criticism of the not-quite-accurate handling, in the docudrama, of Faulk's estranged wife, who drops out of sight midway through the script, whereas she was, in fact, in the courtroom for at least part of the trial.

David Rintels is the writer of *Fear on Trial*. He also is the respected president of the Writers Guild West. Rintels told me, "It's been a bitter, galling experience for me to be accused of falsifying facts. I had to tell a story condensing six or seven years into a little less than two hours, which means I could just barely hit the major highlights. I did what I think all writers should do—present the *essence* of the facts and capture the truth of the general story. As it was, CBS didn't come out looking too good, even though I couldn't include all the details. Attorney Louis Nizer's summation to the jury took more than 12 hours. I had to do it in three minutes.

"As for Faulk's wife, the divorce was so messy that I made the judgment call that it would be better to eliminate her from the latter stages of the story, rather than dredge up painful problems for a lot of people. I stuck to the record, except in intimate scenes for which there was no record—and that's what writers are paid to do. I'll go to my grave believing I dealt honestly with the overall facts."

The defenders of NBC's Sam Sheppard docudrama also claimed the right to winnow out the truth as they saw it, in the interests of necessarily compressed storytelling. The main beef against the film was that it overexaggerated newsmen's outrageous behavior in the courtroom *during* the trial, whereas the U.S. Supreme Court's landmark Sheppard decision had also cited "massive pretrial publicity" as an important factor bearing on the inability of the defendant to get a fair trial.

To Louis Rudolph (who wrote the story and developed the project), it made more sense dramatically to play up visible courtroom disturbances by the press rather than concentrating on the difficult-to-photograph pretrial transgressions by late columnist Bob Considine and others. "It all amounts to the same thing," he told me, "and every word we used in the disturbance sequences came out of the transcript of the trial." He admitted some exaggeration for dramatic effect, and executive producer Harve Bennett added, "We *did* select only certain scenes from the transcript for emphasis—but they were all true."

The truth. There indeed are varying versions of it, as writer Ernest Kinoy found when he wrote the script of ABC's *Collision Course* in which Henry Fonda plays Douglas MacArthur and E. G. Marshall is a credible Harry Truman. Kinoy says he faithfully followed both the MacArthur and Truman memoirs in depicting the events before and after the fateful meeting of the General and the President on Wake Island at the height of the Korean War. "But then," said Kinoy before the program was telecast, "I was faced with the meeting itself, which took place inside a Quonset hut on the island with absolutely no one else present, not even a military secretary. I made up that intrinsic key scene, based on what I knew had happened afterwards when Truman fired MacArthur. The Truman partisans have one idea of the truth of that meeting in the Quonset hut and the MacArthur admirers have their version—so undoubtedly I'll be slammed by both." He was, and apparently with good reason, because the version of the meeting that Truman developed later strayed a good distance from the facts.

John Henry Faulk loved *Fear on Trial*. After all, it was his version of what had happened. Astronaut Edwin (Buzz) Aldrin isn't quite so sure about ABC's interpretation of his inability to cope with life after leaving the space program, even though the film, *Return to Earth,* is a dramatization of his own book and he served as consultant to the TV project. Aldrin said, "On the whole, I'm satisfied with the picture, but condensation sometimes alters the truth. For example, you're left at the end thinking I'm still a mixed-up guy emotionally, when by now I'm actually recovered and coping quite well. Also, there's a romantic scene at the end in which I'm walking down a beach hand in hand with my ex-wife. It never happened that way. In fact, I'd already told her I wanted a divorce and was going to marry someone else."

Brandon Stoddard, vice president in charge of TV-movies at ABC, has his own version of the facts in the Aldrin docudrama. He told me, "In normal film structure, we'd show a man slowly falling apart, destroying his family, but fighting back and recovering. But we didn't do it that way because it didn't happen that way at that time. Aldrin then was a man suffering deep depression and I felt we *had* to show a depressive as he actually is. It doesn't help the film but it is accurate."

Of all the docudrama experts I spoke with, Stoddard made the most sense. He frankly admitted that his network does "actuality" movies

ABC's The Trial of Lee Harvey Oswald *with the "amazing Oswald look-alike, John Pleshette," presented an alternate reality: Oswald makes it past Jack Ruby in the basement (and therefore misses out on a footnote in history as the first man murdered on live television) and survives to be tried for the crime. This is a shot from the film, not the historical event. (Robert E. Thompson wrote the film, David Greene directed it.)*

because they're easier to sell to a potential audience during pre-broadcast promotion "if there are actual names and events that are familiar to people to begin with." He said, "We should not be held to the absolute truth of pure documentaries, because we're in the business of making *movies,* and audiences watch movies to be moved, to get involved with characters who live and breathe and whom you like and don't like. I'm not a reporter. If it's pure documentary you're looking for, the news department does it better. Docudramas get much higher ratings. I consider them to be historical fiction as opposed to history—and historical fiction always far outsells history at the bookstores."

Stoddard added, "On the other hand, we are very aware of the terrible danger and responsibility involved in doing our kind of historical fiction. By using dramatic license, we can take a point of view that could affect the attitudes of millions of people. For example, we have *21 Hours at Munich* in development. It's about the massacre of the Israeli athletes by Arab terrorists at the 1972 Olympics. Since we have to tell at least part of the story from the point of view of one of the Arabs, we can't create sympathy for him. We *must* get the message across that with acts of terrorism, no one wins in the end. I'm not sure it will work, and if it doesn't, we'll yank it as a docudrama."

The problem is that, given the success of the docudramas, no one in the industry is ready yet to openly label their product "historical fiction"—except possibly in the rare case of a *Legend of Valentino,* in which the truth was *so* distorted that to do otherwise would have been ridiculous. Thus, CBS's *Helter Skelter* begins with actor George Di-Cenzo saying, "You are about to see a dramatization of actual facts in which certain names have been changed. But the story is true." The story is *not* all true. At the very least, because of pending lawsuits, certain fictional adjustments had to be made.

Television experts in the academic community are justifiably disturbed. One such expert is psychologist Dr. Victor B. Cline of the University of Utah, who pioneered in studies of the effect of TV violence on children. Dr. Cline told me, "The very real danger of these docudrama films is that people take it for granted that they're true and —unlike similar fictionalized history in movies and the theater—they are seen on a medium which also presents straight news. No matter how much they call these movies 'drama,' they're really advocacy journalism. They can't help reflecting the point of view of the writer or the studio or the network. I think they should carry a disclaimer to the effect that the story is not totally true but based on some of the *elements* of what actually occurred."

But, as we learned from Orson Welles' panicking the country with his radio version of *War of the Worlds* in 1938, even that won't prevent people from believing what they see on television.

VICTIMS

9. THE MYTHOLOGIZING OF CITIZEN PATTY

by James Monaco

This *MORE* piece was written in October 1975, the middle of the Patty Hearst affair. The case has become increasingly complicated still, as the recent illustrations show.

A dozen books, three movies, a profusion of cover stories, assorted posters and buttons, several classic photos, an affidavit, even a tape transcript—just like P's, with [obscenity] deleted: these are the highlights of a rapidly growing catalogue of Pattiana. And media exploitation of the Patty Hearst Story, now in its twenty-first month, is far from over. At present, we're entering the second stage in a pattern of development that has become familiar during the last ten years: the story begins as hard news, then gets progressively soft around the edges as pens and cameras sketch in the background ("Life at the Texas Book Depository," "The Watergate Cookbook"). The second stage is commentative, focusing not on the story but on the story about the story (P yields center stage to Woodstein). Eventually, the third stage is reached: the story (and its story) are absorbed into the general stream of fact and fiction known as folk history: fan clubs are formed to discuss arcane theories and trade bits of information; anniversary articles ("Five Years Since the Tragic Murder," "The Flower Children: Where Are They Now?") are locked into future books; and pundits wax eloquent upon Significance and Historical Effect. By this time few people really care about validity or veracity. The "facts" of the first stage like the analyses of the second have become undifferentiated bits of raw material—factoids, to stretch Mailer's useful term a little—which are available to all interpreters, whether they consider themselves novelists or historians, to use as they please in their retellings of the tale.

Condemning this process of mediaization is tempting. Fortunes will be made—are being made—in the Patty Hearst Industry. For example, Roger Rapoport, a young San Francisco journalist, signed with Steven Weed for a six-figure advance. He bought a house, installed Weed (his story) in a studio in the back, only to discover that Weed's view of the story was quite different from his own. Weed quit, suing Rapoport for "sensationalizing" the couple's sex and drug habits. All Rapoport was eventually able to realize was $15,000 from a countersuit and a piece in *New Times* (March 21, 1975) about his experience with Weed (the story of the story). His agreement with Weed forbids him making any further use of the material. A novelty distributor told Dick Brass of the *New York Post*: "You just get me the rights to a good, clear picture and I'll have 100,000 'Tania for President' badges out in a week." It's not only outsiders who see dollar signs. The *Boston Globe* reports the rumor that Patty's father hopes to share in the profits from her own story in order to recoup some of the $2 million spent on the food give-away program.

Yes, there is money to be made. What else is new? It's not the merchandising of Patty Hearst that's particularly interesting, but the mythologizing of her Story—the reason there *are* profits to be made. There is no specific, intrinsic single element of the Tania saga that suggests it should be especially profitable. Most kidnappings are good for a book or two, but no more; they haven't been inordinately saleable since Leopold and Loeb first demonstrated that money isn't the only object. Nor is the Symbionese Liberation Army the only colorful guerrilla group in operation. Bank heists may be big news in France these days; not here. Fugitives? There are a dozen Weatherpeople—big news in their time—who have been surviving underground successfully since Patty was a child.

What raised the SLA-Patty Story to the level of myth was the extraordinary combination of these elements, together with thematic and dramatic twists that give it special intrigue: the small band of urban guerrillas with the symbolic name, committed to the tactic of violence; the major characters—black ex-cons and upper-middle-class young whites who had developed a romantic/mystical attachment to them; the almost melodramatic conversion of the hitherto apolitical heiress to one of the mythic fortunes of the power structure; the effective media events staged to gain the necessary public forum; the brutal deaths of most of the group in a flaming western shoot-out. If a novelist came up with a plot like this it would be judged a bit ripe; must *all* the angles be covered so thoroughly?

In fact, a novelist did produce a fictional version of the story, published a full two years before the "real" event. Grove Press's *Black Abductor,* a porn novel by an engineer from Southern California who has written over 200 pulp novels, sold moderately well when it was released in 1972. Its heroine, a young woman named Patricia who lives with her boyfriend and is a senator's daughter, is kidnapped for political ransom by a mixed group of revolutionaries—black and white, male and female. There is a lot of sex. In the end she joins the group. It must be the first case of "pre-event novelization."

So, if the Patty Hearst Story hadn't happened it not only would have had to be invented: it was. But it is not only the strongly symbolic nature of the story that suggests this necessity—journalists and film-makers, after all, are adept at supplying symbolic interpretations for even the simplest events. It is the fact that the characters inside the story think this way, as well. You don't name your group the "Symbionese" Liberation Army, you don't invent a seven-headed cobra symbol, you don't decide to capture Citizen Kane's granddaughter, you don't hold her for ransom for food rather than money, unless you are painfully aware that politics in the mid-seventies is a matter of imagery and iconography. It is no longer so important for something to have happened; it is mainly important for something to have been reported. Haskell Wexler described this phenomenon brilliantly in 1969 in his film *Medium Cool,* still a masterpiece about the relationship between film, news, and reality. "You put him on the six, the ten, *and* the twelve o'clock news," insists a black militant talking to a TV reporter about the subject of the story, "then he be real." We can even go back to Jean Genet's *The Balcony* (1959) for more abstract theories about our increasing distrust of reality and our preference for media.

Deadened by the massive assault of fiction *cum* reality in print, on film, and on TV (especially the "cool medium") we tend to trust the record of the event, even if it is staged, rather than the event itself. Jane Alpert and Pat Swinton, for example, shared a series of events— political bombings—some years ago. Alpert gave herself up last year and is now serving time. Her colleague, Swinton, was caught a while later, tried recently, and found innocent. Swinton's jury preferred to believe a different interpretation of the story the two women had once shared.

With the Patty Hearst Story we have arrived at a point where all concerned—actors, reporters, and audience—have a considerable sophistication about this new realm of the factoid, halfway between fiction and fact. There are a number of groups doing much more useful, more effective, and more admirable radical political work, but when the stories of the early seventies are turned into history chances are it will be the Symbionese Liberation Army that dominates the narrative, through sheer force of celebrity. For better or worse, the fictions they have staged will transcend the "real" work of organizing, education, and political action. Naturally, the media people recognized a good story when it was offered them. Just as naturally, the audience picked up on it. Not only was it a good "read," but one could read it so many different ways, so rich was the material the SLA troupe offered us.

The nature of that material bears further discussion. Documents are the stuff of stories and Patty and the SLA have provided an unusual range of proto-literary documents. The affidavit, for example. Ignore for the moment the question of what relationship the affidavit bears to Patricia Hearst's own experience during her ordeal. Chances are even she couldn't answer that question. The affidavit works literarily. Notice, for example, how it alludes to the use of drugs, thereby suggesting a blanket excuse for the whole story and at the same time provides—almost offhand—the element of confinement in a dark closet for weeks. That sort of confinement—even for a day—can lead to altered states of personality, a psychological fact that one of Patty's filmmakers (Bob Roberts) discovered doing research many months ago and incorporated into his version of the story (*Patty*). The affidavit suggests one explanation for Patty's state—drugs—while we discover another—the confinement. The first is a red herring, the second the *real* reason. Because we "discover" the real reason we make a personal investment in the validity of the whole narrative.

In another nice twist, Patty has given us—apparently unintentionally—the tapes recorded in jail, which make an interesting contrast not only with the affidavit but also with the tapes Tania recorded to communicate with the media audience while she was underground. The transcripts of the jail tapes which have been published read uncannily like those of "P," "E," "H" and that whole crew who made this format famous not so long ago: Patty, like P, is hiding something. P, like Patty, created his own complicated persona and then didn't know what to do with it; both were overwhelmed by their own images.

There are other intriguing raw materials: SLA's political communiqués, Patty's messages, the photographs of the bank holdup, FBI documents, lists of personal possessions (there's room too, for a story or two on Emily Harris' extensive wardrobe). All of these are provided directly, by the SLA events. But others can use the elements of the myth in their own way. The novels and films are obvious; possibly the most creative use of the myth however was the curious *Dog Day Afternoon* episode acted out in "real life" by one Ray Olsen in Greenwich Village, October 1975. Taking his form from Sidney Lumet and Frank Pierson's movie which itself was based on an incident that took place in Brooklyn several years ago, Olsen cornered ten hostages in a storefront bank, demanding in return the release of Patty, the Harrises, and, as he put it, "that Oriental woman [Wendy Yoshimura]." Olsen ensconced himself in the tiny branch bank for eight and a quarter hours and made wide use of the media attention riveted on him. He had voluble telephone conversations with local rock disk jockeys and an editor of *High Times* magazine (the drug journal), got angry when he heard on the radio that he was robbing a bank (he wanted to make it quite clear that money was not the object), and gave up at 11:15 p.m. just in time to be covered live on the 11 o'clock news. (One of the cops on the specially trained hostage squad had suggested this opportunity to him.) The networks were there with their minicams and scored what I take to be a first: live coverage of a hostage media ploy.

More germane, perhaps, are the photos and drawings of Patty that have become familiar during the last year and a half. Here is where we can see most clearly the range of significances that various media attach to the Patty Hearst Story. The first five images give us various versions of the SLA icon. This is the "Tania" shot staged by the SLA itself to announce visually Patty's new revolutionary personality. The SLA shot (1) is satisfactory, but the reenactments of it are better. In (2) we have Sarah Nicholson's version of Patty; in (3) Judith Bergan's. "Tania" dominates the frame more effectively in both and the camera angle (low) makes Tania seem both more powerful and sexier. In the Nicholson version, the cobra logo stands out better. Meanwhile, Bergan (3) humanizes Tania: the backlighting on her hair and right side glamorize her, the gun is de-emphasized and the doorway at once reinforces the image and frames her. The *New Times* cover drawing (4), meanwhile, is both more stylish and more generalized. The shadow to the right of the face and the downward curve at the corners of the mouth make artist Miggs Burroughs' Tania harder, more abstract. The driving tension of the first three images is between our sense of Patty Hearst as the petite, pampered rich kid and the tougher revolutionary costume we see. But in the *New Times* abstraction, that tension is gone and we are left with the much more simplistic, undramatic, conventional image of the woman militant, hair blowin' in the wind.

Image (5), abstracted slightly by the scan lines of the bank's surveillance video camera, is perhaps the most intriguing of this set of Tanias. Image (1) was staged, directed, and photographed by the SLA, and distributed by them. Patty Hearst was being directed in her new role. Image (5), however, is an improvisation. The SLA had staged it, but the bank shot the scene, and the FBI acted as distributor. Interestingly, this is the one major image of Tania to appear before her trial in which she is looking backward. The SLA and the filmmakers had the intuitive sense to photograph her looking "forward," to the right; but in (5), Patty/Tania has been caught hesitating, not quite so sure of her revolutionary objectives. The posture, a slight crouch, also adds to this sense of indecision. We can assume that the video record of the robbery also included frames in which Patty was looking forward. The FBI chose carefully which image to release for publication. Don't look back, Patty, they may be gaining on you.

The next four photos show an even more divergent range of interpretations—yet they are all of Patricia Hearst as herself rather than "Tania." It's significant that the candid shots of Patty herself are more various than the staged shots of Patty and the actresses who play her. (Patty often looks less like "Tania" than Judith and Sarah do. Sarah, her producer says, was once picked up by the police as a Tania lookalike.) Gordon Clark's cover for *Newsweek* (6) softens the features, the lines of the face lack the tension they once had, the raised fist is clear: this is the positive, sympathetic image of our heroine. The *Time* mugshot (7) is, of course, the negative. What is read here is the hardened, sallow sneer of the criminal. Printed in black and white, the photo's flat grayness also distances us.

Most fascinating, however, is Paul Sakuma's AP shot (8) which *The New York Times* ran three columns wide in its issue of September 20, 1975. There is real mystery here. The costume is precisely the same as in the *Newsweek* shot, yet the shirt neckband seems stretched, the shirt seems too large, the glasses seem bigger (and darker), the eyes are lost behind them, the hair is mussed, the handcuffs are shown (making the gesture of the fist seem futile), and the smile is extraordinarily ambiguous, as she bites her lower lip at the same time. Sa-

FIVE IMAGINED TANIAS

1.

2.

3.

1. *Patty Hearst as Tania, photo by the Symbionese Liberation Army. The photo was received by a San Francisco radio station in April 1974, and is now distributed by Wide World Photos, a division of the Associated Press.*

2. *Sarah Nicholson as Patty/Tania in* Patty, *directed and produced by Robert L. Roberts. (Photo: George Bernard)*

3. *Judith Bergan as Patty/Tania in* Abduction, *written and produced by Kent E. Carroll, directed by Joseph Zito. (Photo: João Fernandes)*

MAY 3, 1974 /60 CENTS · THE FEATURE NEWS MAGAZINE

NEW TIMES

The struggle
to win back
Patty: her
boyfriend
tells the
inside
story

California's
biggest drug bust

Paolo Soleri builds a Brave
New World in the desert

"Tania" Hearst

4.

4. New Times *version of the SLA Tania icon. (Artist: Migg Burroughs)*

5.

5. *Patty as Tania by Hibernia Bank surveillance camera, San Francisco, April 1974, and released by the FBI. (Courtesy of Wide World Photos) This was Patty's first public performance as Tania in a leading role. (The SLA didn't know it, but "Tania" turns out to be a fictional creation of the CIA's domestic dis-information program.)*

6. *Patty in captivity (and therefore photographable) took on two basic images, one essentially euphoric, the other apparently tragic. Newsweek's September 29, 1975, cover (photo: Gordon Clark) presented the isolated close-up of the euphoric Patty, the new star with the attractive tinted glasses and pearly smile.*

7. *Time's Patty cover, same issue date, takes the opposite tack. (Photo: San Francisco P.D.)*

ork Times

LATE CITY EDITION

Weather: Variably cloudy today, warm and humid tonight, tomorrow. Temperature range: today 62-81; Friday 59-88. Details on Page 67.

SEPTEMBER 20, 1975

30 CENTS

PATRICIA HEARST IS REFUSED BAIL PENDING HEARING

Magistrate Names Lawyers for Harrises—$500,000 Figure Set for Each

LEGAL SPARRING BEGINS

Miss Yoshimura Released to California Authorities—Fourth Suspect Held

By WALLACE TURNER

Patricia Hearst leaving San Mateo jail for a bail hearing at San Francisco courthouse

Cold Trail' Led to the Fugitives

8.

9.

8. AP photographer Paul Sakuma's shot of Patty, taken at the same time as the Newsweek *cover shot, reveals an entirely different side to the media personality.*

9. *Months later, the media had a convicted criminal to deal with and image-making became more difficult.* Newsweek *(March 29, 1976) suggested the new, more ambiguous and complex reality with this rough halftone screen.*

10.

11.

10. Patty as comic-book heroine. New Times *(March 21, 1975). Drawing by Bill Nelson. The story about the story.*

11. Patty as art object. Jamie Putnam's full-page illustration for Rolling Stone *(October 23, 1975).*

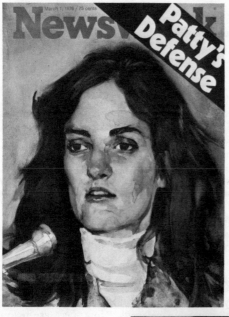

12.

13.

12. *Patty as a gothic novelist's dream. Bert Silverman's cover water-color for* Newsweek *(March 1, 1976).*

13. *The aftermath: Patty as soap-opera heroine on* The New York Times Magazine *cover (April 3, 1977).*

kuma's Tania is far more complex than the others; she is not fully in control of the situation as they are. The image, the expression, is strangely reminiscent of the preteen cartoon idol, Alfred E. Neuman.

Newsweek's March 29, 1976, cover (9) literally brands Patty "Guilty!" with tough stencil print. The very rough halftone screen (a 13 line per inch grade, rather than the usual 133) analyzes the image into its elemental components and makes us much more aware that we are not, either literally or figuratively, looking at Patty herself, but at a media reproduction. Patty has been translated into the code of the press. The colors of the image (the word "GUILTY!" is in white, the *Newsweek* logo in yellow, and the photograph itself in dark orange and black) also suggest the brashness of the yellow-journalistic charade that was Patty Hearst.

Now the point of all this is not to suggest that these photographers were carefully composing insightful and telling portraits, nor that their editors chose these shots for specifically ideological reasons (although in the cases of SLA and *Time,* this is obviously true), but rather that the fictional materials are malleable: we can read them any way we want.

If they seem to clash, that's our problem as readers. In truth, there is no such woman as Patty Hearst any longer. She ceased to exist in February of 1974 when she became a celebrity. Now there are many Pattys, and Patty/Tanias, and Tanias, defendants and revolutionaries, SLA militants and loving daughters, fugitives and homebodies, feminists and bankrobbers, acid freaks and cute kids, affidavit-swearers and tape actors. If she was brainwashed by the SLA, she was also brainwashed by the Hearsts. She doesn't even employ her own lawyer. Choose your brainwasher and any action of hers from now on becomes immediately explicable within the bounds of whichever particular Patty Story you prefer. The Hearst family have been image-builders— icono*plasts*—for three generations. Patty's grandfather just about invented a war, quite an accomplishment. The SLA are new to the game: all they've done so far is to invent a Tania. But the Hearsts and the SLA are well matched: a productive if stormy marriage of mythmakers.

The romanticization of Patty began early on, with *New Times'* cartoon cover of March 21, 1975 (10). In October of that year, *Rolling Stone* ran a portrait by Jamie Putnam (11) which remains the most effete attempt to mold the image of Patty in sentimental terms. Putnam's painting parodied Patty as the heroine of Andrew Wyeth's pop classic, "Christina's World." Did *Rolling Stone* mean to suggest she, like Christina, was a cripple?

As the Patty persona became increasingly complicated with the approaching trial, the news media found it necessary to simplify it in more traditionally fictional ways. *Newsweek's* March 1, 1976, cover (12) gave us a soft-featured, romantic heroine seen from a relatively low, and therefore heroic, angle, who would not have been out of place on the cover of a gothic novel: heroine Patty bearing up stoically under the slings and arrows of outrageous fortune. One of the last media images in the continuing Patty saga, *The New York Times Magazine*'s cover for April 3, 1977 (13), suggested a beaten Patty, fuzzy, grim, tired, and—like many of the post-arrest Pattys—no longer optimistically looking ahead, but rather facing backward. Since we tend to read images from left to right, these Pattys turn in on themselves, suggest narrative dead ends, rather than opening up to the infinite possibilities beyond the right-hand margin of the images.

Perhaps the best way to describe all the Pattys we now have at our disposal is to use the parallel narrative technique that Orson Welles employed in his portrait of her grandfather thirty-five years ago. There was no single Kane in the mythic American movie; there were many, and all of them were set in the framework of mediated reality—the newsreel. "If the headline is big enough," Kane declared, "it *makes* the news big enough!"

Pattiana

BOOKS

Avery, Paul, and Vin McLellan. *The Voices of Guns.* New York: Putnam's, 1976.

Baker, Marilyn, and Sally Brompton. *Exclusive! The Inside Story of Patty Hearst and the SLA.* New York: Macmillan, 1974.

Belcher, Jerry, and Don West. *Patty-Tania.* New York: Pyramid Books, 1975.

Bryan, John. *This Soldier Still at War.* (Joe Remiro and the SLA.) New York: Harcourt Brace Jovanovich, 1975.

James, Harrison. *Black Abductor.* ("Prenovelization" of the Hearst kidnapping and transformation. Source for the film *Abduction.*) New York: Grove Press, 1972. Reprinted as *Abduction.* New York: Dell, 1975.

Pascal, Francine, and John Pascal. *The Strange Case of Patty Hearst.* New York: New American Library, 1974.

Payne, Les, *et al. The Life and Death of the SLA.* New York: Ballantine, 1976.

Pearsall, Robert B. *The Symbionese Liberation Army: Documents and Communications.* Atlantic Highlands, N.J.: Humanities Press, and Forest Grove, Ore.: International Scholarly Book Services, 1974.

Reeves, Kenneth J. *The Trial of Patty Hearst.* San Francisco: Great Fidelity Press, 1976.

Ritz, Rosalie. *The Lady and the Lawyers.* San Francisco: Anthelion Press, 1976.

Weed, Steven, and Scott Swanton. *My Search for Patty Hearst.* New York: Crown (cloth) and Warner Books (paper), 1976.

Also: The two most highly publicized book exploitations of the Hearst affair—those by columnist Shana Alexander and *Rolling Stone* writers David Weir and Howard Kohn—have yet to see the light of print. Alexander's contract with Viking is still pending more than three years after it was signed.

FILMS

Abduction. 1975. Director: Joseph Zito. Writer/producer: Kent E. Carroll. Cinematographer: João Fernandes. With: Judith Bergan, Dorothy Malone, Leif Erickson, David Pendleton, Gregory Rozakis, Lawrence Tierney. Rating: R. The most reputable of the filmed versions of Patty's story. Harrison James' Grove Press book served as the basis for the film.

Patty. 1975. Producer/director: Bob Roberts. Writers: Bob Roberts, Judy Smyth. Cinematographer: Henry Smolowitz. With: Sarah Nicholson, Lenny Montana, Turk Turpin. Rating: X. A hard-porn version of the story to counter Carroll and Zito's soft-porn film.

Snatched. 1975. Producer/director/writer: Robert Mitrotti. Cinematographer: João Fernandes. With: Jody Ray, Rebecca Brooks, Robert Furey, Phil Bendone. Rating: R.

TELEVISION

As yet Patty and the SLA have not reached the small screen, although Paddy Chayefsky suggested the potential of such a show in his film *Network,* in which a group not unlike the SLA stars in a show that does wonders for Faye Dunaway's career.

10. THE KENT STATE GIRL: AN AMERICAN TRAGEDY

produced by Suzanne St. Pierre, reported by Morley Safer

In January 1977, CBS's *60 Minutes* ran this incisive report on the present condition of MaryAnn Vecchio, a young woman who was iconized in the famous Kent State photo of 1970. Vecchio's saga is considerably simpler than Hearst's, but no less significant.

MORLEY SAFER: This is the story of a small American tragedy that we learned about because of a greater American tragedy. On May 4th, 1970, four students were killed and nine wounded when National Guardsmen opened fire on the campus at Kent State University. By May 5th, this photograph had been flashed from the small Ohio campus to every newspaper in the world. Later, it would win a Pulitzer prize. To millions of people it represented something—this moment of grief for an American coed, MaryAnn Vecchio, as she wept over the body of an American student, Jeffrey Miller.

[*Sounds from automatic camera.*]

The photograph may have become a symbol of the tragedy of Vietnam, and the tragedy of America. In fact, MaryAnn Vecchio was not a coed at Kent State, not a war resister, not symbolic of anything. MaryAnn Vecchio was a fourteen-year-old runaway, hitchhiking from nowhere to nowhere, who found herself that afternoon on the campus at Kent State.

[*Film footage of National Guard at Kent State—shooting and sirens.*]

How come it was you, kneeling over that boy?

VECCHIO: I guess I just—I just cared for him. I didn't really at the time know what death was. I— You know, except for my grandmother I'd seen in a funeral. But I've never seen a person get shot. And I just was scared. And after I realized what happened, I had—I had just ran —just kept running.

SAFER: How did you get to Kent State? Why did you go to Kent State?

VECCHIO: It was somewhere out of Opa-Locka.

SAFER: But you didn't even know you were going there?

VECCHIO: Right. It—it— I guess, in my— At the age I was, it didn't really matter where I went. You know, it was just the fact of going and traveling and meeting people. And I just left a little earlier than some people.

SAFER: Somewhere out of Opa-Locka. Opa-Locka sits and decays on the edges of suburban Miami, neither prosperous nor poor. It is a place that just happened. Fifty-odd years ago someone had the bright idea of building an Arabian Nights community—one of those ideas that seemed fun at the time. But now the fantasy flakes away on the flat plain of southern Florida. There are hundreds of Opa-Lockas in America. And in the sixties there were thousands of MaryAnn Vecchios. A fourteen-year-old nobody, caught up in the drift of the sixties. And on May 4th, 1970, in the split second it takes to snap a picture— [*sounds of automatic camera*]—from Tokyo through Moscow, through Paris and London and Washington and Opa-Locka, MaryAnn Vecchio became somebody.

PHILLIP VITELLO [*lawyer*]: She was a runaway before. She's had social problems before. She was a maladjusted kid before. But in all her limited experience, she was not prepared for the deluge of newspapers and wire services and magazines and authors that descended upon her in a quest to embroil her in this political tragedy at Kent State.

SAFER: That picture had made MaryAnn Vecchio a material witness to murder. Her lawyer was Phillip Vitello.

VITELLO: The Special Commission from the Ohio Grand Jury questioned her. And they asked her what a Communist was. And she said, "Well, everyone knows that's a bad person."

SAFER: The tragedy of Kent State and of MaryAnn Vecchio was now becoming absurdity. The then-governor of Florida wondered what part she played in a conspiracy.

GOVERNOR KIRK: I would like the Justic Department to determine if there is a nationally organized conspiracy, of professional agitators. And moreover, if such a conspiracy does exist, how does it relay information? And does it attempt to attract and lure fourteen- and fifteen-year-old girls?

SAFER: She suddenly became something worth interviewing. The networks sought her out. It was as if this fourteen-year-old could answer the questions to Kent State. And she even tried.

VECCHIO: Everybody's dying, because we're killing ourselves. And yet the people over at Vietnam, they get—they're charged with manslaughter and murder and things like that. And yet they're not being, you know—anything to do with it. I can't explain it that much.

SAFER: And if she was worth interviewing, she was worth hating. Show me some of the letters.

VECCHIO: Here's one saying, "You hippie Communist so-and-so!" Let's see . . .

SAFER: "You hippie Communist bitch! Did you enjoy sleeping with all those dope fiends and Negroes while you were in Ohio? The deaths

John Filo's Pulitzer prize-winning photograph of MaryAnn Vecchio
and the body of Jeffrey Miller, "a symbol of the tragedy of Vietnam,
and the tragedy of America." Interestingly, the sixteen other figures in
the photograph are surprisingly disinterested. There's little sense of
drama in their postures. None of them are looking at Miller's body
(although the young man with the headband, second from left, is looking at the photographer taking the picture). They are walking slowly in
various directions, or standing, looking off into various distances. The
drama of the shot is the direct result of Vecchio's Pieta-like posture
(even Miller's body is visually undramatic). The irony of the photograph—and the quality which makes it a rich image of political
realities—lies in this seemingly undramatic setting. It wasn't the way it
was, but it looks as if Miller and Vecchio's symbolic tragedy is taking
place almost privately, in the midst of a society that cares even less
than it sees. (Photo: John Filo, for the Valley News Dispatch, Taren-
tum, Pa.)

of the Kent State Four lies on the conscience of yourself and other subhuman rabble-rousers like you." Unsigned.

VECCHIO: Most of these were unsigned.

SAFER: You got these when you were—what?

VECCHIO: Fourteen. Things like "Mary, you dirty tramp, it's too bad it wasn't you that was shot. Your kind make it look bad for all teens. A good teen." "What you need is a good beating with the strap, beaten until you bleed, good red blood."

SAFER: The Vecchio family kind of enjoyed the publicity, the notoriety. A West Coast outfit went into the MaryAnn Vecchio T-shirt business. Her father got a court injunction and tried to get a piece of the T-shirt action himself.

You know, when I read the MaryAnn Vecchio story, I read the newspaper clippings and I look at the old film and the magazine articles, and I come away with one very strong conclusion: that you were used. In the sense, the photographer used you. Television used you. We're using you right now, I suppose. The governor of the state used you; said that at fourteen you were a part of some Communist conspiracy. Your own father used you; got a lawsuit, trying to get a piece of the action on the MaryAnn Vecchio T-shirts.

VECCHIO: Well, I think the only reason why he did it was to—to help me get some money, because he was tired of everybody else using me.

SAFER: What do you think—I don't know how to phrase this. What do you think, put—put your daughter on the wrong path? Was it her home life? Her street life? What?

MRS. VECCHIO: No. It— It was her— And she—she's adventurous. She wanted to see the world, and she wanted to see it ahead of time, which she still does.

Seven years later, protesters attempted to stop the construction of a physical education building on the site of the Kent State shootings. This magnificent AP shot of an unidentified demonstrator made the front page of The New York Times *and many other papers on July 13, 1977. It provides a perfect contrast with the Vecchio shot of seven years earlier; maybe it also signals a change in the politics of the country. The cops are helmeted, but they are humanized by their eyeglasses (and, on the right, moustache), and the unidentified woman, fist raised, but not clenched, looks defiantly, but also hopefully, over her shoulder, up, and off into the future. The muscles in her neck and the folds in her coveralls provide the dramatic tension, but they lead directly to her face which, seen from a low angle, is not only heroic but also surprisingly calm—even content. The iconography of the shot is exhilarating. It is telling us that this arrest—in deep contrast to the shootings seven years earlier—is an act of faith and a positive statement.*

SAFER: Do you think you provided the best home life for your—for your kids?

MR. VECCHIO: Yes, the best. Financially and morally, both.

MRS. VECCHIO: Best-fed, the best-dressed kids. In the—

MR. VECCHIO: They got everything they want.

MRS. VECCHIO: In bed early.

SAFER: Too much perhaps?

MRS. VECCHIO: Not too much, because we're not that rich [*laughing*].

MR. VECCHIO: It's hard for me to figure out if you really had given them too much or given them too little. Really, we didn't give them what you'd call little, but we gave them plenty more than the average kid.

SAFER: Why did they get into trouble?

MR. VECCHIO: Hanging out with the wrong kids.

ROBERT KNAPP [*police chief*]: All the children, except for the youngest, have had their problems over the years.

SAFER: Including going to jail, some of them?

KNAPP: Yes, definitely.

SAFER: Police Chief Robert Knapp knows Opa-Locka better than anyone—all of its secrets—the melancholy accounts of domestic squabbles, of runaway children—all the small tragedies of a small town. And he knew MaryAnn Vecchio well.

Before she ran away, before Kent State, what kind of trouble was she in?

KNAPP: She just wasn't staying at home. Parental supervision was a little on the loose side. She came and went as she pleased.

SAFER: But soon after Kent State, she was in trouble again—at fourteen, a washed-up celebrity and an uncontrollable child. She ran away from school, and ran away from home, and was reported to police by her own family. She was finally placed in a juvenile home.

A minute ago, you were sitting here on this front doorstep, and crying. Why?

VECCHIO: Just leaves me depressed about this place, and that I had to stay here.

SAFER: Here is Kendall—a juvenile home. She was sentenced to six months for running away from home, and eventually she ran away from Kendall. Here they mix truants and runaways with more serious offenders. MaryAnn's cottage has been closed down.

VECCHIO: The people here—they just, you know—I mean, you—you weren't an individual; you were just a number. It's not my idea of rehabilitating somebody. It's just—just a place to stuff you.

SAFER: What about psychiatric help? They even have a psychologist here?

VECCHIO: Right. And I fiddled with some blocks, and some other tests they did—numbers and blots and things like that. But I don't think that's the way to—

SAFER: MaryAnn, what *is* the way? What's the way? Is there such a thing as the right way to deal with somebody who is so unable to get along in society?

VECCHIO: Right. It's hard to say. Giving them attention, and things that they really need.

My room is right over there. You know, I really felt bad about being in here. And I really felt bad about leaving, because I—I was so adjusted to this kind of style that I didn't know what I was going to do. I was scared, too. I'm getting back on the right track, and society's track.

SAFER: The next thing is she's arrested for prostitution.

MR. VECCHIO: Right. It's—it's a hard thing for a parent to believe, but he has to believe it. Let's put it that way, there.

SAFER: Do you believe it?

MR. VECCHIO: Well, if she was in the room, you'd have to believe it.

SAFER: Do you believe it?

MRS. VECCHIO: No, I don't. I believe it's—it's not proven, or anything. She didn't even go to court. So she didn't even go to court for it.

SAFER: Aren't you kidding yourself a bit?

MRS. VECCHIO: No, I'm not.

SAFER [*to MaryAnn*]: How old were you when you first accepted money for sex?

VECCHIO: Oh—seventeen.

SAFER: Every city in the country has its nasty little combat zone, where melancholy pleasures are bought and sold. MaryAnn Vecchio became part of the merchandise—from instant stardom at Kent State to hooker on Biscayne Boulevard.

So the police arrested you once for prostitution?

VECCHIO: Right.

SAFER: Here in Miami?

VECCHIO: Hm-hmm.

SAFER: You paid your fine?

VECCHIO: Right.

SAFER: And what happened? Did you go back on the street?

VECCHIO: No. No. I started working in a—in a health spa.

SAFER: In a health spa? And it's another—

VECCHIO: And it's another term—

SAFER: For—? It's a massage parlor, right?

VECCHIO: Right.

SAFER: Another brothel?

VECCHIO: Well, they don't use that term. [*Laughing.*] So I started working in the health spa, and—and then I got busted.

SAFER: And that was a couple of weeks ago?

VECCHIO: Right.

SAFER [*to MaryAnn's parents*]: Is he quick to anger, Mrs. Vecchio?

MRS. VECCHIO: Yes, very quick. He's Italian, yes.

SAFER: Pretty rough-tempered? Pretty rough-tempered?

MRS. VECCHIO: Yeah.

SAFER: Did you hit her?

MR. VECCHIO: Yes.

SAFER: Were you here when that happened?

MRS. VECCHIO: When he hit her? Yes. He's very quick-tempered.

SAFER: Was that a pretty bad scene?

MRS. VECCHIO. Yes.

VECCHIO: I'm sure, if I have kids, that I'm —I'm not going to hit them, and—because it—it doesn't do any good. It kind of hardens you. It doesn't bother you. You know, therefore, your feelings about certain things stop, and you stop caring.

SAFER: You think that—that she has any chance at all in life, or is it just going to be pretty much a repeat of the past?

POLICE CHIEF KNAPP: Unless she wants a change, it'll be the same thing for the rest of her life.

SAFER: The chances are that, without a Kent State, MaryAnn Vecchio's life would not be much different. But it would be a private failure, not a public one. This story—the story of a nobody who became a somebody—has no great symbolic meaning. MaryAnn is no more a symbol of anything today than she was that day her picture was snapped at Kent State. But maybe she does have a chance. In spite of the fact that she has lived a lifetime between the ages of fourteen and twenty-one, she retains a young girl's dreams of glory—to be an actress, or housewife—to be something. She's enrolled in college now. And she says she wants another chance.

VECCHIO: I never dreamed that it would—it would be like this. It's "Put the Barbie dolls down and grow up!" And that's what happened. And I—I just realized a—a lot of things. And I thought that's what society was like. So I—I did the same.

SAFER: Do you think that you're, in a sense, as much a casualty of Kent State as the four who died?

VECCHIO: A lot of times, yes.

[*Sounds of automatic camera.*]

And that's another thing people don't realize. People— The—the hate mail the people had sent in. They don't—they don't know what I went through, at a very early age.

[*Camera sound.*]

And I think they're just paranoid that it happ— It might happen in their home.

[*Camera sound.*]

SAFER: There, but for the grace of God, goes their daughter.

VECCHIO: Right.

[*Camera sound.*]

11. THE CASUALTIES OF "REVOLVER JOURNALISM"
by James Monaco

Eventually, if you work back far enough, there is a real Katharina Blum at the bottom of this mountain of media imagery. What we have here is essentially a review (from *MORE*) of a film made from a semi-fictional novel that was written and published as a tract against "Revolver Journalism," the very useful German name for the process in which a human being is negated, obviated, liquidated by a viciously fictional media image. The story is not unlike Citizen Patty's: the Baader-Meinhof gang was the German equivalent of American post-sixties radical groups like the Symbionese Liberation Army—but the denouement is quite different. There have been no novels or films in Patty's defense, only exploitations.

Katharina Blum, a self-possessed, independent-minded young woman who makes a fairly good living as a freelance maid/home economist, meets a certain Ludwig Götten, anarchist on the lam, at a carnival party. Once unhappily married, Blum now values her independence so greatly that her friends have nicknamed her "the nun"; but Götten intrigues her. She takes him home, they spend the night together. At dawn, two dozen cops toting submachine guns and sporting eerie plastic riot masks surround her apartment, closing in on Götten. They're disappointed and angry to discover he's escaped their trap. Left only with Katharina for their morning's work, they haul her in for questioning. Katharina is a pretty girl; the cops take a liking to her and treat her rather pleasantly. But she'll have none of it. Through her work she has met powerful people. She's not afraid of the police and she maintains her cool, self-contained poise, and is released.

Within hours, however, the tabloids leap into the case. Werner Tötges, star reporter for *The News*, starts to work his special journalistic magic. For form's sake, he conducts a few perfunctory interviews, then turns his formidable talents to the real job at hand: weaving a saleable fantasy in which Katharina and her lover are seen as vicious, if romantic, Commie anarchists whose very existence threatens the fabric of German society. At first, Katharina is merely angry. Then the obscene phone calls and the threatening notes slipped under the door at all hours begin to wear her down. Even people she considers friends seem to believe Tötges' lurid fantasy: they wink knowingly. Within three days, *The News* has nearly succeeded in breaking Katharina where the police had failed.

After Götten is finally captured (several platoons of paramilitary police stage a helicopter attack on a lonely farmhouse), Katharina sets up a showdown with Tötges. He arrives smiling. After all, hasn't he made "Blumikins" a celebrity? He's hoping to get laid. He suggests this. Blum pulls out a pistol and kills him.

This is the steel-sharp morality tale that filmmakers Volker Schlöndorff and Margarethe von Trotta have fashioned from Heinrich Böll's equally chilling and efficient novel, *The Lost Honor of Katharina Blum.* The film marks a quantum jump for the New German Cinema, the renaissance in film that has been in progress in West Germany since the late sixties. *Katharina* is that *rara avis,* a political film that is as popular as it is effective. Until now, the New Wave of German directors (which includes Alexander Klüge, Werner Herzog, Wim Wenders, and the hyperprolific R. W. Fassbinder, as well as the Schlöndorff-von Trotta team) has been responsible mainly for *succès d'estime.* Their films, made quickly and cheaply, have become film festival favorites abroad, but they've seldom succeeded with popular audiences at home.

Katharina, however, is a box-office smash of the first order. Since its release in October 1975, it has become the first serious German movie in many years to rank among the top-grossing films in that country. Hailed as "a major breakthrough," and "the first West German film in modern times to come to grips with our political reality," it is repeating its popular success story in the half-dozen other European countries where it has so far opened.

In the U.S., however, where the film premiered at the New York Film Festival in 1975, *Katharina Blum* has met, in general, with a confused and flaccid critical response. Why this contrast between European and American reactions? Mainly because Schlöndorff and von Trotta's movie, essentially a political act, is susceptible to a fairly standard set of misreadings of the sort that any political film in recent years has had to contend with: what we might call the "Costa-Gavras Syndrome." There seems to be a primal shared resistance to this sort of movie among the American critical establishment (and that's a shame considering we pioneered the form of the popular political movie in the thirties).

There's also another, simpler reason for *Katharina*'s poor reception. For the most part, Americans who have written about the film betray a woeful lack of knowledge of the contemporary German political situation, out of which the film grew and upon which it comments with such startling effect. Now, German audiences don't need the title-card *envoi* at the end of the film to know that Böll, Schlöndorff, and von Trotta have taken aim at notorious press baron Axel Springer and his infamous and influential *Bild Zeitung.* And they easily see the parallel with the continuing saga of the Baader-Meinhof gang, a real enough group of anarchists whom the Springer papers, using what the liberal weekly *Der Spiegel* calls "Revolver Journalism," have blown up into grotesque antiheroes. Springer employs the lurid melodrama of *Anarchisten-Hysterie*, which has been such a significant element of 1970's German politics (and which has helped sell hundreds of millions of newspapers). But American audiences (and most American critics) do need a little background.

The most widespread misreading of *The Lost Honor of Katharina Blum* suggests that the film exaggerates reality. We have nothing to compare with Axel Springer and his chains of newspapers and magazines which so thoroughly dominate the German press scene. The *Bild Zeitung*, with a daily circulation of 4.35 million, is by far the largest-selling paper in West Germany.*

For years, Springer papers have been engaged in a running battle with the political left. He was a special target of the student movement in the late sixties and he has taken his revenge in the seventies. The *Bild Zeitung*, more than any other newspaper, fanned the flames of hysteria surrounding the Baader-Meinhof gang: after building up the myth, they then succeeded in using it against a wide variety of presumed "enemies of the state" (and real enemies of Springer). If William Randolph Hearst had the politics and temperament of William Loeb and if the Hearst chain had been at its height during the heyday of Joe McCarthy, then we might have something like an American parallel for Axel Springer.

Does *Katharina Blum* exaggerate the virulence of Springer's Revolver Journalism? Heinrich Böll was writing from personal experience. In Kaiserslautern in December of 1971 a bank robbery took place. While the police were still investigating, before any charges had been brought, the *Bild Zeitung* pinned the crime on the Baader-Meinhof gang, and tried and convicted the group in its pages. The Springer papers had a field day, discovering Baader-Meinhof behind every major crime. Doubters were defamed, sympathizers condemned. Nobel prize-winner Böll, like many West German liberals angry at this witch hunt, took to the pages of *Der Spiegel* with a quiet essay on the importance of prudence and the judicial process. Böll immediately became a target for Springer; he was tagged a "Communist sympathizer" and "latter-day Goebbels." As the hate campaign gained momentum, Böll was subjected to the full treatment he describes in *Katharina Blum*: obscene phone calls, threats on his life, police raids on his home. (Armed with machine guns, they were looking ostensibly for Baader-Meinhof gang members. Needless to say, they found none.)

The book was Böll's revenge and an immediate best seller, causing

---

* In addition to *Bild Zeitung,* Springer owns *Die Welt* (circ. 231,000), *Hamburger Abendblatt* (269,000), *BZ* (305,000), *Berliner Morgenpost* (179,000), *Welt am Sontag* (321,000), *Bild am Sontag* (2.36 million), *Hoer/Zu* (3.7 million), and *Funkuhr* (1.6 million). Springer papers have a total daily circulation of 5.3 million and a weekly circulation of nearly 9 million.

Angela Winkler as Katharina Blum in Volker Schlöndorff's film, juxtaposed with screaming headline . . . and Coca-Cola ad.

Springer to drop his best-seller list in *Die Welt* until *Katharina* moved off the list. Volker Schlöndorff and Margarethe von Trotta shot their film version of the book in the spring of 1975. By that time the Baader-Meinhof hysteria had lessened somewhat. Most of the early accusations ended in mistrials. Many defendants were declared medically unfit to stand trial, having been on hunger strikes. Eventually, Baader-Meinhof became something of a non-event in the German public consciousness. Still, Schlöndorff was worried whether or not he could get the film properly distributed in Germany; many conservative exhibitors had threatened to ban all of his films, starting an organized campaign to prohibit the screening of *Katharina*. But he did not expect the kind of reaction he got late in the summer of 1975.

Schlöndorff and von Trotta spend vacations each year at a small farm in Italy, outside of Florence. According to Schlöndorff's brother, a doctor who lives in New York, they awoke at dawn one morning that August to find the farmhouse "surrounded by 50 to 100 Italian police who were searching for a group of anarchist/leftists who had recently been freed from prison by a group of German radicals." The police were equipped with submachine guns and accompanied by helicopters on their four a.m. sortie. They performed a meticulous search of the house and, after some absurd questions about Daniel Cohn-Bendit (the German-born leader of the French student revolt in 1968 who has not been active in politics for years now), they reluctantly left. A warning had been given.

So, no, *The Lost Honor of Katharina Blum* does not exaggerate. But is it still too melodramatic to be an effective film? This was the second most common misreading among American critics, one which is often leveled at films that have a political intent. There are two ways to answer the charge. First, *Katharina Blum,* considering its context, is no more melodramatic than real life. The liberal esthetic insists that black-and-white simplicity is bad while carefully and subtly graded shades of gray better reproduce the valued complexities of reality. The problem is that sometimes those nuanced shades of gray are trouble-somely close to black and white. Such is the case with *Katharina,* a film with heroes and villains. Yet, both the book and the movie clearly avoid wooden stereotypes. Katharina, heroine though she may be, nevertheless displays a quirky, not altogether sympathetic character. Revolver-Journalist Tötges isn't so much motivated by politics as he is by the scent of a hot story. In another film he'd be quite an interesting rogue. If he has to invent most of the Blum fantasy, well, that's where he gets his chance to demonstrate his art. Behind their riot masks, the police aren't all ogres; in fact, one of them—Lieutenant Moeding—is more sympathetic toward Katharina than most of her friends. On the other hand, the Blornas, friends and employers of our heroine and prominent in her defense, are subtle portraits of liberal indecision.

A more difficult barrier for American audiences, perhaps, is the tone of *Katharina Blum.* Vincent Canby, as usual, put it succinctly: "It's cold and bright and has dozens of lethal edges. It's very difficult to like even though it has things to admire." Like the majority of the new German filmmakers, Volker Schlöndorff has been profoundly influenced by Bertolt Brecht's theories of epic theater. Böll writes with a bitter Brechtian irony to begin with; he is master of a sour, glandular prose. And Schlöndorff has translated this tone into cinema. The film holds us at arm's length; there is a strong undercurrent of satire whose object is to allow an audience some intellectual distancing. The purpose is not to alienate us but rather to counteract the propagandistic power of the medium. For Böll, Schlöndorff, and von Trotta (as for Brecht), the aim is not to brainwash an audience but rather to set up the political dialectic, to get viewers involved in the logic of the situation so that they can work it out for themselves. Manipulation isn't the aim; reason is. But this doesn't mean *Katharina Blum* is a cold, unemotional film. On the contrary, the technique, when we understand it, redoubles the passion of the story because it insists we participate in the experience rather than simply observe it. This isn't easy to do—either on stage, in a novel, or on film—which is one reason Brecht's theories are still very much alive now twenty years after his death. They are still very valuable tools for political artists, whose greatest concern is how to transmute rage into action, how to translate the psychological into the political, and *Katharina Blum* is one of the best examples in many years of their continued vitality.

Why all this about esthetics? It's important in itself, of course, but it is even more significant in the context of the subject matter of the film. The dilemma that confronts Schlöndorff and von Trotta, the film-makers, *should* also confront Tötges the journalist: how to deal honestly with an audience. The false moral outrage that the Revolver Journalist and the Springer papers use to such effect is mirrored by the real moral outrage of Böll and the filmmakers. Moreover, both the newspaperman and the filmmakers are involved in similarly iconoplastic activities: they are both building images for public consumption (albeit certainly with different motivations). What kind of honor is it that Katharina Blum loses, anyway? One (minor) misreading of the film sees it as a feminist epic (Schlöndorff and von Trotta were previously responsible for *A Free Woman*) in which Katharina's virtue is besmirched by the *News* campaign while she herself maintains her integrity. But I think the film-makers and Böll have a much more sophisticated sense of honor in mind. What Tötges does to Katharina is to "rewrite" her. The psychological effect is devastating. The "Katharina" she sees in the tabloids—even in the eyes of people she considers friends—is not the woman she thinks herself to be. For such a self-made woman the effect is doubly destructive. It's not so much *what* Tötges makes of her that drives her to mur-der—simply that he does have the power to "make her."

And this is the aspect of journalism that has fascinated filmmakers ever since *The Front Page, It Happened One Night, The Philadelphia Story, Citizen Kane*—these are just a few of the classics that investigate the ways in which private personalities are remade into public personas that often contrast strikingly with their real-life models. No, *The Lost Honor of Katharina Blum* is not a film about "the excesses" of freedom of the press (to dispose of the last of the prevalent misreadings). Like those earlier American movies, it is about a phenomenon particu-lar to journalism. What Tötges does to Blum is "schizogenic": he cre-ates her double. While we may no longer have anything to rival the Springer papers on this side of the Atlantic, this phenomenon should still be of interest. That tension between reality and the report of it is what gives journalism its special esthetic sex appeal. Straight fiction doesn't have it, which is the main reason nonfiction outsells fiction in bookstores today and the best-selling fiction purports to be more or less *à clef*.

Where *Katharina Blum* surpasses the American film portraits of reporters is in providing a political dimension. The real danger of the Springer papers and their Revolver Journalists is that they comprise a fourth estate of exceptional clout. As Tötges can create a new Katharina against whom the real Katharina is nearly helpless, likewise Springer can create a fictional political climate which quickly supersedes real political situations. Yet Katharina does have a measure of power, and so do Böll and Schlöndorff and von Trotta. Such things are difficult

Blum's arrest takes place while she is in the shower. The nudity points up the humiliation. The costumed character to the right, intersecting her body with a submachine gun, is an undercover cop dressed up to look like the police image of a radical.

to measure, but it seems to me that first the novel, now the film, have had a distinct and positive effect. Powerful, direct, subtly ironic, relevant yet complex, *The Lost Honor of Katharina Blum* is quite an achievement.

FOR FARRAH,
WITH LUST
AND ARTIFICE

12. DON'T CHANGE A HAIR FOR ME
by Roger Rosenblatt

It takes a long time to produce a book these days. For months now I have been plagued by the nightmare that no one will quite be able to place Farrah Fawcett-Majors by the time this book is in the stores. She is a supernova, if ever there was one. Within the space of one month in the spring of 1977, FF-M appeared on the covers of three women's magazines, each of which is clearly directed toward a different class (*Vogue* is upper-middle, *McCall's* middle-middle, *Woman's Day* upper-working class). This came after her widely noticed blitz of the gossip and fan magazines, and just before her announcement that she was leaving the show—*Charlie's Angels*—that had provided her with a springboard.

Farrah is a notably assured and conscious celebrity: her own work of art, not the creation of studio technicians and network program directors. The feat would be applauded if *Charlie's Angels* hadn't been such a blatant throwback to fifties sexism, and if Farrah herself hadn't contributed so willingly to the reactionary images of women it gave us.

Roger Rosenblatt's reasoned appreciation notes the paradoxes of the persona, but isn't quite as sensitive to the sexist underpinnings as it might be.

We're in deep now—the age of sexual freedom—up to our adult book stores with their smoky windows, our Fritz the Cats, *Penthouse*s, porno T-shirts, see-through blouses, how-to best sellers, bold rock lyrics, shocking vocabulary, congressional offices, and everywhere else we look, or would like to. All of which is stupid or silly, but suggests a cultural question of supply and demand. Assuming that tantalization is the key to sexuality, that we only crawl for the out-of-reach, then who or what becomes a sex symbol when the picking is free?

According to a lot of people, tens of millions to date, the answer is Farrah Fawcett-Majors. The name alone offers multiple possibilities, from some defunct India regiment to a group of undergraduates in a vocational college. Add a picture and the dreams expand. Farrah has the glow of a star, the first full-fledged sex queen to emerge from the relatively sex-free medium of television since Dagmar in the fifties.

The picture to add is a poster of Farrah in a red bathing suit which at this writing has sold three million copies to equal numbers of children and the aged for two dollars or $2.50 apiece, and is expected to sell ten million. In comparison Raquel Welch's poster has sold two million copies, Marilyn Monroe 1.5, Betty Grable 1.5, and Lindsay Wagner, the Bionic Woman, 400,000. A poster of Lee Majors, the "Six Million Dollar Man" and the husband of Farrah, has sold 500,000 copies, which might make for some nasty domestic competitiveness in a less valuable fellow. But Majors is evidently as happy as the rest of America to hail Farrah, who besides the poster earns a living from ads for Noxzema shave cream (for which she plays a character called "Creamy"), Mercury Cougars, Wella Balsam conditioning shampoo, and Vic Tanny health clubs. She also is one of *Charlie's Angels,* 1977's highest-rated TV show, about three young women who are ordered to solve crimes by John Forsythe's voice. Farrah has been on the covers of *Time* and *People;* and in the week of February 15 alone was on the tabloid covers of *Midnight,* the *Star,* and the *National Enquirer.* Why?

In ten years at the outs, Farrah Fawcett-Majors will be the answer in a trivia quiz or an entry in one of Richard Lamparski's *Whatever Became of . . . ?* series, an Irish McCalla, a Cobina Wright, Jr., or, God willing, a Margaux Hemingway. For the magical moment, however, she is America's pin-up girl, gracing teenagers' bedrooms instead of GI's lockers, and satisfying some inarticulate desires other than our wish to gaze on just another pretty face. Professor Ray Browne of the popular culture department of Bowling Green University told the *Star* it's the hair: "It's sort of windblown and free spirited. But it is a safe sort of free spirit, because the role she plays on TV represents law and order" (a blow to Kojak). Farrah says she's popular because she doesn't wear a bra. Dr. Alan Rosenberg, "prominent New York psychiatrist," told the *National Enquirer* that "innocence and bold abandon are the wildest combination sexually to a man. These two factors, which Farrah has, are enough to make America go bananas."

Psychiatric terms notwithstanding, it is astounding to think of ten million poster-buyers, of fifty million weekly viewers, of who-knows-how-many Mercury drivers and Noxzema shavers, and of sponsors paying $100,000 per minute to be seen with Farrah. The reason, I think, is that Farrah is not sexy, which in response to her eurythmic form, the poster, and the various wet suits in which she poses might sound like an insult. But if this age of ours is as sexually free as it claims, it makes sense to choose an America's Sweetheart who has something other than mere sexuality to commend her. What Farrah has is comedy, comedy built on sex to be sure, but comedy (not wit, not humor) nevertheless.

Long before the advent of Farrah, subtler actresses realized that comedy and sexuality could complement each other. Veronica Lake was a very funny performer. Carole Lombard was witty, not broadly

The Farrah poster, by Pro-Arts, Medina, Ohio. It has now sold more than twelve million copies and has thus become the best-selling poster of all time.

funny, yet as sexually exciting as they come. Jean Arthur's voice was more erotic in *The Devil and Miss Jones* than anything in *The Devil in Miss Jones,* its X-rated namesake. Marilyn Monroe actually became sexy when she started to parody herself in *The Seven Year Itch* and *Some Like It Hot,* as did Ann-Margret in *Carnal Knowledge.*

For a sex queen, self-parody involves as much mockery of the observer as the observed, because the exaggerated teeth and bottoms are meant to embarrass as well as tease, and ease disgrace by making it community property. Only a country deeply embarrassed by sex would put naked girls on calendars—*it's really functional, you see.* The embarrassment is funny, and our sex queens, the best of them, instead of being sources of allure, are always inflated out of reach like Thanksgiving Day balloons, preposterous metaphors of our sly desires, which in fact are as obvious as teeth and bottoms themselves.

When someone like Farrah comes along, then, we have a spot open for her, a cultural zone where we house our most high-priced clichés. Farrah has teeth and a bottom, and her celebrated hair looks like a cartoon of hair, which is appropriate for comedy. But her most appealing comic attribute is that she takes it easy on us, playing the exact opposite of a *belle dame sans merci,* not a Carmen or a Salammbô, not the European Fatal Woman to lead us through a romantic agony, but as *Time* describes her, "a warm, giggly sort of girl," who implies, as Mae West used to hum aloud, "Come on boys; sex won't kill you." It's an assurance we cannot hear too often.

What constitutes sexuality in an age of sexual freedom? The same thing it always did, only more so. The greater the freedom, the greater the fear. The greater the fear, the louder the laugh. So here's Farrah, not witty like Lombard, nor humorous like West or Monroe, but just as funny in her fashion. She doesn't crack jokes; she is one—sitting pretty at pool side, tossing back her celestial curls, and flashing those choppers at millions of boys who, as ever, will wink, hoot, whistle, and elbow each other in the ribs, but will never come up to see her sometime.

13. HAIRDO LIKE STAR'S
SPURS ATTACK
by the Associated Press

Hair is clearly the key to the Farrah phenomenon, and no wonder. It has been a major determinant of women's celebrity images since Mary Pickford's sausage curls. In his pioneering book, *Les Stars,* French sociologist Edgar Morin traces changes in hairstyles from Pickford through Jean Harlow (for whom the term platinum blonde was invented), Greta Garbo, Norma Shearer, and, of course, Veronica Lake. We could expand the catalogue to include Debbie Reynolds, Jackie Kennedy, maybe Barbra Streisand, Joan Baez and Judy Collins, Cher, Dorothy Hamill, and, most recently, Farrah.

You've noticed that there are no movie stars' names after 1955 on this list. The reason is simple. There have been precious few women film stars in the U.S. since that time.

Farrah's hairstyle is, like the persona, a curious, paradoxical contrast: designed to present a free and windblown image, it is actually carefully set and held. The freedom is illusory. But what do I know about hair? Let her hairdresser tell it. Here's a short excerpt from a wonderfully egregious star bio of *Farrah!* by Patricia Burstein:

Hugh York is emphatic: "Length is what men love. Farrah has fantastic hair—just curly enough, just the right amount of wave. It falls about two inches below her shoulders. But let me tell you, she works on that look. You can't get a look like that unless you maintain it. Her hair is not too thick or too thin and has good body enhanced by the streaking."

Then flashing his huge, curious, blue-green eyes. Hugh exults, "Farrah's hair is magic. It makes her the fantastic person she is." And what is a fantastic person in 1977? Well, Hugh York says, "A fantastic person means you can be a major symbol in today's society. And Farrah certainly is THAT!"

Hugh York says that THAT HAIR is Farrah's identity. Even other celebrities could not wear the FF look. "Imagine Shirley MacLaine with a Farrah Fawcett hairstyle?" Already a major Los Angeles

department store, the May Company, advertises "Angel" wigs—
"to get the look you want." But a wig won't do it, because the
whole story behind THAT HAIR is the movement of Farrah's hair.
Free, unbound, windblown. And there's feeling behind it. The
Farrah Fawcett look has flourished all over the country. Besides
the hair, it's that fresh sporty feeling that really spells 1977.

Such a beehive of activity would be enough to make lesser stars
fall apart. But not Farrah, who is unflappable even in the most
frantic of times. Like her lustrous hair, everything seems to fall
into place in her life.

Hugh York, whose hair is silken brown with a matching beard,
says the bottom line is that Farrah knows herself and her hair.
"Farrah knows she has a manufactured look," he says. "She knows
she is packaged like other stars. But the incredible thing is that
she is so natural about it, with it. The clincher was when she became Farrah Fawcett-Majors. She really likes to have her hair wet
and pulled back or blowing in the wind. That's Farrah!"

Hooray for Hollywood!
  But there is, inevitably, the tragic side to this fairytale. The Associated Press ran this story on their wires February 23, 1977.*

---

* We have purposely used a false name for the girl who is the subject of the following story. We have also chosen pointedly not to use the high-school yearbook
photo that ran with the AP story. "Tessie Senmont" became a temporary celebrity
obviously against her will. She should be allowed to return to noncelebrity status
as quickly as possible.

HAIRDO LIKE STAR'S SPURS ATTACK

LINWOOD, Kan. (AP)—Jealousy over a Farrah Fawcett-Majors type hairstyle was apparently the motive for an acid attack on a pretty fourteen-year-old cheerleader here.

The girl, Tessie Senmont, may need skin grafts.

She had arrived for classes Valentine's Day with her light-colored hair done up in the exploding bouffant style popularized by Miss Fawcett-Majors, a star of TV's *Charlie's Angels* series.

Miss Senmont, an eighth-grader, was opening her locker when another girl ran up behind her and dashed nitric acid on her hair, back and shoulders. The burns were treated at a hospital.

The school principal, Bill Chambers, yesterday recommended to the school board in this tiny community west of Kansas City that the girl who threw the acid be expelled.

At the same time, Chambers suspended six other girls he said had talked about the attack with the perpetrator or knew it was coming.

"The hairdo was mentioned prominently in all their statements," Chambers said yesterday.

Chambers says the idea was apparently to damage Tessie's hair so badly she would have to get it cut.

That was the result. Her hair has since been cut and restyled.

"We just thank God every day that she didn't turn her head" when the acid was thrown, Mrs. Kenneth Senmont said.

Tessie's parents operate a 320-acre farm about three and a half miles outside town.

Tessie will say little about the attack. Two of the girls implicated in the alleged plot have been schoolmates since kindergarten. She had considered all of them her friends.

County Attorney Patrick Reardon said yesterday he was considering legal action and might ask for a juvenile court hearing.

Mrs. Senmont was philosophical.

"Even if she has a scar on her back, that isn't going to change Tessie—and that's what they were jealous of," she said.

14. HERS
by Lois Gould

A television celebrity like Farrah is a frighteningly attractive role
model. Lois Gould investigated this aspect of the phenomenon in
her weekly column in *The New York Times* at the height of the
Farrah boom.

Kimberley Ann, nine, has just decided what she wants to be when she
grows up: a part-time cocktail waitress with frosted blond streaks. It is
probably just a coincidence that Kimberley Ann's mother recently
graduated from law school and lopped off her two-tone gold ringlets
right at the dark roots.

Kim's classmate, Janice, who is still eight, has her heart set on
becoming a file clerk who ties up her hair in a severe bun that can be
shaken free, with a single lightning stroke, into a quivering mass of
raven tendrils. (Janice's mother is a securities analyst, with a naturally
frizzled pepper-and-salt pageboy.)

Nina, ten-and-a-half, plans to be a schoolteacher, with a firm grip
and frosted blond highlights. And twelve-year-old Stephanie, the cynic,
intends to become a frosted blond highlight, period.

Clearly, a fair number of feminists' daughters are having "role-
model" trouble. The cause seems to be a sudden and widespread cultural confusion about the difference—if any—between a role model
and a hair model. As I understand it, a role model is an adult person
of your own gender whom you admire and want to be like: a president,
an astronaut, a nuclear physicist, a private eye. Whereas a hair model
is a stunning raven-haired president; a luscious redheaded astronaut;
a blond bombshell of a nuclear physicist; a frost-streaked poster pin-up
of a private eye.

It would be easy to blame the confusion on television's newest rage—
the female "action-adventure" star who can either ride a motorcycle,
toe-tap on a skateboard, shoot straight, do heavy lifting or figure out
how to rap a criminal while wearing a dripping wet bunny costume.
After all, no matter what else these new wonder women do besides

wonders—and part-time file-clerking, schoolteaching, cocktail-waitressing—the thing they all do best is their hair.

So it would be easy to blame TV, but, as one of our stunning, raven-haired ex-presidents used to say, "It would be wrong." The truth is, we have always had a little trouble spotting the subtle line between a heroine and a hairdo. In a highly unscientific recent survey, mothers of nine- to twelve-year-olds, selected solely on the basis of shampoo, color tint and permanent-wave length, were asked the following question: When you were nine- and twelve-year-olds, who was your "role model," and why?

● Seventeen percent answered, "Esther Williams, the swimming star, because she could do fifteen minutes of flawless underwater sidestroke with gorgeous flowers twined in her braided coronet."

● Twenty-five percent named Brenda Starr, the comic-strip girl reporter, on the basis of her sensational headline set in bold-type curls the color of "a five-alarm fire," an "Irish setter," or a *"saumon fumé."*

● Twelve percent had idolized Sonja Henie, the Goldilocks of the ice, because she skated like a windup Christmas angel; her hair and feet set off "matching sparks of white light"; she was an "animated gold sequin."

● The remainder chose a wide assortment of heroines ranging from the Dragon Lady (dangerous mastermind set in a black curtain of silk hair) to Amelia Earhart and Dale, Flash Gordon's dauntless co-pilot, both of whom had their heads in clouds of wispy gold tendrils escaping from under the flying helmets.

Nobody had a role model with non-terrific hair.

Film historian Molly Haskell has noted that the long, sexy tresses of movie queens in the hard-boiled dramas of the 1940's were the female equivalent of a gun—an ultimate woman's weapon in a tough man's world of crime and carnality. The new "action" heroines of the seventies, operating in the same man's world, actually get to wield both weapons—the hair *and* the gun. But it's the same old game: Everything, including the girls, is still owned and operated by the fellow who runs the beauty parlor. Body, soul, gun and frost job, they are strictly *Charlie's* angels.

Armed with this valuable knowledge, I recently watched my first episode of the TV series *Charlie's Angels,* accompanied by two hard-core nine-year-old fans, Nicole and Sandy. Here's how it went:

ME: Tell me about the "angels."

NICOLE: Well, first off you have to know which is which, Sabrina is the smart one, Kelly is strong, and Jill is beautiful. Mostly her hair.

ME: But they're *all* beautiful.

SANDY [*patiently*]: Of *course,* but Sabrina is beautiful *and* smart. Kelly is beautiful *and* strong. Jill is *just* beautiful. Mostly her hair.

ME: Oh. [*On the screen, three women are flashing guns, hair, sexy clothes and dazzling smiles, like armed stewardesses serving plastic*

"Tons of Hair, Acres of Teeth: It Could Only Be a Farrah Fawcett Lookalike Contest" read the headline in People. *A disc jockey in Detroit discovered 280 would-be FF-Ms in no time. These are the fifteen finalists. Farrah not only always looks like herself. She obviously also looks like a lot of other people. (Photo: Ira Rosenberg)*

filet mignon. Pause.] Which would you rather be—the smart one, the strong one, or the beautiful one, with the hair?

NICOLE: Definitely not the beautiful one.

SANDY: Obviously.

ME: Why obviously?

NICOLE: Because even if she has the most hair, she has the smallest part. [*Sandy nods, solemnly.*]

ME: What if you had a choice, I mean in real life? You could be smart and strong—or you could be beautiful. Which would you choose?

SANDY: Why couldn't we be all three?

ME: Well, first off, because hardly anybody gets to be all three. And hardly anybody even gets to have a choice. So I'm giving you a choice. Beautiful but dumb and weak. Or smart and strong, but ugly. Ugly *hair*, especially.

SANDY [*frowning*]: Hmmm.

NICOLE [*cocking her head so that her long mane of naturally frosty curls tumbles gently around her shoulders*]: *How* ugly?

15. COVERING THE STORY
by James Monaco

Not since the heyday of Jacqueline Kennedy has a media star so captured the attention of the nation's magazine art directors. During the spring and summer of 1977, newsstands were plastered with Farrah's face. The effect of the magazines, side by side, row upon row, often suggested an unintentional parody of Andy Warhol's well-known serial portraits of the early and mid-sixties.

Interestingly enough, the teeth and hair never changed from cover to cover. The pose was frozen. In this respect, the Farrah covers are in direct contrast to the Patty Hearst covers. None of the magazines had very much to report on FF-M. This was a non-story if ever there was one. The articles which backed up the selling tools of the covers were of this sort: "Farrah Fawcett Is Lee Majors' Six Million Dollar Baby—And She Loves It," "From Fantasy Femme to the Total Woman," "Farrah-rah! A New Kind of Gorgeousness," "Farrah's Hair and How to Do It." Most were vaguely anti-feminist in the style that has become common in the late-seventies backlash. Of course, as the boom continued to grow, it became more and more difficult to find something to say about the "Unlikely Sex Symbol." The pulp journals turned to the usual inventions: "Farrah Admits to Racial Prejudice," "Why Farrah's Ambition May Be Her Own Worst Enemy," "Farrah and Teenage Boy Spend Weekend Together! The Rumors Lee Can No Longer Deny!" and—my personal favorite—"Farrah's Losing Her Hair! Beauty Expert's Shocking Claim."

Not to worry, however. At about the same time the pulp tabloid *Midnight* heralded this disastrous news, a new little offset publication devoted to bald-headed-women fetishists—*The Razor's Edge* —featured a modified Farrah in its premiere issue.

Magazine business managers have long known that it is the image on the cover, not the articles within, that sells magazines. People, in general, will pay for pictures much more readily than for ideas. For months during the spring and summer of 1977, Farrah Fawcett-Majors and magazine art directors enjoyed a symbiotic relationship. Farrah made it easy to sell magazines; the magazines made it easy to sell Farrah.

Perhaps *New Times* (see p. 111) was the only one to be honest about the relationship.

A

B

C

D

Charlie's Angels *publicity shots. The triangular pose of the three women (A) became the iconographic symbol for the show. Jaclyn Smith and Kate Jackson, brunettes, provide the support for the pyramid structure crowned by Farrah's golden locks. Smith and Jackson usually look rather bemused. No wonder. Farrah never begins a horizontal series of the three women. If she concludes it, she's closest to the camera and we read from Jaclyn to Kate to Farrah (B), or Kate to Jaclyn to Farrah (D). More often than not, Farrah is the center of the design as well as the attention (C). The show didn't start out as a showcase for Farrah; Kate Jackson had been the best-known actress of the trio and early publicity material describes her character, Sabrina, as the leader of the group, "pragmatic and analytical . . . she speaks five languages, is considered an intellectual [my italics] and approaches danger with the calm of the eye of the hurricane." The hurricane, as it turned out, was Jill Munroe (FF-M), "the sports whiz of the group. She excels as an athlete and is an expert in sports trivia. Warm, romantic, and a bit kookie, Jill is a skillful gambler for any stakes—up to and including her life." In the ABC promotional material Kelly Garrett (Jaclyn Smith) represents the low end of this scale of imaginary feminine virtues. She is described as having "common sense developed from first-hand experience. She has worked as a cocktail* waitress, stewardess, and Las Vegas showgirl along the way. Kelly is skilled at self-defense with her hand, mind, or gun." Obviously the working-class figure in this carefully calculated trio.

Since Farrah occupies the middle ground (neither too "intellectual" nor too "physical") it is probably no surprise that her character quickly became the most popular. "Warm, romantic, and a bit kookie," she's clearly the epitome of middle-class feminine virtues, and certainly less threatening than the intellectual and the working girl.

The New York Times Corporation's answer to Time, Inc.'s People had the genius to feature Farrah on the cover of its premiere "test" issue in November 1976, months before other magazines caught on to the Farrah boom. Los Angeles magazine featured Farrah during the spring rush, but chose to emphasize the swim-suited body, while the real iconographic interest in Farrah was quickly becoming the hair.

Vogue, McCall's, Woman's Day, *and* Ladies' Home Journal *neatly cover the scale of class interests from upper middle class to working class. These covers all appeared within a month of each other in the spring of 1977. Notice the remarkable consistency, even when Richard Avedon (Vogue) photographs our heroine. Fawcett knows precisely how to project the same image for the camera, and the simplicity of the persona was in large part responsible for its success. There was no mistaking Farrah, no matter what the medium. Although you can't see it in these black-and-white reproductions, the image-makers were also careful to surround her with blue backgrounds, blouses, and sweaters in order to bring out the blue in her eyes (which ABC publicity material describes as gray). Only the Avedon photo has gray eyes.*

By June, Farrah's face had become so common on magazine racks that product differentiation among the various women's and celebrity gossip magazines was threatened. New Times announced the beginning of the end of the Farrah vogue with this cover which, as it happens, is also the most photographically interesting of the scores of Farrah covers to date. Good Housekeeping, traditionally the most conservative of the women's magazines, tagged along in August with the last of the portrait covers. Meanwhile, more with-it magazines were searching for new Farrah angles. The athletic image was big for a while, as in these New Dawn and People covers from July.

The great Farrah hairdo put-on

(cut it out and try it on)

Meanwhile, Farrah merchandising was moving into high gear. The hairdo was an obvious source of profit; the inevitable celebrity doll is "recommended for children over three years old." The movie gossip magazines, in general financially hard pressed because of the successful competition from the chic celebrity journals such as People and the decline of interest in movie stars, seized on Farrah. By August she had her own magazine, the first issue including "over 200 sexy new fotos!," "Farrah's Special Diet Tips," "In the Kitchen With Farrah—How to Prepare Her Favorite Foods! Plus Her Fabulous Chocolate Chip Cookie Recipe!," and "First Time Ever! Farrah's Wedding Album!"

As the Farrah phenomenon cooled down in the summer of 1977, attention inevitably turned to ancillary topics. TV Guide discussed not the star but the phenomenon as early as May. Us, ever in the vanguard in its losing competition with People, turned to Kate Jackson in June. A magazine bluntly entitled Celebrity tried a two-pronged attack with an article on Jaclyn Smith but a cover of last year's Farrah, Cher. If Celebrity's attitude to the phenomenon seems diffident that may be because it is published by Stan Lee of Marvel Comics fame, and primarily devoted to the exploits of Lee, the first comic book author to gain celebrity status. In August many magazines turned in desperation to the "man behind the women," actor David Doyle. Notice that Farrah's replacement, Cheryl Ladd, takes low position in this inverted Angel triangle.

16. HOW MANY ANGELS CAN DANCE ON YOUR HEAD?

by Klaus Lucka

Klaus Lucka designed and photographed these *Charlie's Angels* parodies for *Esquire*.

THEY'RE NO ANGELS

EXTERMINATING ANGELS

LEAGUE OF ANGELS

PERSONAS

17. FAIRBANKS:
HIS PICTURE IN THE PAPERS
by Richard Schickel

Despite the reams of pop bios, fan mags, and gossip ground out daily about celebrities, the phenomenon has only seldom been studied with acuity. Richard Schickel's slim volume, *His Picture in the Papers: A Speculation on Celebrity in America, Based on the Life of Douglas Fairbanks, Sr.,* is the most thoughtful treatment of the subject I've run across. In the opening pages, Schickel explains why Fairbanks was so important to the history of celebrity and how he controlled the development of his own powerful persona.

To see him at work—even now, over thirty years after his premature death, a half-century, more or less, since he made his finest films—is to sense, as if for the first time, the full possibilities of a certain kind of movement in the movies. The stunts have been imitated and parodied, and so has the screen personality, which was an improbable combination of the laughing cavalier and the dashing democrat. But no one has quite recaptured the freshness, the sense of perpetually innocent, perpetually adolescent narcissism, that Douglas Fairbanks brought to the screen. There was, of course, an element of the show-off in what he did, but it was (and still remains) deliciously palatable because he managed to communicate a feeling that he was as amazed and delighted as his audience by what that miraculous machine, his body, could accomplish when he launched it into the trajectory necessary to rescue the maiden fair, humiliate the villain, or escape the blundering soldiery that fruitlessly pursued him, in different uniforms but with consistent clumsiness, through at least a half-dozen pictures.

Watching him, indeed, one feels as one does watching an old comedy by Keaton or Chaplin: that somehow we have lost the knack, not to mention the spirit, for what they did, and that the loss is permanent. Undoubtedly there are people around to equal, even surpass, Fairbanks' athletic gift. But there is none, one sadly imagines, who could or would orchestrate those gifts as he did, creating out of a series of runs, jumps, leaps, vaults, climbs, swings, handsprings, somersaults, those miraculously long, marvelously melodic lines of movement through which he flung himself with such heedless grace. The problem is that even among the most youthful spirits in the acting game there is no disposition to see the aim of acting simply as taking joy from the job and giving it back—enhanced—to the audience. For actors, like everyone else these days, have grown distressingly sober about their missions in life. Fairbanks, on the other hand, was product and exemplar of an age that, if not quite so innocent as we like to suppose, was nevertheless not quite so grand in its artistic aspirations—especially in the movies, which only a few zealots could even imagine as an art form. There is absolutely no evidence that as an actor—or, to risk a pretentious term, an artist— Douglas Fairbanks conceived of himself as anything more than a fabulist and fantasist. And the idea that he might have held a mirror up to life would probably have appalled him. What he did was hold a mirror up to himself—to endlessly boyish Doug—and invite his audience to join him in pleased contemplation of the image he found there, an image that very accurately reflected the shallow, callow, charming man who lived by the simplest of American codes, and eventually died by it.

Let us, therefore, stipulate at the outset that his artistry—the one thing he was always too modest about—was a given factor in the equation of his personality. Of course, like all marvelous athletes, he submitted to the most rigorous discipline to keep in condition and to perfect those wondrous "stunts" (somehow the word seems too small to describe the miracles of motion he wrought). But the fact is that these, like his basic screen personality, were a natural outgrowth of his character—exaggerations, to be sure, of his natural ebullience and his need to express that ebullience physically, but nothing he had to force or study too hard.

Indeed, it is fair to say that, of the great stars of the silent screen— the ones who pioneered the genres and the characterological archetypes that for so long determined so much film content—Fairbanks probably expressed more of his true self on screen than anyone. Mary Pickford, with whom he was to contract Hollywood's first royal marriage, had created, of course, the classic American girl—spunky, virginal, with a beauty endlessly bathed in golden sunlight—but she was, in fact, a tough, shrewd woman and it would appear that her character began as a fantasy shared by her archetypal stage mother and her first film director, D. W. Griffith, and that it was sustained more by the demands of commerce than by the demands of artistic conscience. Chaplin's Little Fellow was a more complicated construct, and surely represented a part of his complex nature—but only a part of it. William S. Hart, the first great Western good-bad man, came in time to identify very strongly with his screen character, but his real-life Western experience was limited and, before the movies found him, he had been an actor in stage melodramas (notably *Ben-Hur*) that had precious little to do with frontier days in the United States. As for vamps and other exotic sex symbols, from Theda Bara to Rudolph Valentino, they were all

"Melodic lines of movement": Doug in action in The Iron Mask.

largely the products of the feverish imaginations of producers and publicists.

Fairbanks was, on the other hand, always—triumphantly, irritatingly, ingratiatingly—Fairbanks, both on the screen and away from it. Indeed, there is about his career a certain inevitability; one can't quite imagine what he would have done with himself if the movies had not come into existence and provided him with precisely the kind of showcase his spirit and his talents required. Many of his peers might have been just as successful (if not quite so wildly prosperous) as stage personalities. Others, rather ordinary souls beneath the exotic personas that were invented for them, might well have been far more comfortable in routine occupations, leading anonymous middle-class existences. But there was no stage—not even, finally, the movie stage—that could contain Fairbanks' energy or fully exploit his natural gifts. And he was, from earliest childhood, different from other children in ways that no one at the time could quite specify. From his personal history we gain a sense that none of the usual livelihoods would have satisfied him, that he had no choice but to carve his own, singular path in the world.

Indeed, it is perfectly clear that merely acting in films could never have been enough to contain his restless energy. Though that medium was more suited to him than the stage, he still needed more action, more excitement, a greater involvement in the creation of his films and in the management of his career and his image (to use a word not then in vogue) than had been possible for stage-bound actors, or than had at first seemed necessary in movies. The mass appeal of the movies, it must be remembered, had been established for only a little more than a decade, while the star system, the great organizing principle of the industry, was only in the experimental stage when he came to them.

What he had—in addition to his personal magnetism and his delightful energy—was the imagination to organize this organizing principle. How consciously he undertook the task it is impossible to say, but the fact was that, alone of the first generation of superstars (to use another word that came into common usage much later), he had one of those rare personalities that truly flourish best under the light of public attention. Miss Pickford appears to have tolerated it under a tight mask of queenly graciousness. It was part of the price she had to pay not just for economic security but for economic power. Chaplin and Hart were, each in his way, intensely private men. The former, preoccupied with the purification of his art and with the cultivation of respect among the handful of international figures he regarded as his artistic and intellectual peers, mostly shunned public display and, indeed, claimed that his only close friend was Fairbanks. Hart, too, was artistically preoccupied, intent on presenting to the public what he believed was an historically accurate representation of The American West—so much so that he retired from the screen abruptly, in revolt against what he regarded as vulgar commercial pressure to glamorize that history as it was presented on the screen. The other great silent stars who came to fame slightly after this group (Valentino was a notable example) were often either too weak or too unaware of what was happening to them to make more than confused and occasional stabs at the careful management of their public lives and images. They allowed others to handle these matters and quite often discovered too late that they had been wretchedly deceived, even unto the point of destruction. ("A man should control his life," Valentino once said. "Mine is controlling me. I don't like it.")

Fairbanks, however, was different. Only late in life, when his body betrayed him and he could no longer physically do what his spirit commanded, did he demonstrate discomfort over his highly public life and the demands it made of him. Until then he gave every evidence of relishing the attendant confusions of group creation (which any movie necessarily involves); was always, irrepressibly, the leader of that effort; and seemed to enjoy demonstrating mastery over his career almost as much as he enjoyed demonstrating mastery over his body. In short, in the entire history of the screen it is impossible to find anyone with a better temperament for, or a keener instinctual understanding of, what amounted to a new profession—that of being a movie star and a celebrity.

And let there be no mistake about that. This line of work *was* un-precedented. To be sure, there had been great, and greatly popular, stage stars in the United States throughout the nineteenth and early twentieth centuries. Their tours (and the tours of English and European artists capitalizing on their reputations in provincial America) had been major events in the cultural life of the nation. But their relationship to the public had been very different from the relationship movie stars would experience. For one thing, the stage is a less intimate medium (even though the audience is physically in the presence of the actors) because the proscenium has a profoundly distancing effect—no close-ups here. Moreover, the stars of the popular melodramatic and spec-tacular stage (whose audience was quickly taken over by movies) tended to submerge themselves in one or two or three roles (James O'Neill as the Count of Monte Cristo, for example, or William Gillette as Sherlock Holmes), and though they were much admired, they were able to keep their private lives and their public lives quite nearly sep-arated. Indeed, there seems not to have been inordinate public interest in the former. Even the rise of a truly popular press, in the form of mass circulation dailies and large circulation national magazines, did not greatly impinge on their solitude. Content analyses of the major magazines up until 1920, for example, has indicated a singular pre-occupation with political and business leaders and inventors and very little concern with show business figures, although occasionally these individuals were subjects of public adulation very like that visited on movie stars later. (In his excellent study *The Hero in America,* the late Dixon Wecter reprinted a sample of the mail William Jennings Bryan received during and after his 1896 campaign for the Presidency, and it has the same grotesque and pathetic qualities that film-star fan mail would later exhibit.) Which is to say there was a hunger in the land for a more romantic popular hero (Bryan, as the handsome "boy orator," briefly filled the bill before lapsing into buffoonery), and it was this hunger that the movies, quite by accident, began the process of satisfying. It was a process that greatly expanded as more maga-zines (including those devoted exclusively to film personalities) were born, just as radio and, latterly, television provided new and ever-expanding means for image-making, or buffing.

In short, what Fairbanks and the entire first generation of stars had to do, besides play their roles, was to serve as transitional figures in an era of revolutionary change in the media, change that was both creator and creation of a similar revolution in mass sensibility. What happened in this period was that the public ceased to insist that there be an obvi-ous correlation between achievement and fame. It was no longer abso-lutely necessary for its favorites to perform a real-life heroic act, to invent a boon for mankind, to create a mighty business enterprise (on the whole, and especially in America, achievement in the arts was not until recently of any great consequence in the fame game). Beginning with the rise of the star system in Hollywood it was possible to achieve "celebrity" through attainments in the realms of play—spectator sports,

Perhaps one of the most direct signs of Fairbanks' celebrity and its inherent influence in the twenties was the popularization of the suntan as a symbol of chic virility and health. Previously, it had simply been the mark of the workingman. Almost singlehandedly, Doug reversed that image. Here he is seen in The Thief of Bagdad.

acting—and almost immediately thereafter it became possible to become *a* celebrity (a new coinage describing a new phenomenon) simply by becoming . . . a celebrity; that is, in Daniel J. Boorstin's fine phrase, to be "known for your well-known-ness."

This is not to imply that there was anything fraudulent about the achievements of Fairbanks and the other pioneers of this particular industry. Far from it. Many of them were extraordinarily gifted individuals who had to overcome the problem of having absolutely no precedents to guide them in their work. It is suggested that something like a quantum change occurred in the quality of public life during the period, roughly from 1915 to 1925, and that the problem it presented people like Fairbanks was that of keeping one foot firmly planted on the ground of traditional American values and the expectations those values created among their publics while trying at the same time to make a giant step forward into the unknown, into celebrity country, if you will.

Moreover, once the star system—and the technologically expanded media system that fed upon and was fed by it—began to function in something like the modern manner in the 1920's, our definition of reality began to alter. It is not too much to say that we then had two realities to contend with. Daily life, of course, remained—that reality that we experienced personally, using all our senses. Then, however, there was this other reality, the one we apprehended through the media and through the employment of one or at most two senses intensively. The people who existed in this separate reality—the stars and celebrities—were as familiar to us, in some ways, as our friends and neighbors. In many respects we were—and are—more profoundly involved with their fates than we are with those of most of the people we know personally. They command enormous amounts of our psychic energy and attention. It is not too much to say that we have, in about a half-century's time, reached a point where most issues, whether political, intellectual, or moral in nature, do not have real status—that is, literally, the status of the real—until they have been taken up, dramatized, in the celebrity world.

Indeed, it is now essential that the politician, the man of ideas, and the nonperforming artist become performers so that they may become celebrities so that, in turn, they may exert genuine influence on the general public. It is also true that, in recent years, the politics of confrontation, far from being a manifestation of a genuinely radical, revolutionary impulse, have been instead a form of theater, staged by amateur, if clever, actors creating parts for themselves as "leaders," "spokesmen," thus gaining the attention of the media and status as instant celebrities. It is their way of moving over from the realm of ordinary reality to that other reality, that surreality (the word literally means super-reality), which is peopled exclusively by the well known.

The reason for this is simple: It is in this surreal world that all significant national questions are personified and thus dramatized. In time these dramas reach denouement, and when they do the essential decisions facing the nation are made. Or more often, are left unresolved as some new group of personalities, representing some new problem, elbows aside the players (and issues) that previously commanded our fascinated, outraged attention. For the patience of the media is short, and the attention span of the great audience even shorter.

This is not to agree with the proposition that the medium is the message. It is, however, to suggest that the media are anything but neutral, reportorial entities or a simple transmisison belt for ideas. And that qualification implies that, to a greater degree than we allow ourselves to suppose, the quality of celebrity "acting" while in view of the media is a large—perhaps the largest—factor in determining national goals.

18. THE FACE OF GARBO
by Roland Barthes

In *Mythologies,* from which this short meditation comes, and in *Roland Barthes* (about himself), the French structuralist critic has provided an insightful commentary on celebrity and persona.

Garbo still belongs to that moment in cinema when capturing the human face still plunged audiences into the deepest ecstasy, when one literally lost oneself in a human image as one would in a philtre, when the face represented a kind of absolute state of the flesh, which could be neither reached nor renounced. A few years earlier the face of Valentino was causing suicides; that of Garbo still partakes of the same rule of Courtly Love, where the flesh gives rise to mystical feelings of perdition.

It is indeed an admirable face-object. In *Queen Christina,* a film which has again been shown in Paris in the last few years, the make-up has the snowy thickness of a mask: it is not a painted face, but one set in plaster, protected by the surface of the color, not by its lineaments. Amid all this snow at once fragile and compact, the eyes alone, black like strange soft flesh, but not in the least expressive, are two faintly tremulous wounds. In spite of its extreme beauty, this face, not drawn but sculpted in something smooth and friable, that is, at once perfect and ephemeral, comes to resemble the flour-white complexion of Charlie Chaplin, the dark vegetation of his eyes, his totem-like countenance.

Now the temptation of the absolute mask (the mask of antiquity, for instance) perhaps implies less the theme of the secret (as is the case with Italian half mask) than that of an archetype of the human face. Garbo offered to one's gaze a sort of Platonic Idea of the human creature, which explains why her face is almost sexually undefined, without however leaving one in doubt. It is true that this film (in which Queen Christina is by turns a woman and a young cavalier) lends itself to this lack of differentiation; but Garbo does not perform in it any feat of transvestism; she is always herself, and carries without pretense, under her crown or her wide-brimmed hats, the same snowy

solitary face. The name given to her, *the Divine,* probably aimed to convey less a superlative state of beauty than the essence of her corporeal person, descended from a heaven where all things are formed and perfected in the clearest light. She herself knew this: how many actresses have consented to let the crowd see the ominous maturing of their beauty. Not she, however; the essence was not to be degraded, her face was not to have any reality except that of its perfection, which was intellectual even more than formal. The Essence became gradually obscured, progressively veiled with dark glasses, broad hats and exiles; but it never deteriorated.

And yet, in this deified face, something sharper than a mask is looming: a kind of voluntary and therefore human relation between the curve of the nostrils and the arch of the eyebrows; a rare, individual function relating two regions of the face. A mask is but a sum of lines; a face, on the contrary, is above all their thematic harmony. Garbo's face represents this fragile moment when the cinema is about to draw an existential from an essential beauty, when the archetype leans toward the fascination of mortal faces, when the clarity of the flesh as essence yields its place to a lyricism of Woman.

Viewed as a transition the face of Garbo reconciles two iconographic ages, it assures the passage from awe to charm. As is well known, we are today at the other pole of this evolution: the face of Audrey Hepburn, for instance, is individualized, not only because of its peculiar thematics (woman as child, woman as kitten) but also because of her person, of an almost unique specification of the face, which has nothing of the essence left in it, but is constituted by an infinite complexity of morphological functions. As a language, Garbo's singularity was of the order of the concept, that of Audrey Hepburn is of the order of the substance. The face of Garbo is an Idea, that of Hepburn, an Event.

19. AUTO-INTERVIEW
by "Ernest Riffe" (Ingmar Bergman)

The European film world is far less susceptible to the pressures of celebrity than Hollywood. Nevertheless, they exist. In the sixties, Ingmar Bergman wrote two pieces under the pseudonym "Ernest Riffe." The first was a violent attack upon his own work, the second this testy self-interview.

Where do you stand politically?

Nowhere. If there was a party for scared people I would join it. But, as far as I know, there is no such party.

Your religious leanings?

I don't belong to any faith. I keep my own angels and demons going.

Say something about The Shame.

I don't discuss my own films. That would kill the pleasure for audiences and interpreters.

This is going to be a poor interview. I got to get some meat on it. Can we talk about your private life?

No. We can't talk about my private life.

What the hell are we going to do then?

I don't know. *You're* being paid to write about me, not me. If you start crying I don't plan to console you.

If you don't cooperate I'm going to write something terribly unpleasant about you and your film. If I were you, Mr. Bergman, I would watch myself. You're no longer on top. You're on the skids. You need us. We don't need you. You're terribly old. You're not big business. You're not so big in any respect. Face the facts and let's work out an interview in an atmosphere of mutual consent.

Bergman and Liv Ullmann, with whom he had a child in the late sixties, on the set of Face to Face *(1975).*

Ullmann and the Bergman alter ego played by Erland Josephson in a scene from Face to Face.

Excuse me. If I have offended you, I'm sorry. You destroy me. I'm willing to make all the concessions you wish. What do you want me to do? Shall I kiss your ass?

I can imagine greater pleasure. All I want you to do is to say something about your damn, shitty film, which, to be sure, I haven't seen but which according to many sensible people could just as well never have been made.

That's it. Just as well never have been made. You're more right than you understand, you dear dirty darling son. In the drama that washes over us, my cry is just as audible as the chirp of a bird during a battle. I feel it. I know it.

If you're aware of the total pointlessness of your work, why do you continue with it? Why don't you do something useful instead?

Why does a bird chirp from fright. Yes, I know, the answer sounds melodramatic and I see already how the corners of your mouth beneath your weak little moustache turn into an ironic and a very becoming smile. But I have no other answer. No, I have no other answer. If you want to you can note down the whole series of words: anguish, shame, humiliation, anger, boredom, contempt. Do you know what a film is? No, how the hell could you. You're a critic. A film is like a big wheel that one gets started with all the physical and spiritual power that one can muster. Slowly, the wheel starts to move. And its own weight gets it to turn faster and faster. In due course, one becomes hopelessly a part of the wheel, of its motion. That's the way it goes, Mr. Big Shit. Let me conclude our discussion with a punch on the jaw and by wishing you good luck.

20. COMING OF AGE: JEAN-PIERRE LÉAUD

by James Monaco

It's rare enough that an actor is allowed to grow from childhood to adulthood gracefully on the screen. It is even more unusual when that actor manages to capture something of the style of a generation. Jean-Pierre Léaud's close collaboration with Truffaut in the Antoine Doinel cycle of films is, moreover, unique. No American actor came as close as Léaud during the sixties and early seventies to seizing the spirit of that generation. Jack Nicholson, considerably older, caught a thin slice of it. Elliott Gould could have contributed if he had worked more regularly. A number of actors—Peter Fonda, for example—made one or two films that seemed at the time to have something to do with the way we lived then, live now. But, sad to say, there was no one in the U.S. at that time whose work compares with Léaud's.

This essay, which appeared in *Take One,* attempts to trace the development of that unique persona.

François Truffaut thinks Jean-Pierre Léaud is "the most interesting actor of his generation." John Simon, on the other hand, calls him "an eternally callow, crushing bore." Léaud's work has never been especially well appreciated outside of France (as Simon's testimonial bluntly demonstrates). He's certainly not a cashable box-office star of the likes of Jean-Paul Belmondo or Alain Delon. Yet during the next few years it may become much clearer that Truffaut is more perspicacious than Simon—and that Léaud, who has been a committed actor/*cinéaste* for eighteen years now, has during that time carefully and quietly developed a persona that is especially well-suited to the seventies.

Now only thirty-two, he has completed twenty-four films (and starred in twelve of them). He is best known, of course, for his work with Truffaut on the Antoine Doinel films, and throughout the sixties he has intimately identified with the New Wave: first Truffaut, then Godard, then Rivette. In the early seventies, however, he set out to widen his range. In 1972 and 1973 he completed three of his most important films: Bertolucci's *Last Tango in Paris,* Truffaut's *La Nuit*

Américaine, and (most significant) Jean Eustache's *La Maman et la putain* (*The Mother and the Whore*). In each he played roles that were in various ways commentaries on or parodies of his New Wave persona.

Having broken through to a new quantum level, Léaud then took nearly two years off from filmmaking (even as Truffaut did at just about the same time). He has only recently returned to acting, working in two films by young directors: *Umarmungen* (*Embraces*), by the West German Jochen Richter, is a comedy about a ménage à trois in which Sydne Rome and Anny Duperey co-star with Léaud. *Les Lolos de Lola,* the first feature of Bernard Dubois, is a blatantly empty semi-autobiographical investigation of love and marriage, interesting only in that it is a co-production between Truffaut's company, Les Films du Carrosse, and a company composed of the crew members.

A while ago, during his sabbatical from acting, I had a chance to talk with Léaud. He spoke with care and intelligence about his experiences during fifteen years of filmmaking, but we kept returning again and again to the films he had completed in 1972 and 1973, which he regards as an important watershed period. Léaud is not tall; he looks a bit undernourished and sallow (like nothing so much as the cinephile he admits to being, haunting dark movie houses in his free hours, avoiding the beaches and ski slopes). He speaks about film and filmmakers with an animated intelligence and an intensity that stem from a lifetime's commitment.

When he talks, his arms move with the awkward but communicative gestures that punctuate his films, his hands describing intricate patterns in thin air, the blank, Keatonesque pan that is his face breaking into grins of recognition when he discovers a particularly bon mot. He works hard to find the precise phrase and he is remarkably articulate in a specially French way: he has, how you say, the Gallic wit. He appears older, more weary, than his film roles have so far allowed him to be on the screen, but he is entirely capable, if he is bored, of rolling his eyes to the ceiling in that classic, sublimely impatient gesture of Antoine. Like Truffaut, he is Homo cinematicus, he makes small distinction between life and film so that the question he and Truffaut pose in *La Nuit Américaine*—"Is film more important than life?"—is almost moot: they are the same. To meet Léaud "in real life" is only to strengthen an acquaintance that has developed over the years on film. His character is larger, more diverse than the roles he has played, but it is not different. He doesn't act; he is.

"I always wanted to be an actor," he says, "like other kids wanted to be engineers. Recently, I saw the rushes of the screen test I had done for *The 400 Blows.* I was astonished at the image I saw of myself. There is an enormous desire of the fourteen-year-old kid to get the role. Absolutely evident! The personality under the surface is one of the mysteries of film! I was scared stiff, but there are two kinds of fear: the kind that makes you seize up and the kind that fills you with the craziest kind of exuberance. Truffaut was quite as shy as I was, but in a much more introverted way. My shyness makes me aggressive. I

Léaud at age fourteen as Antoine Doinel, Truffaut's alter ego, in The 400 Blows *(1959).*

act entirely by intuition. All that matters to me is the camera that makes me react, sometimes through fear, as in *Masculin-Féminin* for example. Other times it's just the opposite and I forget everything. I have Truffaut to thank for that."

Léaud was very influenced by the "moral character" of Truffaut, he explains. "His moral attitudes concerning life and film were very similar. For a child he was a very impressive personality. No war, no violence, no gross sexuality. He always had something to say about life or film which was of great importance for me." It is just this quality, of course, that Léaud shares with Truffaut: their films avoid stylization and trickery in order to focus intently on the humanity of the characters.

After Léaud's success at the age of fourteen in *The 400 Blows,* he made an interesting but little-known film, *Boulevard,* with Julian Duvivier, and then the second episode of the Doinel saga, *L'Amour à vingt ans,* in 1961. For five years he did not act (actresses may be in great demand at the age of eighteen or nineteen, but actors aren't). He missed the atmosphere of shooting (so lovingly recreated in *La Nuit Améri-*

caine). He needed it physically. "So I had to get back and Godard gave me the chance." Between 1962 and 1966 Léaud spent a period of belated apprenticeship that few actors ever have, working as production assistant (read "gofer") and then assistant director and editor on several films by Godard, Truffaut, and Jean-Louis Richard: *La Peau douce, Mata-Hari, Alphaville,* and *Pierrot le fou,* among others. The experience gave him an interest in the work that was done on the other side of the camera, but he prefers acting and has no plans to follow Trintignant, Karina, Brialy, and the other actors of the sixties who have now become directors.

Godard's *Masculin-Féminin* (1966) gave him an opportunity to act again, and during the following three years he made seven important films for Godard. His major roles during this period—Paul in *Masculin-Féminin,* Guillaume in *La Chinoise,* and Émile Rousseau in *Le Gai Savoir*—although they are not nearly as well known as his work with Truffaut, are of major importance since they define much more clearly than, say, *Easy Rider* or *The Strawberry Statement,* the emerging revolutionary consciousness of the late sixties. Paul is something of a transitional figure between Antoine Doinel's existential childhood isolation and the more social adulthood that awaited Léaud. Guillaume is the second stage of radicalization—a commitment to action. The role of Émile Rousseau (hardly a character, more a lecturer) in *Le Gai Savoir* illustrates the final stage of the process through which so many of us passed in the 1960's. If Léaud had only these three roles to his credit, he would still have to be considered one of the major actors of his generation, a generation which has been very poorly served by American films until very recently, but which Godard and Truffaut (and now Eustache) were fascinated by, and whose lifestyles and obsessions they mined as subjects for their films. They caught the particular sense of alienation, and they understood the politics it led to, but even more important, they could see that the politics was intimately connected with the revolution in sexual roles. Léaud's characters most often seem to be involved in triangular relationships which point out and elucidate the changing moral universe of his generation.

In *Masculin-Féminin,* Paul, who has some sophistication in politics, understands very little about the three women he finds himself living with. He dies of it. In *La Chinoise,* the ménage à trois has become a commune which Guillaume must try to come to terms with. He is not very successful. Émile Rousseau's relationship with Patricia in *Le Gai Savoir* has been raised to the level of dialectic, but it is still a battle. Throughout the latter films of the Antoine Doinel cycle, Antoine must contend with his eternal mystification at womanhood and the intractable experience of marriage. In his first film outside of the Doinel cycle for Truffaut, Léaud as Claude in *Two English Girls* is suspended between the poles of Anne and Muriel in an historical recreation of the beginning of what we call, for want of a better term, the "sexual revolution." Alphonse's highly ethical but destructive passion in *La Nuit Américaine* is one of the finer touches of the film. His recurrent question—"Are women magic?"—although comic in intent, also summarizes his existential dilemma through this series of films. As Tom in *Last Tango in Paris,* a relatively healthy foil to Marlon Brando's self-pitying Paul, Léaud exists on the edge of the film and, from Bertolucci's point of view, serves mainly as comic relief. Alexandre in Eustache's *La Maman et la putain* is squarely at the center of the film, on screen for most of its three and a half hours, and balanced painfully between the "mother" and the "whore" of the title.

In all his major roles, then, Léaud has (intentionally or otherwise) developed characters who are essentially the products of an obsessive interest in the new sexual politics. So very few American films during the sixties came anywhere close to dealing with the knotty problems of modern sexuality, that Léaud's accomplishment seems even rarer and more valuable from our own perspective. As Bogart summarized the experience of most of us who were young in the forties, so Léaud has helped us to understand the lives of the young in the sixties. Like Bogart, he has also provided an ironic model which viewers of his films relate to instantly and which they can use almost therapeutically within their own lives. Bogart's quiet irony and self-sufficiency are very attractive parts of his persona. Likewise, Léaud's manic protestations and awkward but deeply felt reactions to pain and love provide us with weapons we can use to fight off the pain and absurdity of our own lives. More than any other actor of the 1960's, Léaud has symbolized the generation who are, according to Godard, "the children of Marx and Coca-Cola."

Two of his three most recent roles recapitulate that experience, while the third—Alexandre in Jean Eustache's *La Maman et la putain*— marks a new beginning for Léaud and—just possibly—an entirely new factor in French Cinema. Léaud as Alphonse in Truffaut's *La Nuit Américaine* has a chance to work a little against the grain of the Antoine Doinel character that the two of them collaborated upon over a period of eleven years. Where Claude in *Two English Girls* was more passive, more controlled than Antoine, Alphonse is much freer, more active, and more brashly and dangerously romantic. Truffaut appears in the film as the hard-of-hearing director Ferrand, who "keeps the script moving." According to Léaud, "he wanted only to talk about practical problems of filmmaking. He put the sentimental problems on me." The division of labor is significant; the central fact about the long collaboration between Truffaut and Léaud has been just the manner in which Léaud has been able to translate the barely audible but nevertheless deeply felt emotions onto film, leaving Truffaut the director free for "practical problems." As Léaud understood early on, the shyness which united them expressed itself in opposite ways, Léaud being much more aggressive than the introverted Truffaut.

While Alphonse was an important role for Léaud because it was "another step away from Antoine," he probably had higher hopes for his participation in Bertolucci's *Last Tango in Paris.* Here was a chance to work with a "hot" director on a large project. Yet despite the finan-

Léaud as Doinel grown up, in bed with Christine (Claude Jade), his wife in Bed and Board *(1971).*

cial success of *Last Tango,* Léaud does not appear to be particularly pleased with the film nor with the experience of making it. His character, Tom, is marginal, interrupting the central interest of the relationship between Brando's Paul and Maria Schneider's Jeanne. For someone like myself who thinks that Brando's performance and the film itself are both self-indulgent and temporizing and that the attitude of both Bertolucci and his alter ego Paul toward Jeanne is narcissistic and sexist, Léaud's brief scenes in the film bring it some life and wit. Léaud begins his critique of the film, as is his manner, with a positive and liberal view of it, but then continues to indicate the serious problems he had with this project: "Like Truffaut says, *Last Tango* is interesting because every time a man is asking questions about love it's always interesting. It might have been more interesting, however, if we'd stayed inside the room. People are most interested in what is going on inside that room, and the film would have had more unity.

"Without being conscious of it, I must have felt something equivalent about the way the film seemed to be pulled in two different directions. Bertolucci wanted to speak about himself—the film was partly autobiographical—but he was embarrassed to cast a character close to himself in age, so he split himself between Brando, who was older, and me. He took the sexual obsession and gave it to Brando and I became the part of himself that was the adolescent filmlover. I tried to play the

Léaud and Jacqueline Bisset in Truffaut's Day for Night *(1973).*

part with a little bit of humor. I was thinking also of that slow Brando
manner. I wanted to act quickly and accent the stylized gestures because
I was not given enough time to analyze the character. The part was a
little bit difficult because the audience always wants to get back to the
room. Besides, everything is absolutely improvised. We would write it
in the morning with Bertolucci. My only frame of reference is that I
used to be a film buff.

"It was difficult, in another way, for me to work in Bertolucci's film
because Brando refused systematically to work on Saturdays. (Maybe
he was marching for the liberation of Indians!) Me, I had to work
every Saturday so that the crew wouldn't waste time. Maybe the sympathetic thing to say is that there was a clash of styles—Italian, French,
and American."

Like *Last Tango in Paris,* Jean Eustache's *La Maman et la putain*
deals with the reconstruction of sexual habits; like *Last Tango, La
Maman* takes place mainly in one bedroom. But where Bertolucci's film
is flaccid and improvised, Eustache's is tightly written and witty; where
Bertolucci (with an implicitly Roman Catholic sensibility) deals only
with the destruction of the old mores, Eustache, on the other hand, also
analyzes for us the new mores that are beginning to replace the old
ones. *La Maman et la putain,* more than any other recent French film,
gives one a sense of new beginnings, fresh departures. At the same

time, it is thoroughly evocative of the elements of the styles and concerns of the New Wave that made the films of Truffaut, Godard, Rohmer, Rivette (and Bresson) so valuable during the last fifteen years. Eustache draws a little something from each of his predecessors, but the synthesis he makes is entirely his own. The film is three and a half hours of intense dialogue (and monologue), which is both rich with resonances of the past and at the same time clearly a very relevant film about the way we live now, the way we make love. As Alexandre, Léaud is caught in a tangle of relationships with three women, just as he was seven years previously in *Masculin-Féminin*. Godard's film was, however, an objective, slightly bemused study of people in their early twenties—a generation which, Godard explained at the time, was like a foreign country to him. Eustache's film, while it speaks of the same generation, now about thirty, is far more subjective and ironic. Most important, moreover, are the tremendous changes which have taken place in the sensibilities of that generation. The new lifestyles have become institutionalized, and the people have been vulcanized by the politics of the intervening years—in America, mainly Vietnam, but in France, the revolution of '68. Alexandre, in the course of this intense film, proposes romantic marriage to Gilberte (Isabelle Weingarten) but is turned down. He discovers Veronika (Françoise Lebrun) to take her place, a woman who, as she explains, "Screws a maximum of guys." All the time, meanwhile, he is living with Marie (Bernadette Lafont). As similar as it is to his previous roles in terms of content, Alexandre is "something completely new and different" for Léaud. He speaks of the film with admiration, even love:

"There is always a moment in life when a man asks himself questions about sex, and that's always interesting because the answers are always different. For myself, I like very much *La Maman et la putain*. Eustache had written a text that was detailed and extremely beautiful, word for word, and I had to put it back on the screen with a kind of natural feeling. He had written the part especially for me, and I fell into my age again—twenty-nine or thirty. Anything which had to do with adolescence I had to forget and leave behind. Since there was no improvisation, I found I had to work for the first time in films as I do on stage. The text was written out and I had to give it back. I was trying to be as natural as possible, but I had to follow this very strict line given by the director, although I was still using my own small personal technique, which mainly consists of finding the image of a director and following that. (It usually happens within the first three days of shooting that I can tell where we are going.) Given my preference, I would rather have the director provide some ideas and some words, leaving some room for the actor in between. Most of the time it works like that, but I am full of thanks to Eustache for writing that part for me. It's more pleasant when you can give back in your own words the author's ideas, but the tensions we were under were productive here, I feel. Besides the difficulty with the extensive script, there were tensions for other reasons. It was Eustache's first long feature film and a director

Léaud, once again in bed, with Bernadette Lafont and Françoise Lebrun in Jean Eustache's The Mother and the Whore *(1973). A disproportionate number of scenes in New Wave films took place in bed, a quaint fact which Eustache is lovingly parodying here.*

in that position has to discover a lot. We were limited by the four-week shooting schedule and we had a lot of problems with the film stock itself which were multiplied by the limitations of the shooting schedule: we were doing shots of four or five minutes each, and retakes would have taken too much time. But with all that, it was like participating in a very intimate adventure. We were all old friends.

"At the same time the film is very close to life, and there was a special atmosphere on the set which colored our feeling, which is good, because it gives a special psychological colorization to the film. It was the most difficult work I've ever done in my life. It was the true work of an actor. Yet there were no special psychological difficulties for us with the subject of the film because you couldn't get lost in it. We had no time. The only way we could express it was to play it. The film is finally a structure of monologues, and the most important character is words. It's maybe the first time that you hear women talking the way they really do, and it's difficult to imagine that a man could understand this the way Eustache did. The film is deeply political without

being explicit. There is a sentiment—a sense of loss—that is very political and that exists at the center of the film. Eustache feels that very
much. Even though Alexandre is the pivot of the film, I think Eustache
was thinking equally about the roles that Françoise and Bernadette play
(and about Françoise and Bernadette too). There was never really
any attention focused on me, it was always the three of us. And after
all, Alexandre is not a brilliant homage to men! I like Bernadette's
character very much. She plays with a special strength and intensity.
It is a very noble character and very true. I like the film very much."

There is not much doubt, looking back over the list of Léaud's films
during the past ten years, that he has, with the great help of Truffaut,
Godard, and now Eustache, become an actor who doesn't simply serve
time on the screen, but rather collaborates actively with his directors.
It is no accident that Truffaut's *L'Enfant sauvage,* in which the teacher
learns as much as the student, is dedicated to Jean-Pierre Léaud. If he
prefers not to direct films himself it is only because he is perceptive
enough to know how much important work there is to be done as an
actor. As Antoine, Paul, Guillaume, Émile, Claude, Alphonse, Tom, and
Alexandre, he has created a subtle and various persona that explains
much about his generation. In his understanding of that subject among
actors, he is almost alone, sad to say. He represents for many of us the
actor as surrogate, not portraying a whole gallery of strange, distant,
and objective characters (in a way that calls attention to the actor's
art) but rather conscientiously and regularly illustrating our own
deeper selves, subjectively holding the analytical mirror up to our own
natures. That is really useful and interesting work.

For Léaud, "the position of an actor is very difficult because you are
always waiting for someone to give you a script. I'm extremely impatient; I have to make a film as soon as I sit still. An actor has to rediscover everything if he stops working. I haven't any idea what I will
be doing in the future; I only hope I get as good films as I have recently." If he does, we can continue to expect that he will illustrate
with wit and a very rough charm the progress of the "children of Marx
and Coca-Cola" into their rapidly approaching middle age.

21. WOMEN AND THE POLITICS OF ACTING
by James Monaco

If there hasn't been an American woman film star of sufficient magnitude to set a hairstyle since Debbie Reynolds, it's safe to conclude that there have been even fewer actresses whose work attracts us. The French attitude during the same period of time has been markedly different. Like Léaud, most of these women lead relatively normal lives. They are workers rather than stars and their celebrity is channeled into the job of acting.

Since this piece was written for the *Village Voice* in late 1975, Marie-France Pisier has set about the task of becoming an international star. She picked up a role in a major Hollywood melodrama *(The Other Side of Midnight)*, perfected her colloquial English, and can now be seen chatting with Johnny Carson quite as if she had been born a Hollywood starlet. She still hasn't lost her sense of herself, however.

One of the most striking differences between French and American movies for the last fifteen years has been the relative importance of women. Simply put, most American movies are still stuck somewhere back in the desolate fifties when it comes to women's roles. The usual structure of a contemporary American film is a triangle—two men and a girl—and the woman turns out to be superfluous as the two buddies ride off into the sunset at the last fade. The situation is so absurd that we congratulate a latter-Day Doris movie like *Alice Doesn't Live Here Anymore* as a "feminist" phenomenon just because its central character is a woman, even though it tries to persuade us—not so subtly—that women who think about careers, about going off on their own and leading independent lives, are at best silly and will eventually see the light and settle down with a quiet hero like Kris Kristofferson. *Mahogony,* setting box-office records, teaches us the same old repressive lessons in a black setting. As far as movies are concerned, the women's movement of the last eight years might just as well have never existed.

But in French movies, things are different. Women characters never suffered the kind of repression that clamped down hard in this country after the Second World War and hasn't yet lifted. Think of the New Wave of ten or fifteen years ago. Where would Godard have been without Anna Karina? Or Truffaut without Jeanne Moreau? Chabrol has depended upon his vital artistic relationship with Stéphane Audran for fifteen years now; Jacques Rivette's entire career rests on the work of the groups of actresses he has organized for his films; and Eric Rohmer's movies are about nothing if not the relationship between stronger women and weaker men.

Having grown up with roles that many American actresses would trade Beverly Hills mortgages for, French actresses are now demanding even more sophisticated parts and, more important, a greater share of power in the complex process of filmmaking. To a large degree they are succeeding. The stars of the early New Wave—Anna Karina, Jeanne Moreau, Delphine Seyrig—have now moved behind the camera and are directing films as well as acting in them. Younger actresses, meanwhile, have developed a variety of strategies for realizing their full potential. I recently spoke with five of them about their plans and their attitudes toward their craft—a profession, by the way, which plays no small part in determining how the rest of us perceive the world.

Canadian by birth, Alexandra Stewart is a witty, ironic, and voluble woman whose roles seldom exhibit those qualities. Most of the time she's hired to play a cool, statuesque, blond stereotype of the sort she parodies in Louis Malle's *Black Moon*. She is properly ironic about the type-casting, and despite the limitations of the parts she has been able to act in an extraordinary variety of movies—sixty or seventy over the last fifteen years—where, she says, she has had the freedom to develop her craft that she never would have had "in the big Hollywood films where the roles of the women are completely uniform and blah and boring." (After *Exodus* in 1960 she appeared in only one other major American movie, Arthur Penn's experimental *Mickey One*.) Stewart is a prime example of a common European phenomenon that has no significant counterpart in the American film industry: the actor with the well-developed reputation who prefers to put craft before career. She often works with young directors making their first films—which is usually more helpful to the film than to the "star" persona of Alexandra Stewart. Older by a few years than the other actresses I spoke with, she is also more sanguine about the profession. She is interested in moving into the technical end of the business (where the power is) but she hasn't yet made her move. Nothing like the bourgeois stars who are older than she, Stewart is also not as militant as her younger sisters.

Juliet Berto, not yet thirty, got her start when she was eighteen in Godard's *Two or Three Things I Know About Her,* quickly did four more films for Godard (including *La Chinoise* and *Weekend*) and worked with such directors as Alain Tanner and Nadine Trintignant before reaching a peak with Jacques Rivette's fascinating *Céline et*

Alexandra Stewart, by Maureen Lambray.
Copyright © 1975.

Juliet Berto, as she appeared in Rivette's
Céline et Julie vont en bateau *(1974).*

Julie vont en bateau. The experience with Rivette and the troupe of actors in that film (as well as his earlier, legendary *Out One*) was climactic for her as an actress. Rivette is the Peter Brook of French film and something of a saint to actors because of his concern and respect for them. "Without getting into psychodrama," Berto says, "the experience of that film was very rare and very important. I got a new image of myself, a constructive one." She has already written two screenplays for which she is trying to raise money and has shot a short film, a portrait of an American jazz musician. After a half dozen major films with Godard and Rivette it's no wonder Berto has become impatient with acting. "I want to return to zero so I can go further," she says, quoting Godard: "I want to shoot."

Marlène Jobert, in her early thirties, also began with Godard (in *Masculin-Féminin,* 1966) but unlike Berto moved on into more popular cinema. In 1969 she played opposite Charles Bronson in *Rider on the Rain,* René Clément's huge financial success, which guaranteed her a position as one of France's top box-office draws. During the next two years she completed six films (including Chabrol's *Ten Day Wonder* and De Broca's *Touch and Go*) only one of which, Maurice Pialat's brilliant *We Won't Grow Old Together,* fully satisfied her. She considers it her best film. In 1972 she quit cold for two years while she reassessed her position. Having reached a point where she was considered the number-two female star in France (just behind Catherine Deneuve) she found she still couldn't get what she considered to be decent roles. She spent six months straight at the movies, getting a delayed education in the classics, and then developed a plan. Unlike Stewart and Berto she had no interest in working behind the camera, so the only way for her to gain some power was to get involved in the financial end of the business. She worked out a scheme in which she would co-produce her films, putting up the money necessary to get a project off the ground and using her name and box-office reputation to raise the rest. Nothing unusual here—Belmondo, Delon, American stars have been doing this for years—except that now it was a woman who had financial control and, more important, her aim was not to find vehicles for herself and hire submissive hacks to direct them, but rather to seek out talented filmmakers who were having difficulty financing their films and bring her economic clout to an equal partnership. The first product of "M.J. Productions" was Swiss director Claude Goretta's *Pas si méchant que ça,* in which Jobert not only does not have the central role but even plays a character who's not entirely admirable from a feminist point of view. It was enough for her just to work with Goretta. Jobert is no longer interested in becoming a star; she simply wants to do the best work as an actress that she can.

Marlène Jobert is the last young French actress who came anywhere near being sucked into the star system that has damaged the artistic careers of such once-promising actors as Delon, Belmondo, and

Marlène Jobert.

Deneuve (while at the same time making them very rich). Anyone under thirty seems to be immune to the lures of big money, Borsalino hats, and Chanel No. 5.

Marie-France Pisier decided to be an actress when she was ten. At eighteen she starred with Jean-Pierre Léaud in Truffaut's *Love at Twenty,* the second episode of the Antoine Doinel saga. When Truffaut returned to the story six years later he brought back Pisier's character (Colette) for a short scene. In the interim Colette had married and had a child. But Pisier had done something quite different. She had picked up not one but two graduate degrees—one in law (1965), another in political science (1968). Since then she has written occasionally about such subjects as censorship and feminism for *Le Monde* and several magazines. (Her thesis subject had been the role of women—in film and in life—years before the subject became popular.) She has also completed half a dozen movies and three television series. Why the advanced degrees when she had wanted all her life to be an actress? "When my mother met my father she was studying medicine. When they got married she dropped everything. When she got divorced all she could do was be a secretary." This lesson was not lost on the rest of the family: Pisier's sister is a university professor of law with several books about politics—Marxism in particular—to her credit. Her brother does research in pure mathematics.

Aside from the pair of films with Truffaut, Pisier's film work is little known in the U.S. (although that should change with the release of *Céline and Julie* and André Téchiné's *French Provincial* in which she stars with Jeanne Moreau). In France, however, her name is the proverbial household word ever since she acted a major role in *Les Gens de Mogador,* an extraordinarily popular twelve-episode television program a couple of years ago which dealt with the lives of three generations of women between 1860 and 1914.

Pisier watches the sexual politics of French film (both on and off the screen) carefully and senses a new, more hopeful mood now. She points to the selection of three films by women for the official program at Cannes in 1975 and the useful and prolific work being done by a group called "Psychoanalyse et Politique" whose publishing arm, Éditions des Femmes, is quite active. "Now there is a movement to do things," she says, "rather than just talk about them." In time, she too plans to direct. Her first project is a script called *Stolen Comedy* that takes the classic triangle of two women and one man and inverts it, giving the women the primary roles.

Isabelle Adjani, who carries Truffaut's brooding, complex *Story of Adele H.* singlehandedly, is the kind of phenomenon that comes along once in a generation. In the last year she has been the subject of a firestorm of publicity as she achieved smashing successes first on television, then theater, then film. Born the year Truffaut made his first movie, before she turned twenty Adjani had been asked to join the

Marie-France Pisier, by Sylvia Plachy. Copyright © 1975.

Isabelle Adjani, by Maureen Lambray.
Copyright © 1975.

permanent company of the Comédie Française. She turned them down. "They wanted me to be bound to stay there for twenty years. I found it an incredible proposition," she states with some wonderment. Her rejection of the most prestigious French theater troupe caused something of a scandal—one that was unwelcome mainly because it came too early. She was not yet confident enough to make good use of the media spotlight in which she found herself.

Adjani really represents a second generation of young French actors and actresses—one that has grown up after the events of May 1968, and has benefited by the struggle for independence of the generation (now about thirty) that came before. For them the star system is completely ludicrous—not even a temptation, according to Adjani. Do the young actors feel contemptuous of Belmondo and the stars of his generation? "Contemptuous? They just despise them!" she exclaims. Adjani belongs to an informal group of a couple of dozen young actors and actresses who have achieved some success but are not yet (except for Adjani) well known. The group meets every once in a while to discuss ways of changing the system that exploits them as "workers in film and theater" and endlessly analyzes possible cooperative structures which might allow them to make films differently. Most of their ire focuses on the large Paris agencies who control the lives of their clients—"We are trying to find a way of not being indentured," says Adjani. Nothing concrete has come of these discussions so far but that doesn't worry her. She thinks the process is more important than the result—a political theory straight out of late sixties Godard, whose films are among those that most affected her when she was younger.

Having been only the second from this group to gain some fame (Gérard Dépardieu was the first), Adjani at present is busy learning how to deal with it. "I'm very embarrassed," she says. The interesting thing will be to see whether she will be able to maintain her healthy skepticism about her profession or whether the embarrassment will turn to acquiescence as the torrent of publicity wears her down. So far she has chosen her projects carefully. After first gaining some fame in Claude Pinoteau's *The Slap* she was offered dozens of similar parts. She turned them all down. Her next film will be with André Téchiné. In it she plays a young, intelligent working-class woman, the main character in a detective story. Imagine a similar film in an American context. Not likely.

Ten years ago the attitudes of Isabelle Adjani—and the others—toward their profession would have appeared strange indeed. Wasn't the whole idea of acting to become a star? (Unless you failed; then you were a "character actor.") But, at least in France, all that has changed now. Adjani has the stunning appearance and real talent that rightly appeal to starmakers and stargazers, but she has something else as well —a skeptical intelligence and a sense of herself that some people might find even more attractive. Stewart, Berto, Jobert, Pisier, and Adjani aren't isolated cases; they have a lot of company in the French film world: actors like Dépardieu, Léaud, and Philippe Léotard, and actresses like Bulle Ogier, Bernadette Lafont, Françoise Fabian, and Dominique Labourier. For these people celebrity is simply beside the point; it's more exciting for them to *act* than to *star*. They mark a new phase in film history in which actors take their place in partnership with auteurs.

22. DRUGSTORE REVENGE: DEATH AND TRANSFIGURATION IN THE HOLLYWOOD FIRMAMENT

by David Thomson

English critic David Thomson is the author of *A Biographical Dictionary of Film,* a singlehanded reference work which is unique and invaluable for its succinct, sharp, intelligent analyses of hundreds of star personas. No other writer is half as aware as Thomson of the precise and subtle ways those personas influence our image of ourselves.

There is, as there has always been, the coloration of religious ritual in star personas, so it is no surprise that in the end we sacrifice them, literally or figuratively. In this piece written especially for *Celebrity,* Thomson investigates this morbid attraction.

The week after the 1977 Oscars were presented, a stunning and insolent color picture was printed in *Time* magazine. Terry O'Neill had been up early the morning after that ritual orgy of applause and self-tribute, so much franker now that winners are permitted to applaud themselves and their own bounty—this is the gift to stars of humble game shows. The photographer—seemingly?—happened on the delectable and magically provided Faye Dunaway. It may not have been the lady herself—she would have been weary from exhilaration—but her dawn appearance. We are used to the separation of imagery and substance.

His picture of her was suffused in the copper-sulphate light of swimming pools under sunless skies. Faye sat in a white recliner, on the tiled promenade of a calm azure oblong. She was wearing an ivory-colored housecoat, agape from mid-thigh, showing one lean leg crossed over the other and high-heeled shoes with slender straps emphasizing the ankle. The pool stretched away behind her and rows of other recliners were respectfully empty. A table attended her, its pedestal buried in the discarded morning papers, all shouting death and glory—Posthumous Oscar for Finch. On the top of the table was what appeared to be a rather homely breakfast and the golden phallus given her the night before: Oscar at attention, arms folded, face blank, the discreet, ever-erect god of the drugstore kingdom, the magical authority that only one girl a year has to turn her into a goddess—like Dwan in *King Kong*, tethered for her big break and golden shot.

The enigmatic Faye sat back, symbiotic with the luxury of triumph, risking daft splendor to have a "still" of it, her graven face just suppressing the nervous grin—serene, assured and, like all movie creatures, simultaneously public and withdrawn. I adore the girl, but there was a sheerness to the picture, an overweening perfection that made some mean wretch within me mutter, "Just you wait, my lovely."

That was the voice of the small-town drugstore: an elastic community made to embrace all the faithful of the Church of Hollywood. All of us who watched the movies were those left behind to vegetate in provincial listlessness and censorious discontent. Escape from European hardships, the space and plenty of America, and the consequent riot of advertisers, confidence tricksters and hype merchants ensured that America become a land of aspirants, believing in better things and asking "Can't we dream?" But the Europe forsaken had impressed strict moral, social and religious codes, and no one overthrew them without guilt. And in America, the winning of freedom, room and tumble-dryers was so strenuous, and the holding on so desperate, that the public quickly became conservative and neurotic, just as it had been puritanical and angry from its earliest days—protestants stumbling on Eden instead of a looked-for purgatory.

The dreamers therefore loathed themselves for fantasizing and stored massive rancor, envy and punishment for the most reckless protagonists of the great romance. "Just you wait, my lovely" is the promise of revenge for the lowly, ignored and ugly, and it has as much intensity and nobility as the resort to vengeance in Westerns and gangster movies. The persistent right of retribution is encouraged in nearly every genre of the cinema where tit for tat, or an eye for an eye, is the dynamic of so much narrative action, the cause and effect that legitimized violence and competition.

In the American drugstore, the millions sat in trusting but insecure communion with the fountainhead of its religion. There is a counter where the sweet and sour staples of diet are provided: malteds, coffee and a doughnut, hamburgers or hot dogs, ice cream and soda. The drugstore also sells cosmetics, medicines and placebos; it is brimful of things to make you feel contented and look better. The atmosphere is local, superficial and cheerful. But there is access for things from the wider world, carried on the road that hisses past only a few yards from the door and which, according to legend, connects L.A., N.Y.C., and this festering center of the universe—Sugar City, Colorado; Correctionville, Iowa; Hell, Michigan; Hope, Arkansas; or Hot Coffee, Mississippi.

Those names are boastfully far-fetched, and if the last sounds least likely, that in fact is where Stella Stevens comes from. I don't know how she made the great journey westward, and in those conversations with Johnny Carson or Dinah! Shore, addressed to unseen millions, our lacquered celebrities so often slide over the transition, leaving the drugstore addicts to recall the day when an opal and ginger convertible lingered and drove off with the pretty blonde who had served the malteds for a year or more but who all along, they had known, was a tramp, no better than she should be, from the wrong side of the tracks, headed for no good. Otherwise, why would they have kidded her about going out for some real fun one night, or gazed slyly when her stacked body reached up to fill the shelves?

The counter-girl's sparkling thighs, or the crescents of her freckled breasts are prototype delights of the movie experience. They allow the customer to be a voyeur: he is permitted to look and enjoy; he is free to imagine what he cannot quite see and what he would do with it, given the opportunity; and he walks away armored in the self-righteousness that scolds and disapproves of her for letting him look. (What is a starlet? A girl who wants to be a star and will let anyone.) He wouldn't allow his own woman to prance around in a clinging dress like that, and he won't be surprised if this little whore ends up flaunting herself on the screen for millions. Nevertheless, if a tourist comes by and stops at the drugstore, the local will proudly confide that that very girlie, now dwelling in pools and hot lights and featured in the movie magazines that another girl arranges in the racks . . . "Oh yes, sir," he'll say. "She's from this town, you know." And he and the other drugstore vultures can believe they're not lost, that their existence is substantiated. "Pretty as a picture she was. We always knew she had it in her. Coffee used to keep hot from her looking at it. Right."

The tribal legend may exaggerate the central place of the drugstore, but the legend is desperate for a center. The drugstore is a location recreated endlessly in the movies—sure evidence of the industry's awareness of how the audience wished to honor the soft center of their culture. Once in a while the drugstore dream worked—one day in a hundred years—as often as Brigadoon came back to life. Still, Lana Turner was "found" in a drugstore, albeit one in Los Angeles, way to the southwest of her original home town, Wallace, Idaho. Within a few years she was famous as the "Sweater Girl"—thick lips, sleazy eyes, bodily hunks of blond hair and perpetually held breath to fill the sweater, allowing only little signs of speech. In 1946, in burning white, she was the bored waitress-wife in a highway diner who gives John Garfield a murderous hard-on in *The Postman Always Rings Twice*. Turner's celebrity was flagrant and lowdown. She was a broad: indolently sensual and contemptuous of moral stigma. She went to bat for slum girls on the make, and when nice guys pinned up her picture—and pin-ups are the icons of the timid and polite—none of them doubted that she was too extreme to introduce to mother. Turner merged imaginatively with the movie tart, pleasurable but not socially acceptable, tacky sister to the sweet, modest girl men marry. Years later, every public expectation and suspicion was fulfilled when Turner's private life splashed messily onto the scandal sheets and her teenage daughter killed the mother's lover—a hood called Johnny Stompanato, till then the nearest anyone had come to the transfiguring kitsch of "Sylvester Stallone."

The drugstore grew cozy with glee, for Lana Turner had always been a blatant offense to the tribe's dogma that only class and restraint endured. (In a free enterprise system, "class" grows up as an excuse for those who cannot make it.) Small-town voyeurism easily balanced the hypocritical indulgence of peeping at naughty girls and marrying the demure. While puritan energy nursed all the zeal required of a witch hunt. The movies themselves are from the wrong side of the tracks— shady, corrupt and fraudulent, and always threatening to lead the young and earnest astray. But the movies offer prudes the chance of sin without involvement, illicit pleasure without unmentionable disease or scandal. So the wicked movie house was permitted, a licensed brothel. And to tame its rawness, codes and regulations guaranteed that its messages always ended up conventional and genteel. Thus, the honest, integrated and decent are smiled upon with happy endings, while the grasping, messy and depraved are sent to perdition—just so long as they give us moralists in the dark a sip of all three first.

Censorship was not an effective control system. It was a drugstore compromise—like the Surgeon General's stern advice on every packet of cigarettes—not one is missed. It had the effect of making innuendo and suggestiveness as tender as pimples one longs to burst. Before the Hays Code, girls could be naked under slips, chemises and blouses—all in shiny silks—and seemed fragile, delicate and transient as flames. But censorship insisted on the bulwarks of engineered bras and sweaters, so that Lana Turner and Jane Russell gave the impression of being slowed and nearly suffocated by sexual repression. Censorship in the movies was the clearest proof of prurience relying on awful temptation. "Hands off," it told the voyeur, and turned sex from a fond practice to a spectator sport. No one handled it as well as Howard Hughes, who designed a bra that would proffer Russell's twin engines to the gulping camera, and then deliberately withheld *The Outlaw* for five years to persuade everyone that shocked censors were impeding the passage of Jane's pillowy breasts—the most significant obstacle to high-powered superstructure until New York City denied Concorde.

Jane Russell's humbling has not been cruel—mercifully, for she always seemed a merry, good-natured girl. But drugstore philosophers were aroused by the sight of her in the hayloft and by the publicity lines wondering "How would you like to tussle with Russell?" Jane asserted her own respectability by speaking for herself sometimes, and by a devoted campaign to adopt children. But thirty years after *The Outlaw*, drugstore lechers had a last laugh when Jane turned to TV commercials advocating bras and girdles for "us fuller-figured girls." Nothing is as humiliating for stars as having to beseech the camera to buy—so says drugstore opinion, overlooking the indignity of being addressed with such steady blandishments that you can hardly purchase anything that has not been glazed with absurd promises which only a fool would swallow and a madman digest.

The Jane in the hay was at least an imitation of the wanton, but Playtex Jane was domesticated by a sunny living room—her Tarzan has a hernia, hobbies and a respected position in the local community—actually not far from the lifestyle of the screen's young Tarzan. He was always a very decorous noble savage. Class, regularity and bourgeois virtues descend on nice guys and their condominiums with all the stupefying weight of a fair-sized bit of the rock.

The few truly wild or messy spirits who got into movies were house-trained if they were to last. Consider for a moment the career of James Cagney. In the early thirties, he was an astonishing insurgent glamorizing a randy, nihilistic vitality and sneering at the "safe" dream of Americana—he was the confidence trickster or gangster who exposed the sanctimonious humbug that reigned in the drugstore. His energy was irresistible and sometimes demonic: he hit women in the face with grapefruit; danced if he got bored with walking; punctured lying homilies; killed with enthusiasm; and when executed himself, ridiculed the moral example with beautiful, extended death throes. At his most exciting, he was the spirit of an alarming urge to abandon ordinariness, the wild one breaking out and scattering dead forms. Revolution! The drugstore stalwarts of law and order shuddered in their sleep.

Many people and institutions felt endangered by his mockery of the dutiful paths to pious success, not least the studio that made money from his films. Drugstore duplicity rose to its peak when profit-making companies hurried to the bank with the proceeds from movies that treated banks as if they were dollhouses. By 1935, Cagney's dynamism was neatly reassessed, and he was cast as a plainclothes cop instead—still snarling, wisecracking and shooting, but blessed by a badge and prime motives. This adoption of violence by screen law-enforcers was commercially crucial, for it saved face and made entertaining slaughter worthy, as witness the many lovely bloodlettings by Clint Eastwood's Dirty Harry in the name of injured innocence.

A fascinating step in Cagney's rehabilitation is *The Strawberry Blonde,* made in 1941, and so charming a period piece that its conservatism is disguised. Cagney plays "Biff" Grimes—a name as terse and belligerent as those he had worn in gangster films. He is a rough diamond, not too smart, but genuine, the salt of the screen. He wants to be a dentist—perhaps the supreme authority figure for drugstore cowards who submit to the dread of regular check-ups. He has a friend, Jack Carson, louder, smarter and dishonest. They go on a double date with Rita Hayworth and Olivia de Havilland. Rita is the strawberry blonde, fabulously dressed and burnished with light, but as hard as the parasol on a Dresden figurine. She is a calculating flirt and opportunist. De Havilland—all warm, sincere eyes—is less fancy, but more hallowed: she wears her nurse's uniform. Cagney is infatuated with Rita, but loses her to Carson's carpetbagger bravura, and settles for domestic, gentle and adoring Olivia. Carson makes Cagney a stooge vice-president in his construction business and when buildings collapse it is Cagney who goes to jail, the honest fall-guy.

He perseveres in prison—where once Cagney seethed with breakout fever—and continues his dentistry studies. His diploma reaches him through the bars of his cell. On release, he goes contentedly to a small practice, a plain home and the chance to walk Olivia in the park on Sunday afternoons. One such outing is forestalled by an emergency: Carson is bellowing with toothache and at the mercy of any dentist at home. (Revenge again, and Cagney pulls his tooth without mercy or anesthetic.) Carson's success is severely put down by the movie, as if to say cheats never prospered. He is gross and whining—the stereo-typed corrupt alderman. His marriage to Rita has degenerated into the inescapable company of selfish rivals who despise one another. The strawberry blonde has gone very sour and anyone could have left the cinema congratulating himself with his limited lot and the anodyne treat of a strawberry sundae at the drugstore. The straight and narrow is there, out of sight, but as fundamental as railway lines for the loco-motive force of society.

Today, Cagney lives in placid retirement, recipient of the American Film Institute's Life Achievement Award, hugely respected and crust-ily reactionary—to judge from his autobiography. Olivia de Havilland works occasionally and is a handsome, gracious lady, married to a diplomat and radiating charm. But what of Rita? Her stardom was brief, heady and outrageous, and she had to suffer for it. Her beauty, originally, was shocking—a redhead: warning lure to drugstore con-noisseurs of female character. Rita was only a brittle charmer in *Straw-berry Blonde,* and wholesome glamour in *Cover Girl.* But *Gilda* made her, and there she writhed in a black satin sheath, withdrawing from elbow-length gloves as she sang—or mimed—"Put the Blame on Mame." The kept woman on screen rushed into notoriety in the late forties. Divorced from Orson Khan, she was the blond reptile in his *Lady from Shanghai.* She played classical sexpots—Carmen, Salome and Sadie Thompson—and she went off with another Kahn, Aly, to the rapturous disapproval of fan magazines and indignant gossips.

Eventually she came back in disgrace, and that flashy appearance was dulled to show it. Her career withered and the press sighed over a middle-age of unhappiness and booze. Then, in 1977, clinching come-uppance and drugstore "I told you so," alcoholism overtook her inde-pendence, and her business affairs were consigned to the control of the Orange County Public Guardian's Office.

Suspicious hatred runs so rampant in the drugstore that someone will wonder if Rita's wreck is not just another publicity stunt: "Those movie stars—they got no shame." And if Cagneys and de Havillands are to enjoy a prosperous, undisturbed retirement, then some Ritas must serve as sacrificial victims.

All the tears shed over Garland and Monroe are mixed with glycer-ine crocodile drops—this is not unreasonable, for artificial tears are a property of the movies. Judy was a babe in arms with Mickey Rooney, the life and amber soul of nostalgia's St. Louis. In those days, her big Louis and every paternalist in America could relish her and marvel at such cuteness. But once she was her own self, battered from an arduous adolescence, late for work, overweight and her system going clang clang clang from narcotics, then Louis' studio dismissed her and the world entered into harrowed witness to the disordered last decades of her life. Many would have helped if they could have; there was no overt malice. But the agonizing performance of a derailed star was in her character and ours—it is hard to think of Garland, past thirty, as anything other than a martyr to sentiment, indiscipline and the winsome fluff. We watched her, waiting for error and disintegration. We had purchased the dishonest comfort of her youth and were forced to endure the willful disasters of middle-age cut off from reassurance and stability.

Marilyn, too, was doomed if there is any logic to promotional adoration lavished on someone innocent of its cunning. She was as daringly low class as Jean Harlow had been, a hot chili baby trying to be cool, and keeping her panties in the icebox in hopes of the sort of sophistication Grace Kelly modeled. When found, dead, she was also naked, and the public nodded in deep appreciation of a hot little strawberry who had yearned for the cool shelter of a baked Alaska called dignity. The sensational and unrestrained often die young or vanish—Mae West is the exception, and she was as knowing as she is now hallucinatory.

Men too have been rebuked for their morning glory. Charlie Chaplin was repudiated by the public that had once rhapsodized over his vulnerability. Scandal hovered near him, just as it had demolished the career of Fatty Arbuckle. Keaton was described in the movie magazines as a forlorn deadbeat. Perhaps all of them contributed to their own downfall. Fatty did throw the fatal party. Charlie uttered half-baked ideas and fell for sharp girls. Buster let his fortunes be controlled by others. But all of them tempted the fickleness of the public, and love of celebrities is on a hairtrigger; it turns to resentment and rejection with a speed so horrible it is explained only by the initial envy and animosity toward those who escape the drugstore.

Errol Flynn, his friends now say, was a cheerful, amiable drunk and womanizer. The public consumed him for fifteen years as an adventurer and ladies' man—he even played Don Juan, though gilded by penicillin. Then they fell upon him in the yellow press, in scandal magazines and reports of litigation. Before he died, he played John Barrymore in *Too Much, Too Soon*. It was an intriguing contest, for both actors drifted away in a haze or stupor, uncertain whether they were drunken hams or masters of themselves, humoring the vicious public's interpretation of them as debris.

Some humiliations were quick and savage. The unnaturally beautiful Montgomery Clift went to pieces in a car accident and was visibly jittery thereafter. George Raft is picked up by a heartless Jerry Lewis in *The Ladies' Man* and tangoed into the shadows of oblivion. He is a pathetic reminder of fame's caprice. Given a first chance when in the employ of gangsters, his screen success came from playing hoodlums and in later years he was harried by police and taxmen for alleged links with actual underworlds. George himself always looked nonplussed. He regularly refused good parts, and perhaps he was equally unastute with mobster chums. He is a tragicomic victim of our knowledge that, up there, nothing is real—he was a dull actor, and we have conspired to tease the unconvincing man that he might have been a Mr. Big.

Death is the greatest manifestation of public hostility: the star may never understand that, but once he is gone the public knows that he had to die for being so superb, so awesome or so lovely. Like Dracula, once pinned down, the imperious rapist turns to dust and decay. Or, like Dorian Gray, he must make peace with the picture of himself where every alleged flaw and every mark of aging is recorded. Valentino and Dean died of real enough causes, but with such public impact, and in ways so consistent with their careers, that one could believe the drugstore willed them dead, and they crumbled like men stricken by voodoo prayers.

If the cinema is a mockery of religion, then surely there is a grisly order in these huge celebrities dying for us—only that redeems our insignificance. In *Network,* Howard Beale, the mad prophet of the air, is so aghast at decadent times that he drops "dead" at the end of every tirade. The film leaves the question nicely open as to whether this is Beale's big finish to a show-biz act, or a frantic zealot impelling himself into trances. Whatever the answer, death's appeal is infectious and the network has him truly killed when the show begins to bore viewers. Beale dies on live TV as, and only when, his performance has made death implausible.

When Peter Finch—the movie's Beale—himself fell dead between the release of *Network* and Oscar night in March 1977, was there ever any doubt that the superstitions uniting movie cabals and drugstore would award him the Oscar? This was death enshrined as the proper destiny of stars, and novel centerpiece for the Oscar show with the actor's widow giving tearful thanks and Finch's serene absence rivalling that other ecstatic proof of stardom—the twenty-year living death of Howard Hughes. In "real life," Hughes achieved a state of withdrawn possibility where all the youthful majesty was atoned for in the riddle of "where is he now?" or even "is he now?" Whether wondering about Hughes, or watching the 1977 Oscar night, we were rocking in credulous rhythm, reassured that our resentful power still reached out to the stars.

THE SELF AS ART

23. ADVERTISEMENTS FOR MYSELF
by Norman Mailer

In the late fifties, Norman Mailer had the savvy notion of stringing together an anthology of occasional pieces, juvenilia, lost short stories, and fragments of failed novels with a running personal commentary on his even then very self-consciously orchestrated career as heavyweight novelist and general cultural pugilist. The book, *Advertisements for Myself*, became an emblem for Mailer's rising career thereafter.

No collection celebrating celebrity would be complete without a few words from Mailer who, with Andy Warhol and Richard Nixon, has been the top-ranking artist of career persona for the last twenty years.

The prose that follows appears rather tame for Mailer if you know his more recent adumbrations on the theme. He hasn't yet discovered the glories of the third-person memoir. In fact, there's even a curiously reserved quality to these two abridged advertisements for himself. But remember the year: 1958.

First Advertisement for Myself

Like many another vain, empty, and bullying body of our time, I have been running for President these last ten years in the privacy of my mind, and it occurs to me that I am less close now than when I began. Defeat has left my nature divided, my sense of timing is eccentric, and I contain within myself the bitter exhaustions of an old man, and the cocky arguments of a bright boy. So I am everything but my proper age of thirty-six, and anger has brought me to the edge of the brutal. In sitting down to write a sermon for this collection, I find arrogance in much of my mood. It cannot be helped. The sour truth is that I am imprisoned with a perception which will settle for nothing less than making a revolution in the consciousness of our time. Whether rightly or wrongly, it is then obvious that I would go so far as to think it is my present and future work which will have the deepest influence of any work being done by an American novelist in these years. I could be wrong, and if I am, then I'm the fool who will pay the bill, but I think we can all agree it would cheat this collection of its true interest to present myself as more modest than I am.

[Mailer then goes into a little turn about his fifteenth anniversary report to the Harvard class of 1943 which segues into a paean to Hemingway, after all the model for the novelist as macho hero that Mailer has chosen as his basic persona.]

An author's personality can help or hurt the attention readers give to his books, and it is sometimes fatal to one's talent not to have a public with a clear public recognition of one's size. The way to save your work and reach more readers is to advertise yourself, steal your own favorite page out of Hemingway's unwritten *Notes from Papa on How the Working Novelist Can Get Ahead*. Truman Capote did it bravely when he began, and my hat is off to him. James Jones did it, and did it well. Kerouac would deserve ears and tail if he weren't an Eisenhower gypsy. I, in my turn, would love to be one of the colorful old-young men of American letters, but I have a changeable personality, a sullen disposition, and a calculating mind. I never have good nor accurate interviews since I always seem to get into disagreeable situations with reporters—they sense no matter how pleasant I try to be, that I do not like them—I think the psychological requirement for working on a newspaper is to be a congenital liar and a compulsive patriot. Perhaps I should hire a public relations man to grease my career, but I do not know if I can afford him (not with the size of the job he would have to do for me), and moreover I would be obliged sooner or later to spoil his work. While there would be hardly a limit to how lovable he could make me in the public eye it would be exhausting for me to pretend to be nicer than I really am. Indeed, it would be downright debilitating to the best of my creative energies. So I do not care to approach the public as a lover, nor could I succeed for that matter. I started as a generous but very spoiled boy, and I seem to have turned into a slightly punch-drunk and ugly club fighter who can fight clean and fight dirty, but likes to fight. I write this not solely out of self-pity (although self-pity is one of my vices) but also to tell the simple truth: I have not gotten nicer as I have grown older, and I suspect that what has been true for me may be true for a great many of you. I've burned away too much of my creative energy, and picked up too slowly on the hard, grim, and maybe manly knowledge that if I am to go on saying what my anger tells me it is true to say, I must get better at overriding the indifference which comes from the snobs, arbiters, managers, and conforming maniacs who manipulate most of the world of letters and sense at the core of their unconscious that the ambition of a writer like myself is to become consecutively more disruptive, more dangerous, and more powerful. It will be fine if I can write so well and so strongly as to call my shot, but unfortunately I may have fatigued the earth of rich language beyond repair. I do not know, but it is possible. I've been in too many fights, I've been hit on the head by a hammer, and had my left eye gouged in a street fight—and of course I'm proud of this (I was a physical coward as a child), and so I'm proud I learned a bit about fighting even though the cost may end as waste. There may have been too many fights for me, too much sex, liquor, marijuana, Benzedrine and Seconal, much too much ridiculous and brainblasting rage at the minuscule frustrations of a most loathsome literary world, necrophilic to the core—they murder their writers, and then decorate their graves.

[He concludes the first advertisement with some general comments on the collection and a political clarion in defense of "courage, sex, and consciousness."]

Second Advertisement for Myself

Once it became obvious that *The Naked and The Dead* was going to be a best seller, and I would therefore receive that small fame which comes upon any young American who makes a great deal of money in a hurry, I remember that a depression set in on me. I was twenty-five, living in Paris with my first wife, Beatrice, and I had gone through a long leaky French winter in which I discovered once again that I knew very little and had everything still to learn. So I think I probably had been hoping *The Naked and The Dead* would have a modest success, that everyone who read it would think it was extraordinary, but nonetheless the book would not change my life too much. I wished at that time to protect a modest condition. Many of my habits, even the character of my talent, depended on my humility—that word which has become part of the void in our time. I had had humility breathed into me by the war. After four serious years of taking myself seriously at Harvard, the army gave me but one lesson over and over again: when it came to taking care of myself, I had little to offer next to the practical sense of an illiterate sharecropper. Sometimes I think courage is the most exhaustible of the virtues, and I used up a share of mine in getting through the war with my lip buttoned, since it took all of me to be at best a fair rifleman. No surprise then if I was a modest young man when it was all over. I knew I was not much better and I was conceivably a little less than most of the men I had come to know. At least a large part of me felt that way, and it was the part in command while I was writing *The Naked and The Dead*.

But once free of the army, I came back to some good luck. My first wife and I had saved some money during the war, and I did not have to work for a year. She believed in me and my family believed in me, and I was able to do my book. *The Naked and The Dead* flowed—I used to write twenty-five pages of first draft a week, and with a few weeks lost here and there, I still was able to write the novel and rewrite it in fifteen months, and I doubt if ever again I will have a book which is so easy to write. When once in a while I look at a page or two these days,

I like its confidence—it seems to be at dead center—"Yes," it is always saying, "this is about the way it is."

Naturally, I was blasted a considerable distance away from dead center by the size of its success, and I spent the next few years trying to gobble up the experiences of a victorious man when I was still no man at all, and had no real gift for enjoying life. Such a gift usually comes from a series of small victories artfully achieved; my experience had consisted of many small defeats, a few victories, and one explosion. So success furnished me great energy, but I wasted most of it in the gears of old habit, and had experience which was overheated, brilliant, anxious, gauche, grim—even, I suspect—killing. My farewell to an average man's experience was too abrupt; never again would I know, in the dreary way one usually knows such things, what it was like to work at a dull job, or take orders from a man one hated. If I had had a career of that in the army, it now was done—there was nothing left in the first twenty-four years of my life to write about; one way or another, my life seemed to have been mined and melted into the long reaches of the book. And so I was prominent and empty, and I had to begin life again; from now on, people who knew me would never be able to react to me as a person whom they liked or disliked in small ways, *for myself alone* (the inevitable phrase of all tear-filled confessions); no, I was a node in a new electronic landscape of celebrity, personality, and status. Other people, meeting me, could now unconsciously measure their own status by sensing how I reacted to them. I had been moved from the audience to the stage—I was, on the instant, a man—I could arouse more emotion in others than they could arouse in me; if I had once been a cool observer because some part of me knew that I had more emotion than most and so must protect myself with a cold eye, now I had to guard against arousing the emotions of others, particularly since I had a strong conscience, and a strong desire to do just that—exhaust the emotions of others. If there I was, with two more-than-average passions going in opposed directions, I was obviously a slave to anxiety, a slave to the fear that I could measure my death with every evening on the town, for the town was filled with people who were wired with shocks for the small electrocution of oneself. It is exhausting to live in a psychic landscape of assassins and victims: if once I had been a young man whom many did not notice, and so was able to take a delayed revenge—in my writing I could analyze the ones who bestow the cold tension of self-hatred, or the warmth of liking oneself again, to whichever friends, acquaintances, and strangers were weak, ambitious, vulnerable, and in love with themselves—which must be of course half the horde of my talented generation.

This was experience unlike the experience I had learned from books, and from the war—this was experience without a name—at the time I used to complain that everything was unreal. It took me years to realize that it was my experience, the only one I would have to remember, that my apparently unconnected rat-scufflings and ego-

Advertisements for each other. *James, born sign of Scorpio, had been at home when the news came about Mailer. The great author had replied in the affirmative to a more or less whimsical invitation from Scorpio's publishers to attend a small party they were giving to celebrate the publication of his first book. No one knew why. True, the affair was scheduled at the French Embassy, well-noted for superior cocktail-party collations. That explained the presence of Sylvia Miles, perhaps. (She was there, of course.) But why Aquarius? The book being celebrated was entitled* The New Wave: Truffaut, Godard, Chabrol, Rohmer, Rivette. *Perhaps Aquarius misread; did he think those heavies would be in attendance? Or maybe it was a sign, a strange and magnanimous gesture from the Champ. "An author's personality can help or hurt the attention readers give to his books," he had written years ago, "and it is sometimes fatal to one's talent not to have a public with a clear public recognition of one's size." Notice the shadow Scorpio casts. Mailer had better watch it.*

gobblings could be fitted finally into a drastic vision, an introduction of the brave to the horrible, a dream, a nightmare which would belong to others and yet be my own. Willy-nilly I had had existentialism forced upon me. I was free, or at least whatever was still ready to change in my character had escaped from the social obligations which suffocate others. I could seek to become what I chose to be, and if I failed—there was the ice pick of fear! I would have nothing to excuse failure. I would fail because I had not been brave enough to succeed. So I was much too free. Success had been a lobotomy to my past, there seemed no power from the past which could help me in the present, and I had no choice but to force myself to step into the war of the enormous present, to accept the private heat and fatigue of setting out by myself to cut a track through a new wild.

Now of course this way of describing my past has a protective elegance. I could as well have described the years which followed the appearance of *The Naked and The Dead* by saying that I traveled scared, excited, and nervous, ridden by the question which everyone else was ready to ask and which I was forever asking of myself: had this first published novel been all of my talent? Or would my next book be better?

24. *MAX JAMISON*
by Wilfrid Sheed

Wilfrid Sheed's Max Jamison is a model of the critic as personality. He is also, into the bargain, a rough copy of John Simon, of all the well-known critics working today perhaps the possessor of the most elaborately and caringly constructed celebrity persona. One remembers the episodes fondly: Simon ripping into Jacqueline Susann on a late-night talk show (as if Jackie could support such criticism); Simon making a habit of bitchy, at times hysterical, personal attacks on actresses' physiognomies; Sylvia Miles paying him back for them all by dumping a plate of food over him at a New York Film Festival party in the early seventies.

All this turned Simon into something of a celebrity—"the man you love to hate" as the tagline goes. And eventually he had won the prize: a first-string spot as film critic on *New York* magazine. But at times it must have been discouraging. Despite his vaunted Ph.D., despite his Old World accent, despite his relatively good looks and bespoke suits, Simon was stuck for what must have seemed an eternity writing for the little magazines. It's true he moved into the theater critic's chair at *New York* early on, but that was beside the point. No one has given two thoughts to stage critics since Alexander Woollcott last came to dinner forty years ago.

Meanwhile, the likes of Andrew Sarris, Pauline Kael, even— preserve us—Rex Reed were becoming household names. Simon's quest ended in success. The venerable Judith Crist was fired from *New York,* and the film chair finally was his in 1975. He settled into it quickly and proceeded to mellow. Perhaps he shouldn't have relaxed the persona quite so much: new owner Rupert Murdoch switched him back to theater from film at *New York* in the autumn of 1977. Sheed's Jamison is not an unsympathetic fantasy on the Simon character (and in fact enough changes have been made so that the book is hard to call a *roman à clef*). Max is painfully aware of his construction. At one point, after his second wife Helen has scored with a sharp riposte, Sheed notes:

> The critic in him saluted. This was the truth. But wasn't it also
> the truth about anyone who amounted to anything? You built a

personality, a style, and you were trapped by it. Otherwise you were a slack-faced nobody.

It's true. Sheed's Max comes to a bad end: he has a breakdown, gets put out to pasture teaching at a rural college, eventually returns to live out his days in the pages of the small magazines nobody but other writers reads.

In this chapter, Jamison wrestles his persona to a draw.

And now the running battle with irony was on. Irony was the thing that must go, if anything was to change. Yet he found himself posing the question with irony. To wit: that Saturday night was a good time to start changing your life. If you did it with the speed of Scrooge, you could be all straightened out by Monday and no one the wiser.

Facetiousness shook him like ague. What were the standard ways of losing your old self? Start with the pleasant ones. Depravity, defilement were ever popular. Getting drunk, dissolving through bright-colored rooms, gay bars, dyke bars, transvestite propositions, down into the grayer tones, until the kaleidoscope straightens and shakes you out on the street. At the feet of some cop. Secondary characteristics: face, eyes blurring, brain silting up, foul taste, self-contempt. "Arrest me, officer, I am the lowest of men." Very popular indeed a few years ago, but rather cornball now. Too predictable. What actually happened was that you wound up tottering in front of some men's-room mirror saying, Well you certainly made a chump of yourself tonight, Jamison. Self-loss had to include more surprises than that.

How about something a little more contemporary—getting high on drugs, rising instead of falling? Battling the wily teenager, coming to grips with the dreaded hippie? Jamison in Night Town, dancing to twitching lights and brain-cracking music. White-faces grinning in a circle. Old man shaking with palsy to a Watusi beat. Old man dancing himself to death while tribe looks on. Head aching, eyes running now: not losing self, but confirming it. To let himself be laughed at for one whole evening: what crud that would scrape away.

The worst of it was that he knew his mind would still work the old way, under whatever weight of marijuana or booze. He had trained it to. It only knew the one way of working. E.g., instead of dismantling himself in front of some impassive bartender, he would wind up arguing with the man about his favorite movie; or he would sit there silently and think about bartenders; or about teenagers; or about Max Jamison thinking.

He was in love with the way his mind worked, and he was sick of the way his mind worked. The first thing that struck you about it, wasn't it, was the blinding clarity, like a Spanish town at high noon. No shade anywhere. Yet not altogether lacking in subtlety. Very fine filigree work in the church. This was the mind they were asking him to blow.

He sat on his bed, leaning his weight on his hands. Exhaustion was another thing you could do. Walk all night, alongside silvery rivers, dank canals, inland waterways, until you arrived in Schenectady, all gray and wasted. This man does not remember his name. Knows the names of all Greta Garbo's movies, but does not remember his own name. Claims to be George Jean Nathan, in his more lucid moments.

Hah. No exhaustion, no heat of day or shock of battle could keep Max Jamison from remembering his own name. That was the whole point. He could spot "Max Jamison" in a forest of words, hear it in the roar of the crowd. He *was* his name, in a way that non-writers could never understand. Its appearance above an article meant that he was about to read something dazzling. A reference to it in someone else's writing meant an automatic quickening of interest, the invasion of a marvelous fresh point of view. A slur on it was like an insult to Helen of Troy, never to be forgotten.

He had a hunch that if he could forget his name, the rest would slip away without effort. But a writer and his name are not easily parted. On his deathbed, where a decent man would be calling on the saints, Jamison would be mumbling his own name faster and faster— not with one of your peaceful smiles either, but feverishly, to insure the maximum of mentions before closing shop; his name, like the pennies on a dead man's eyes, would be useful coin in the next world.

We exaggerate, do we not, Max. The name was just another chain on his leg that had to be patiently filed through. The name and the identity. Be very clear about this. He could not go on as he was. He could not present the old Max to another woman. He could not go through the obscene ritual of giving and receiving, first fascination, then disgust, and retiring to his mirror and falling in love all over again. You could argue whether his life up to now had been wasted (he thought not, but it wasn't important). But it certainly would be if he could urge it no further forward than this.

Did he *have* to go on repeating himself? Was that what personality meant? There must be many people who just never noticed they were repeating themselves. His sisters, for instance. But "Know thyself" was the name of Jamison's racket; he must poke and prod like Oedipus until all was unstuck. In spite of all Sophocles had told him, he had supposed he was *choosing* to act like Max Jamison: because he liked the way Max Jamison acted. Fat choice he had had. Putting your eyes out with a hot poker was supposed to change your luck. But even then he saw an endless sequence of Eves and Helens—girls that he would disappoint and girls that would disappoint him. It was sewn into the lining of Jamison's personality that he would flunk a certain number of women for their human deficiencies; but that others would flunk him for his, and because he gave the same course year after year. The problems were not disconnected, of course. Flunk or be flunked. Race you, professor.

The regular American thing would be simply to become a nice guy. Have you noticed how Jamison has mellowed? But there were ugly precedents for that. Critics who mellowed lost their teeth and never got them back. Fritz Cunningham was an outstanding example. Killer Fritz, readers would moan for him to stop. "Don't hit that play any more, you brute," they screamed. But when he did stop, and after they got over their first delight at his conversion, they began to say, "Have you noticed how dull Fritz has gotten?" Then, when he tried to resume his old ways, he could not recapture his bite, his fangs were false and loose.

And even a regular human being who became a nice guy was usually a sorry sight, like a reformed alcoholic, gray, wistful, played out; worse, flabby and weak as a kitten; and finally, if one could ever arouse him, deeply resentful. Becoming a nice guy was a weaselly evasion—no change of self was involved, just a closing down of certain outlets, a contraction. The enclavement theory of personality. Max might have to resort to it yet, to end his last day in peace; with a woman he would simply not permit himself to loathe. But first he intended to blow the works—if he still could.

How about some kind of mysticism? He supposed that some brands were better than others. The correspondence-course ones—Zen, yoga— well, how could you face your friends? The classic brands—Hinduism, old-line Buddhism—were all right if you weighed ninety pounds and had the bones of a bird. But you could not really separate religion from culture, and he knew it. It was what you ate and how you dressed and what language you used. An American Buddhist was ridiculous. An American who cultivated the best from all the world's religions was a simpering toady.

It seemed he had burned most of the bridges that led away from his current personality. That was why he loved it so. Christianity? Ah, Christianity. That old thing. All the same, he might try a retreat in a monastery sometime. Contemplation should be left to the professionals. If he spent three days with his own thoughts he would become more and not less himself. He didn't really have thoughts any more, only sodden doubts and anxieties, which bound him like heavy wet bandages, with his name embossed on them in shit. Better to listen to some old fool chanting about how they crossed the Red Sea and made a perfect fool of Pharaoh, and about gardens of myrrh and aloes, and the cedars of Lebanon. Get a fellow's mind off things.

Do not be put off by the irony, gentlemen. It is just a question of style. I am really a very serious man. I have fallen into certain habits. Style—good Lord, would that have to go, too? The harsh short sentences (what is the sound of one tooth biting?). The graceful longer ones. Languor and lazy amusement. Majesty and moral indignation. The whole bright colored bag of tricks.

—But gosh, Mr. Jamison, sir—those aren't tricks, are they? I mean, they sound so real, when you do them.

—Well, I don't like to break your heart, honey, but of course they're tricks. What do you suppose writing is all about? Come to think of it, I'm not really Max Jamison—

And with that, he ripped off his rubber nose and flung it into the audience. "You see, my dear, I am really—" But she had already wandered away, and in a moment the theater was empty. Nobody cared who he really was.

Yeah, Fat Lady, how about that one? How was he going to make a living if he changed his style? It was enough act of faith to presume that there was a real self under his big bad one; but to suppose there was another style under there as well—that was madness. Consider, once again, Fritz Cunningham, the prototype of the writer who monkeys with change. Fritz had altered his style, under pressure of psychoanalysis, but the result had been sheer disintegration. Max could picture the doctor saying, "Ja, you are showing off here, you are kissing your big toe there . . . and this is a flat lie," until all color, all idiosyncrasy were gone. It is really rather neurotic to try to avoid clichés, Herr Jamison: an attempt to set yourself apart from your peers.

A really good spiritual director would probably tell him to give up writing altogether. It was all tied in with his character and was doomed to the same repetitions, the same cycle of narcissism and contempt. You'll never get well if you go on writing, little Hans Jamison.

He went to the kitchen and yanked an apple out of the icebox. Returned to the bed and began to chew it, over the wastebasket. Getting sick of one's style was old stuff for writers. At least it proved you had one. Some juice ran down his sleeve. He could see himself compromising on all this. Remaining the same in his work, and changing himself in his free time. A lot of people did it that way. Honestly.

Mahatma Gandhi and Albert Schweitzer had a good laugh at this point. You Americans! You want to do something about that bag of liquid cement you call a soul—and you want to do it in your spare time. Ho, ho, ho.

Sorry, fellows. I understand that it should be the work of a lifetime and that it involves, at the very least, leaving town. But I have an opening Monday and a deadline Tuesday and a lecture date, and Helen's going to want twice as much money to support that sponging leper of hers—love of life comes high. And I want to see the kids. And, well, just look at that calendar, will you?

He threw the core into a nest of screening notices. Didn't know what to do, really. He had seen through so many people's spiritual efforts, seen through and mocked every single choice he could think of now. He must simply roll out the list again and see if he'd missed anything. The temptation was to say, Well, you certainly took a good hard look at yourself, didn't you, Max, and go to sleep on it. But then he thought back to the afternoon, the two women, Helen and Eve, the pillars that bounded his present world, and he knew that he mustn't slide into facetiousness or irony or fatty tolerance, but must take some hard road out of here.

So he started to think, more slowly this time, of the world of drugs and prayer and of various styles in solitude. Max Jamison was really an old man coated in sand, with a raven on his wrist. He sat at the floor of his cave, and another old man with a cowl, and no face, came up and said, "Sweep away the old man, sweep away the sand, and think about what's left. That's contemplation for you, sonny."

Blah, what a burner on you, Jamison. Any high-school philosophy major could tell you what you're doing wrong. You're using the soul of Max Jamison to change the soul of Max Jamison. The instrument *delicti* to change the instrument *quasi nisi*. Fat chance, fellow.

Next he ran through all the advice he had received from the nation's playwrights on how to live. All the fags and whiners, the promising Negroes and the brutally candid Englishmen, who had undertaken his instruction for the last few years. And he thought what a load of crap it had all been, what a sack of sophistries. And even when real wisdom popped up, his mind did something peculiar to it, known as criticism, which rendered it sterile and safe for the public.

What about the ideas he had learned in college, with his mind like a switchblade and the zest for learning that Dad or someone had imbued him with, what about those ideas, huh? Irony had killed them all. One by one. Or they had killed each other, Sartre killing Freud, Max killing Sartre—oh, always something else would come along shortly, but just behind that, the knife. Records are made to be broken. I used to be profound once, honestly. Then Mother died, and I had to give it up.

"If you would just forget those words, man, and listen to your body"—he received advice by mail, too, advice by air and sea and every means known to man of carrying advice. All rushing help to Max. Forget words—easy for you to say, Ellie Watkins of Flagstaff, Arizona, who never knew them. Ask Casals to throw away his cello and listen to his body, and see what his answer is.

But what a waste of time anyway, advising a critic. For years, we are paid to take a position, like bare-knuckle champions; and you cannot slip your advice to us swiftly enough to keep us from flying into our stance and clobbering you. Before you have choked out your pitiable comments about forgetting words, I will have told you of the role of language, of how it is not some extra to humanity but the precondition of humanity, and—blah de blah-blah. I bore myself. I don't know whether I believe it any more, or even what I mean by it. But those are the things I say.

I can't help it. Max said these words out loud. There must be some way of changing, some blinding pain, tearing of skin, wearing down of brain. Some wild obliterating scream. On impulse, to make some sort of gesture in that direction, Max got off the bed and lay on the hard floor for a minute in his shirt sleeves. And felt like a damn fool.

25. PRIVATE LIVES
by John Leonard

Until it began its strange metamorphosis into *"The* New *New York Times,"* the gray lady of Forty-third Street was the last remaining bastion of the values of objectivity and sobriety that used to characterize the old journalism. In the mid-sixties, when the *Times* removed the square Gothic period from its nameplate, it was news. By 1976, however, traditions were crumbling like freeways in *Earthquake.* The first signs were ominous: feature photos (the weather, tourist events) worked their way onto the front page of the Saturday edition, then spread to weekdays. Coverage of soft news—food, consumer goods—doubled.

By the fall, the transformation was irreversible. The hundred-year-old elegance of the eight-column format gave way to the open spaces of six columns, and the new feature sections were born. No matter what the names of these sections ("Living," "Weekend," "Home," "Fashion") the focus was essentially the same from day to day: soft news, consumer goods, self-help pieces, and arts coverage, all with a personal touch that is remarkable in light of the *Times'* traditions.

The superego of the nation's newspapers whose motto was "All the News That's Fit to Print," was now delivering a lot else besides —so much else that a number of critics thought the news was dangerously camouflaged by the flurry of features. The turning point may have occurred on November 14, 1975, the day the *Times* printed food critic Craig Claiborne's notorious $4000-dinner story on the front page. The reaction was violent. Nevertheless, lifestyles and consumer features proved enormously profitable. The metamorphosis was complete.

One of the major characteristics of the *Times'* old-journalistic objective style had been the strict avoidance of the first person. Reporters, when they couldn't avoid talking about themselves, resorted to nineteenth-century circumlocutions like "this reporter," or "an observer." So when John Leonard began his "Private Lives" column for the weekly "Living" section, he decided to "call him

Eric. Or Dmitri." Leonard had worked this way before. During the early seventies, while he was editor of the *Times Book Review,* he also wrote regularly about television under the name Cyclops.

"Private Lives" came about almost by accident. Leonard had been asked to take over the recently revived "About New York" column in the fall of 1976. He agreed, but only if he could write what he wanted. At the time, he was in the process of moving into a new house and remarrying, and so "About New York" was really about John Leonard. The reaction to "Private Lives" has been extraordinary. Partly, no doubt, this is due to Leonard's intense, carefully controlled, sometimes quirky style. There hasn't been such a distinctly identifiable personal voice in a newspaper column since Jimmy Breslin broke out of sports ten years ago. Mainly, however, the response has been to the striking novelty of seeing personal journalism about emotions in the hitherto uniformly gray pages of the *Times.*

Leonard, a novelist as well as cultural critic, has led the way in the novelization of the newspaper. The new style may not give us much information about the balance-of-payments problems of Tanzania, but it does provide a number of other truths. First Mailer, then Breslin, now Leonard have rewritten the rules of fiction and reporting, and each has done it in a highly personalized, immediately identifiable voice. There are problems with Leonard's style. He himself has written about how difficult it is to be bittersweet week in and week out. But the self as art has seldom been better represented than in "Private Lives."

1

Call him Eric. Or Dmitri. We have to call him something, and he has never been satisfied with his real name, which is like Bill or Pete or Tom, a thin name, almost a pronoun, all edge, lacking a dimension, no muscle, no hair, no fat pads. Dmitri he associates with the calisthenics of the soul in nineteenth-century Russian novels. Eric he associates with those sexy television commercials for Scandinavian cigars in the early 1960's. Eric sounds serious and sincere, while not being quite so gloomy as, say, Soren.

Anyway, Eric had to go to Chicago. On the whole, he preferred never leaving New York. And if he had to leave New York, he wanted to go to some other imperial city, Paris or Rome or Baghdad, where the citizens knew that they were at the center of things. But it is sometimes necessary—no one had ever explained why—to go to Chicago, which teems with people wearing plastic identification badges pinned to their lapels to remind themselves of who they are supposed to be.

Having concluded his business in Chicago, Eric presented himself early at O'Hare Airport for what he thought of as re-entry. Would New York this time have discovered in his absence that it could get along without him? There was time to buy a book, a sort of print pill one takes to dissolve the sense of dislocation. And so he made his mistake. It is easy to say in retrospect that he should have purchased a copy of *The Hite Report* and found out how American women really feel about sex.

But Eric wasn't sure he really wanted to know how American women really felt about sex; it seemed an invasion of their privacy. Besides, the mystery of Woman was one of the few things he worshiped, along with the energy of New York and the prose of John Cheever. Instead of *The Hite Report,* he bought a paperback collection of John Cheever short stories called *The Brigadier and the Golf Widow.* Thus equipped, he was ready to be airborne, the mind a particle on the jet stream, the body strapped down for the inevitable steamed steak and the consolations of alcohol.

There was a delay on the ground. Why is there always a delay in Chicago, and never a delay in Paris? Eric read. By mere chance—and there is nothing more terrible in this world than mere chance—what Eric read was a story of a man whose gift, or trick, for getting along in life inexplicably deserts him. Now, this is characteristic Cheever: dark currents in the swimming pool, skeletons in the liquor closet, domesticated desperation, plaintive Sisypheans on a plastic slope, losing their grip when luck, or charm, runs out.

But Eric was disquieted. The man in the story hadn't a clue as to why the world suddenly mistrusted or actively disdained him; why, for instance, on going to a cocktail party in the luxury apartment house of friends, he was directed by the doorman to the service entrance. How had he managed before? He couldn't remember, although he was trying to even as he returned at night to his suburban estate and his own dogs devoured him.

Luck, charm, chance, dividends from trust funds, accidents of birth, the roll of the dice of the genes, fingernails of DNA, credit cards of a blameless personality—all canceled. Your license is revoked. You have been found out. According to the C.I.A. or Ralph Nader or Sigmund Freud or Hua Kuo-feng or *The Hite Report* or God, you are now and always have been unserious and insincere. At last in the sky, and rather shaky, Eric asked the stewardess for two of those little toy bottles of Scotch.

The stewardess hated him.

Why? He hadn't asked for extra ice. He'd said please. Courtesy was his coin, and inoffensiveness his style. But she hated him, and he knew it. In the lamp of her loathing, he was paralyzed, like a rabbit on the road at night in the lights of a truck. He tried, and failed, to hate her back. (He admired stewardesses; they are competent.) You are constructed of nylon and plywood, he thought. But she wasn't. Except in her dealings with him—a Scotch bottle snatched away before it had been entirely emptied, the steamed steak upside down—she was the personification of perkiness, Mary Tyler Moore on rollerskates.

Good Lord, it had happened. Cheevered, just like that, as though his life were an anecdote to which he had forgotten the punchline, and they sneered. The approval of strangers was crucial to Eric; he survived because of it. Which is why he made sure to have exact change for buses, was a conscientious overtipper in taxicabs and restaurants, talked to women at dinner parties about their children, knew how to be sad when it counted, showered once a day, remembered to say I love you.

He should have known he had been Cheevered when the last ten twinpacks of seven-and-a-half-ounce Wise potato chips turned out not to be as crisp as he preferred. He had imagined a breakdown in quality control at Berwick, Pennsylvania. Instead, they were out to get him. And if airline stewardesses and Wise potato chips were out to get him, what about New York? He would, he knew, come back to a block on which every garbage can but his own had been emptied by sanitation workers with Mafia connections; to a Chinese laundry that had been taken over by Albanians or Arabs; to a zip code that added up to an audit of his psychic tax returns; to children who had figured out that he was a coward; to a wife who was reading *The Hite Report.* Devastated, he punched the button for the stewardess.

"You are hostile," said Eric. "Yes," said Samantha. "How have I offended you?" said Eric. "You boarded," said Samantha, "with a youth-fare ticket, and then you ordered Scotch, and I don't like people who cheat." "Wrong," said Eric; "I haven't been that young for sixteen years, and you can check it out."

Samantha checked it out. She had mistaken his identity. So, perhaps, had he. She fetched him a third Scotch, on the wings of whatever. And then he was home, and young again.

2

In California, Dmitri thought of Wilfrid Sheed. On the face of it, that was ridiculous. The idea of California and the idea of Wilfrid Sheed are inconsistent, almost contradictory, like Uganda and Proust. But Mr. Sheed, a friend of Dmitri's who writes novels, wrote one once called *Max Jamison,* in which this passage appears:

"He was in love with the way his mind worked, and he was sick of the way his mind worked. The first thing that struck you about it, wasn't it, was the blinding clarity, like a Spanish town at high noon. No shade anywhere. Yet not altogether lacking in subtlety. Very fine filigree work in the church. This was the mind they were asking him to blow."*

* See pp. 172–173 for more of Jamison on this subject.

Dmitri would not have described his own mind as being anything like a Spanish town at high noon. It was more like Hong Kong or Shanghai before the war, cluttered and overcrowded, full of discrepancies and swamp gas. It was, nevertheless, the only mind he had, and in California they wanted to mess with it.

He went to California to present a paper at a symposium on "The Ambivalence of the Hickey in Fiction by Feminists Living Between Central Park West and Riverside Drive." Why is it that when John Kenneth Galbraith flies to California, he gets to sit next to Angie Dickinson, whereas when Dmitri flies to California he is manacled to a businessman who is mad at New York? The businessman was mad at New York because we won't let the Concorde stop here. If we let the Concorde stop here, for refueling, the businessmen could make it from London to Los Angeles in five hours.

That people might fly against the clock from London to Los Angeles in five hours, giving them an extra day to do mischief, is one more compelling reason to shoot down any Concorde that gets anywhere near us. With slingshots and taxicab drivers, if necessary.

There was a car waiting for Dmitri in Los Angeles. This is because it is necessary in California to drive for two hours, whether one wants breakfast or a chiropractor. Thus the illusion of progress is sustained. For Dmitri, it was two hours north to Ojai, where golf links lay like a rug in the lap of the mountains, God had arranged for a squeaky-clean sky, and bungalows festered. In California, there is no last resort.

See the brave athletes hurl themselves at electric buggies and drive— for two hours, of course—to the burning tee. See the tennis courts, like runways for Concordes. See the swimming pool, a sheet of undulant tin, around which are sprawled the idle and the fricasseed. Why is everybody wearing linoleum? If God looked down from his squeaky-clean sky, what would he think? They are, in their crayon colors, expressing some deep sullen mystique of abstract vapidity, some non-representational fatigue.

Not for the first time, it occurred to Dmitri that leisure may be a bad idea. Certainly leisure suits are. Seneca came to mind before Wilfrid Sheed did: "Who has more leisure than a worm?"

As symposia go, this one went. If you've been to one plenary session of a conference on how to improve the world, you've been to them all. For his opinions, Dmitri was abused, and it was probably good for him. New Yorkers wear smarty-pants instead of linoleum, and deserve an occasional kick in their surliness. It was, however, in the workshops that they tried to mess with Hong Kong.

The workshops were really encounter groups. Each group had a leader, only the leader was called a "facilitator." Dmitri's facilitator was a young man with kind eyes, a kind beard and kind sandals, who spoke so softly that one wondered whether his pilot light had gone out. Whatever one said to this agreeable person, he'd reply, "Beautiful, just beautiful." And when everybody in the group had said something, he'd sum up: "What I am hearing a lot of in this room is . . ." And they *were* in a room, instead of outside around a sand trap, because the beautiful things they said a lot of had to be recorded on tape, and the microphone, like God's necktie, hung from a squeaky-clean ceiling.

Dmitri was innocent of encounter groups. "Beautiful" was an adjective he reserved for his wife, sunsets, Bach and Earl Monroe. He was accustomed, moreover, when in small groups convoked for world-improving, to the white noise of gin and some pretzel nuggets. He was therefore astonished to be asked, while staring into his tenth Styrofoam cup of Styrofoam coffee, to describe his sex life.

Descriptions of his sex life he reserved for his wife and Bach. What was he supposed to say? "Very fine filigree work in the church"? If he wanted to make it public, he would write a novel, like the feminists and everybody else. But he didn't want to make it public, which seemed the direction in which the group was blundering, because the next proposal was that they get into some heavy touching.

Well. The idea was that one member of the group would close his or her eyes, and the other members would touch him/her, and he/she would try to guess whether the toucher was a he or she. Dmitri abstained. He no more wanted to be pawed by a bunch of strangers, however agreeable, than he wanted to reduce the music and mystery of love, the strange connection and the golden trust, to group-chat, self-advertisement, anecdote. Next stop: the bathtubs of Esalen, which is not a Spanish town at high noon. He was urged to shuck himself of his inhibitions. What on earth for? He had spent most of his life acquiring them; inside their picket fence there was sanctuary, no microphones, a redeeming giggle. He imagined the polymorphs around a libidinal pool, ascertaining itch: off, then, with the linoleum, and let us go to water-bed.

Are we Tinkertoys? A nice man at Ojai had spent an inordinate amount of time trying to come up with a nonsexist word to describe someone with whom you have a "significant emotional relationship." He arrived, after at least two hours of driving, at "attaché." So maybe we aren't Tinkertoys: we're luggage on a Concorde. Dmitri suggested, instead, "sidekick." No one was amused. And so, with his inhibitions and his sense of humor, he went home to a private life.

3

It will happen by accident. No one will have warned you. Why should they? They have their own erotic depths and nasal passages to worry about. You will leave the safety of your typewriter, the sanctuary of your home—and perhaps a provocative book, only half read, on genetic engineering or how to process cannabis in a Cuisinart. Going out is a way of not watching *Scenes from a Marriage* on public television. What you expect is an unlacing of the mind among loose friends. Off with the boots of duty! Let us talk small, gnaw chicken and risk a giggle.

But this is not to be. You know it is not to be at the door of your friend's apartment, which is opened by one of those servants rented for the evening from a bat cave in surprising Queens. He will hide your raincoat, sneer at your bluejeans and fetch you a drink. It is, then, a serious party. At serious parties, New Yorkers are not expected to fetch their own drinks: having to move from one side of a room to the other would cramp us in our seriousness.

On the other hand, bat-people tend to pin you into conversational corners. You can't, when some aggressive gnome starts in on psychoanalysis or astrology, excuse yourself to freshen your drink. The fresh drink materializes at your elbow, like a character defect.

Nor are you able to employ what is known in select circles as the Michael Arlen gambit. The Arlen gambit is to arm yourself at the bar with a couple of your own drinks. Two-fisted, then, you can make your escape from any ambush by maniacal bores: "I'm sorry, I really would like to hear more about the basic engram and operating thetanism, but Duchess Pittsburgh is waiting for her toddy of goat's bile." (It is, to be sure, a tricky gambit for smokers. Both hands occupied, what are you to do with the burning weed in the middle of your food-hole? If only ears had thumbs.) A bat-person isn't going to fetch you two drinks at the same time, not unless he steals your ashtray.

You allow your eye to graze on the pasture of those present, and your bonhomie evaporates.

Can celebrityhood be said to glower? As if behind sandwich boards advertising their own famous names, they sit on sullen stools. It is wall-to-wall pout. See the famous TV anchorman, the famous magazine editor, the famous newspaper columnist, the famous courtesan. There are several novels, a Broadway play, half a Cabinet, two banks, one football team, a jazz musician and an Englishman. They are waiting for the latest edition of themselves, for the reviews, for Lefty and Godot, for an energizing principle.

There are too many celebrities and not enough sycophants. Such a discrepancy will be hard on the husbands and wives of the illuminati. Somebody has to grovel and sigh. Somebody has to be shouldered aside so that oaks may huddle before they're felled. This is more than serious. This is power, baby. This is the sort of party where you have to decide whether you are important enough to wait for the other fellow first.

Careers, like camels, hunker down to snooze with a wary eye on which way the fan is blowing.

You have been here before. It is always a mistake. It was a mistake three years ago, schlepping out to the Hamptons because you had never been there before, and how unworldly it was not to have seen the famous artists and writers behaving like debauched gazelles. And so you ended up in Sag Harbor as an uninvited guest at a stranger's birthday party, for which they imported Bobby Short.

Upon you they laid lobster and a grape of France and a, What's-your-angle, sapajou? For yourself, you apologized. For the fifteen minutes they were famous, they famed and famed and famed. We end up, as Kurt Vonnegut has said, licking the boots of psychopaths.

The sad fact is that, taken singly, celebrities are interesting; in herds they low. It is a collective goiter; you want to give them a pill to reduce the swelling. Why are they driven to perform? In our art and science, the magic of our money-making, our sneaking politics, we adumbrate and counterfeit. A self is suggested. An image is projected.

Our children know better, but what a burden it is to pretend to be what we have made, to try to live up or down to an idea of us arrived at in some committee meeting or in desperation. It was, after all, just one idea among many.

What a trial to be Norman Mailer, Billy Carter, Farrah Fawcett-Majors; to have to grow a personality along the lines of one you invented, the one that sold; to have to compete with other fabricated personalities, inflations of cunning, blimps of ego; to jostle at a power party. The more one distends, the more easily one is bruised. Friends would have forgiven you, instead of expecting a performance. You should have stood in bed, buttering your toast.

Suppose you are not clever, except at a typewriter. Suppose you are not sensitive, except in the middle of the night a month later. Suppose your generosity is theoretical, your courage wholly literary, your fast-ball lacking jumping beans, your heartbreak is psoriasis. Suppose, deep down, you suspect that you are dull, and your public works are a form of vengeance. You talk a good poem, and think by numbers. Once upon a time, I was interesting; then Mother died and I had to give it up.

Friends ought to know who you really are, and invite you to dinner anyway. It needn't be served in a room where the walls are always white, the steel always stainless, the chicken always two hours late and the children stuffed into some hamper. Nor need it be oversubscribed with by-lines who deep down in the Cuisinart feel just as fraudulent as you do, who do not at dawn presume to be wise. There is no wisdom; there are only punchlines.

26. THIS HALF, GO OUT THERE AND MAKE STATEMENTS!

by Roy Blount, Jr.

Novelists have been celebrating themselves for years now, but the self as a work of art has only recently arrived in the sports world. In his *Esquire* column in April 1977, Roy Blount took note of the transformation.

Feature this: A pitcher dissipates only lightly, gets to the park on time, avoids fistfights with his mates, keeps his head in the game, always gives at least one hundred ten, one hundred twenty percent. Only one thing: he insists on wearing his late father's beat-up old fishing hat on the mound.

"You can't wear a *fishing hat* on the mound!" cries his owner, and the umpires, and the commissioner himself.

"Why not?" the pitcher asks quietly. "People," he adds with a smile, "wear baseball caps fishing."

"Nobody in the entire history of organized ball has ever worn a fishing hat on the mound!"

"Ah," says the pitcher.

Or this: A pass receiver hauls one in for a touchdown but when he enters the end zone he does not stop. He goes on to circle the entire field, holding the ball aloft, juking and springing into the air every few strides and engaging front-row fans in rudimentary dialogue, until at length a crotchety team physician fells him with a tank of oxygen.

One account begins, "Chicago edged the Lions 27-26 in Detroit Sunday to clinch the N.F.C. Central crown, as Bear wide receiver Freemason 'Sweet-Tips' Teal brought off a refreshing commentary upon the supposed finality of 'scoring.'"

Another wire service reports: " 'Wide' as applied to receivers was a cliché until Sunday, when Freemason 'Sweet-Tips' Teal opened the idea of wideness up and let it breathe, as the Bears edged . . ."

Sound incredible? It may be the coming thing in big-time athletics.

Consider: When Dave Cowens, at the height of his trend-setting powers as an N.B.A. center, left the Boston Celtics on an indefinite leave of absence without pay early in the 1976–77 season, he shook everyone to the roots. Who ever heard of a man like that opting out like that? He didn't have personal problems. He wasn't holding out for anything. He's got *red hair,* for Christ's sake. It was unaccountable. Then came the follow-up quote from Pete Maravich of the New Orleans Jazz:

"Dave Cowens did what I had been thinking about doing for some time now. It's funny in a way, because Dave beat me to the punch. Now I can't do what he did."

Maravich has, however, done this: he has put Cowens' step into perspective. Cowens may protest that he is "just a guy who quit his job," but a field in which things must not be repeated is not a job. It is not a trade. It is not a craft. It is an art. *Expression* is now the need of big-time athletes' souls.

Winning is no longer enough for them. (Especially in years when it looks like they might not even take the division.) Nor is money enough —now that, in these days of free agentry and renegotiation, there is so much of it. Sports stars now, it is becoming increasingly evident, want to make a *statement.*

Thus Reggie Jackson signs not with the Montreal Expos, who offer him more money, but with the New York Yankees—because, as Yankee owner George Steinbrenner puts it, "When we were walking around town last week, a couple of kids came up to him, kids who didn't have a dime. And he told me later, 'We can do something to make those kids feel better.' " (Not give them a dime, but give them a World Series winner.)

A grand and also a very allusive gesture. What is Reggie doing here but paying an *hommage* to the Babe's promise of a home to a hospitalized kid—and also, further and more tellingly, turning Shoeless Joe on his head: the kid comes up to *this* Jackson and says, in effect, "Say you're the edge, Reg." And this Jackson does not turn away.

Let us look again at the Cowens move. Only six feet eight in a position that had seemed to require seven feet, Cowens had already proved that less can be more, had established a new style of play, just as in the late nineteenth century Toulouse-Lautrec had proved that *painters* needn't be tall (pace Anthony Quinn and Charlton Heston), at least in the demimonde. But by this year Cowens had done that already. He was repeating himself.

Then, I think, he heard about artist Robert Rauschenberg's aesthetic coup of the fifties: erasing a drawing by De Kooning. Cowens, though, had long been negating other people's work with his aggressive defense. He had even been upstaged in that department, imagistically, by a lesser player, Marvin Webster, whose flair for blocking shots had earned him the sobriquet "The Human Eraser." Cowens decided to carry this concept further, to turn it in upon itself. He would erase his *own* work. Suddenly, the Celtics were without Cowens. Or rather, a phantom Cowens was on the floor forty-eight minutes a game, glaring in his absence, non-performing inimitably. Within three weeks of his departure, a headline in the *Boston Globe* referred to the UN-COWENS ERA.

Imagine Maravich's vexation: Maravich, whose passes—bounced through his own and opponents' legs, *rolled* the length of the floor, etc. —are so creative that nobody *including the intended recipient* is ready for them. And yet it is clear when the ball bounces off the teammate's head that he *should,* ideally, have known the pass was coming, would have if his imagination had been as rich and quick as Pete's. For years, Maravich has been like Bobby Fischer trying to play team chess. It is a hell of an act, one that many critics prefer to ordinary effective basketball, but Maravich has by now rung all the changes on it. He has of late even been toying with ordinary effective basketball. The more inspired stroke, though, would have been withdrawal. Like James Agee belatedly leaving Time Inc., Maravich could have built a myth of the hoop-artist-better-than-his-context, going on to various nearly realized free-lance projects implying what might have been achieved if only the context had held up its end.

But Cowens—ironically a quintessentially functional, winning, "team" player—beat Maravich to the punch; left him holding the ball. Cowens leaving the Celtics, a class act which he had to a great extent defined, is like E. B. White in the late thirties taking off from regular employment at *The New Yorker,* which he had seemed essential to; going off into the country to do some things on his own. ("He's out right now on a tractor," Cowens' mother told a reporter, "bush-hogging, clearing some ground.")

For some time now we have been hearing athletes say things like, "I don't want to be thought of as just a goalie." (Or "just a Supersonic," or "just a person with incredible quickness," or even "just Professor Up There Novotney.") "I want to be thought of as a human being." It is not much of a jump from there to "I want to be recognized as a person of vision."

There was Ali—vaunting, rope-a-doping, making himself up as he went along. There was Wilt, missing free throws in rather the same way that Theodore Dreiser dangled modifiers. An early earth artist was Richie Allen, writing cryptic words ("Mom," "Coke," "No") in the basepath dirt with his foot. Baseball perhaps had its Duchamp in Jimmy Piersall, who circled the bases backward after hitting a home run. But Piersall was before his time. Baseball thought he was not an innovator but crazy.

Ten years ago, basketball would have thought Cowens was crazy. But today even crusty Celtics general manager Red Auerbach concedes that the eccentric, no-nonsense Cowens, who lives in a modest apartment over a toy store, has his own way of doing things and that he knows what he is doing.

Never apologize, never explain. Surely it will not be long before other N.B.A.'ers will be off on new departures. The concept of "moving without the ball" may be extended—dancing without the ball, moving without the ball *or shorts,* moving without the coliseum. . . .

As usual, the owners, administrators and legislators of sport (except for the N.C.A.A., which has cannily suppressed spiking and dunking for years) have misperceived the threats posed by the new independence of players. The danger is not that they will sell themselves so freely and dearly to various high bidders as to destroy the respective structures of their sports, but that they will begin to express themselves so freely in what Rauschenberg has called the gap between art and life (as opposed to the gap between center and left, or the gap between tackle and end) that ball games will begin to look like half-time shows conceived and directed by John Cage.

Hockey will be staged on gelatin. Baseball on ice. Quarterbacks will begin to experiment with form—standing behind the guard, for instance, to see what happens when the center's snap sails straight up into emptiness. Antonioni has given us tennis without the ball. Writers of free verse, according to Robert Frost, have given us tennis without the net. Ilie Nastase may give us tennis with golf balls. Who knows?

It behooves the custodians of sport, then, to start thinking of ways to accommodate the artist in the athlete. Efforts may be made to channel the new impulses into off-the-field activity: theater groups, leather craft, bizarre private behavior.

But changes are also going to have to take place on the playing fields to allow for experimentation and the development of varying styles. Heretofore the picture of a sport has been cast almost entirely in terms of points scored—a sort of intense, or perhaps reverse, pointillism, the new sports critic might suggest. Henceforth more attention will be paid to the different *modes* of sport. An all-star game between baseball's nine best sluggers and its five or six *worst* pitchers. Surely the judging of lay-ups in terms of quality—form, brio, hang time, degree of difficulty—along the lines of Olympic gymnastics scoring is long overdue. Why should Julius Erving get no more points for a whirling triple-pumping behind-the-back two-hand slam dunk than Phil Jackson gets for an inelegantly coordinated tip-in? Football referees might award yardage for fresh, well-articulated insights and provocations (anybody can simply call the man across from him a fag) at the line of scrimmage.

Inevitably, of course, the new wave in sport will be co-opted. Owners will see the commercial potential in expressiveness and will begin to pay players not for statistics but for magicality, for *je ne sais quoi* quotient. A Dick Stuart, who is brilliant in the role of the terrible defensive first baseman, will be encouraged more than the solid but uncreative Gold Glover. Players who have built careers on just meeting the ball and always throwing to the right base will be asked at contract time, "So where is that at? Why couldn't you once ask for a trapeze at the plate so you could 'swing from the heels'? Why don't you ever throw to the hot dog vendor? You're not *mercurial,* you're not *alive to the moment* out there." Coaches will begin inculcating the Three I's: Inspiration, Imagination, Impishness. Clutch hitting as such will be out—Tommy Henrich was doing that in the forties. Choking and then calling for a microphone to tell the crowd about it—how it felt, what you saw your parents doing when you were six years old, which probably had a lot to do with it—will be in.

Dave Cowens, of course, terminated his leave of absence after two months. I think this was a failure of nerve. "I was taking a lot of flak from many circles," he said—he who has given and withstood so much flak around hoops. You would think he might have found some way to emulate Dante, who stayed in exile and consigned all the circles to hell. Or he might have waited until the sports pendulum had swung to the ultimate in expressionism. And then come back and kicked ass.

27. WHAT DID I KNOW, AND WHEN DID I KNOW IT?
by James Monaco

Richard Nixon was the *2001* starchild of celebrities, the apotheosis of the self as the work of art.

The Ex-President is sitting in the tape room of the Ex-Presidential Western White House. That is not strictly its name. The Press calls it "the western home of the ex-President." The Ex-President likes to call it "Casa Pacifica." This appeals to him. He appreciates the pun: *Casa Pacifica,* "House of Peace"; *Casa Pacifica,* "House by the Pacific." He can't remember whether or not he recognized this pun during the term of his Presidency. He is not sure at what point in time he became aware of this particular play on words—although he surmises that his appreciation of the phrase dates from well before the great event of the Resignation (as he always prefers to call it.) He thinks it makes a nice point about his Presidency, the ambiguity of it—peace, the ocean. He has had much time for reflection of late; that was part of the game plan; and he revels in the role of the "X-P." He has come to understand that it provides a necessary complement to "P." "P" was decisive, active, so "X-P" must be contemplative and serene.

He spends much time here in the tape room in the evenings, the boxes of ordered reels lining the walls; the Uher 1500 sitting in splendid isolation on the carved oak table in the middle of the room (no, not *the* Uher 1500, but one very much like it); the quadrophonic speakers standing like sentinels, each in its corner; the electric fireplace, all brushed copper and brass at one end of the spacious room; the powerful, quiet air conditioner with the digital controls (made specially for him by the Friedrich people of San Antonio) at the other. He runs the tapes for hours, sometimes taking down a favorite, at other times striking out in new directions on this voyage of reflective exploration.

One of the pleasurable little tasks he has set for himself as he listens and re-listens to the tapes is to discover, if possible, references, clues, allusions, internal evidence that might indicate at precisely what point in time he *did* understand this pun on Casa Pacifica. "What did the President know and when did he know it?" He mutters the rhythmic catch phrase to himself, smiling. It would be a simple matter to search his memory for the answer to this little question, but the Ex-President refuses to do so. He knows that he knows when he knew it, but that's not the point, not the point at all. They never understood that. What matters is the *tapes,* what do the *tapes* say. The art of the tapes transcends reality, must transcend even the great art of the Presidency he had so carefully constructed. The tapes are the record: mute and inviolable, saying everything and nothing. The Ex-President loves the tapes inordinately; he worships them.

This evening he has chosen one of his favorite reels with which to begin. It is one of the ones that was printed and he generally enjoys listening to the tapes for which transcripts are available more than the others, although the others, of course, are often far more nostalgic, more historically thrilling. But the Ex-President does enjoy catching the errors between transcript and tape. This particular tape is specially important to him and he has had a cassette copy made of it and often takes it with him when he is taking one of his long, lonely walks on the beach in front of his house.

It is a very short tape but the Ex-President likes it even better for that. He has memorized its rhythms.

He is also fond of it because it is of a telephone conversation rather than an office conversation. He has learned, while listening to the tapes, that telephone conversations are of generally better quality than the rambling, often disjointed recordings of office meetings. He has theories about why this is so. It isn't only that the voices are much clearer on the telephone tapes. More important is the special energy of the conversations: in the phone tapes, people speak with more art, more authority. They are performing for an audience, the listener at the other end of the wire, and this gives the phone tapes a special power that the office tapes seldom show.

This particular tape which X-P has chosen to begin the evening's entertainment involves a conversation between Lawrence Higby and "Bob" Haldeman on April 15, 1973. "P" appears only briefly, at the beginning.

P: For Mr. Haldeman?

OPR: Yes.

P: Mr. Haldeman, Mr. Higby wants you.

LH: Hello, Bob.

H: Yeah.

LH: John Dean just called me. He had a message he wanted to relay to the President through you. He would not speak directly to you.

H: All right.

LH: One. I hope you understand my actions are motivated totally out of loyalty to you, the President.

H: Wait a minute.

[*X-P turns up the volume slightly and edges forward in his chair; this is a beautiful part coming up.*]

LH: Totally out of loyalty to you and the President.

H: Yep.

LH: And if it's not clear now—

H: Uh, huh.

LH: —it will become clear.

H: Wait a minute.

LH: Two. Erlichman requested to meet tonight—

H: Yeah.

LH: But I feel inappropriate at this time.

H: Just a minute. Okay.

LH: I am ready and willing to meet with you, meaning the President, at any time to discuss the matters.

H: Just a minute.

LH: Three. I think you, meaning the President, should take your counsel from Henry Petersen who I assure you does not want the Presidency hurt.

H: Hmph.

LH: That was the end of his message. He was calling you from his home, the operator said.

H: From his home?

LH: That's what the operator said.

H: How long ago was that? Just now?

LH: Yes, sir.

H: Okay. Thank you very much.

LH: Yes, sir.

Punch; stop; punch; rewind. The Ex-President shakes his head slowly. A shiver of appreciation runs up his spine. That's what it's all about, he thinks to himself. Here he is, the *Ex*-President, listening to the tape of Haldeman listening to Higby reading the statement Dean had read to Higby to give to Haldeman to give to the President. Beautiful! First Dean writes it down, then reads it, then Higby writes and reads, then Haldeman writes and reads and the President listens. And the Ex-President listens. Seven or eight levels. X-P is not sure whether Dean's quote of Petersen adds another level or two. If it does, there would be ten. If he adds the future framework of his memoirs, that would make eleven. During the years, now, that the Ex-President has spent listening to the tapes, he has never found a higher instance of media complexity.

The reference to Henry Petersen's concern for the Presidency makes the experience complete for X-P. Now in the process of writing and taping his memoirs, he has toyed with the idea of writing three separate but parallel volumes: one about the President, one about the Presidency, and one about the Ex-Presidency. They had never appreciated him for the artist he was; maybe now he could suggest to them just what it was he was about. But he rejected the idea eventually, sadly. They would only dismiss it as further equivocation. He nevertheless feels sure posterity will understand.

What X-P especially likes about this particular tape is Dean's irony. He realizes now that Dean was one of the very few, during his Presidency, who really understood what he (P) was doing—and who could do it himself. " 'Henry Petersen does not want the Presidency hurt'!" Sure, but what about the President? X-P had often wondered whether Haldeman's "Hmph" at that point indicated that Haldeman appreciated the twist Dean had given that remark, or whether he was merely indicating his annoyance at the formal equivocation. Admittedly, that is what hit you first. But X-P, attuned to these matters from long days, months, years at the recorder, understands the subtleties of the tapes.

He has already catalogued most of them by degree of media complexity: they fall into three broad categories:

(1) Those in which P and the others were acting for posterity.

(2) Those in which they were acting for each other.

(3) Those in which they seem not to be acting at all. (These were usually identifiable by the long silences, interrupted occasionally by the buzz of the intercom or the low hum of the TV.)

There were times, of course, early in his Ex-Presidency, when his faith had wavered; once or twice he had even come close to believing that the tapes had been a mistake. But that was past now. He understands that things had happened only as they must and—most important—that it was far better to have failed—and captured the experience —than to have succeeded unrecorded. Now, in the mellow years of his Ex-Presidency (a term he believed he had introduced to the language), he vastly enjoys re-examining his great work of art, "The Thirty-seventh Presidency of the United States" ("Hail to the Chief!"), and he is at peace with himself in Casa Pacifica.

And he is very happy to have the tapes. Six crises had gone unrecorded, lost forever "down the dark backward and abysm of time." But the seventh, the Presidency, was frozen in tape: not for an age but for all time. He had designed it; he had executed it; he had recorded it.

He would interpret it. And he knew that someday—not soon, probably, but eventually—someday others would recognize him for what he was: not, as the clichéd popular view had it, a disgraced hack politician, but rather a great antihero of contemporary politics, and— without parallel—the first politician ever to exercise full control over the record, the only thing that counts in the end. In fact, he was an artist first, a man of action only second. He had revived the art of fiction by living it (just like in the Renaissance! he thought) and soon others would see this. He had been both author *and* hero of a colorful and historic Presidency. The *man* did not matter: the petty failures, trials, and suffering counted for little in the face of the great art work. Had he not himself explained in the stirring conclusion of his moving farewell speech that,

> The greatness comes not when things go always good for you; but the greatness comes, and you're really tested, when you take some knocks, some disappointments, when sadness comes. Because only if you've been in the deepest valley can you ever know how magnificent it is to be on the highest mountain.

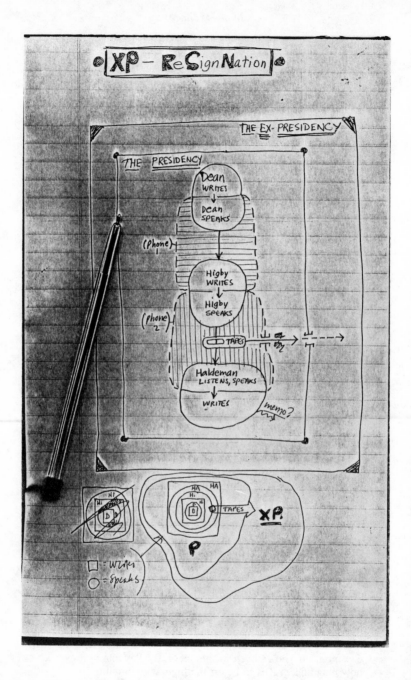

No, the man counted for very little in the vast scheme of things: *Ars longa, vita brevis.*

The Ex-President drowses in the Ex-Presidential easy chair. The serene smile reappears. He has often practiced this look of serenity since the Resignation, and now he can do it easily and well—even in his sleep. The widespread journalistic characterization of P's mood during the last tumultuous days of his Presidency as "serene" is one of the brightest memories for him of that point in time. He remembers his earnest discussions with his wife earlier in that week when they decided what the proper tone for him to adopt for the transition to the Ex-Presidency would be. "The Lion at Bay" had been suggested as a potential image, but P had felt this smacked too much of Richard III and he did not want that comparison to be made. "Cosmic sadness" was popular among the staff, but P felt there was something undignified about that pose. Then he remembered the look on the face of Chairman Mao as they wheeled him out of the room after having been shown to P on his Historic Trip to China . . . that was it! Serenity.

The mask had served him well ever since and had, in fact, become the major motif of his Ex-Presidency, together with a touch of overarching sadness. (P thought: *Weltschmertz,* K would have called it.) His long, lonely walks on the beach at sunset were much commented upon and often photographed. His letters to Heads of State (*never* to Heads of Government) had just the right note of forlornness.

X-P is proudest of the walks on the beach, remembering as he does with not a little envy those artsy but famous photos of John Kennedy on *his* beach. He was confident that he had beaten Kennedy soundly in the record now. (That amateur!) The sharp, poignant reality of Watergate would long outlive, he felt, the puerile fantasy of Camelot. Yes, Kennedy had become a martyr, but that persona struck X-P as ultimately simplistic. Kennedy was only the *object* of the myth. He

It is not generally known, but P was also a pioneer of xerox art. Here, a rare example of his work. Notice the phallic juxtaposition of the pen, just delicately touching the fine line that separates the Presidency from the Ex-Presidency. P wasn't at his best when speaking words, but he had a linguist's appreciation for their signification. Many of the extant note pads are covered with rebusal jottings (such as "ReSignNation") often involving P's initials. Some scholars believe he was fascinated with the letters "XP" because of their resemblance to the Greek "Chi Rho," an earlier heroic letter-symbol for a character to whom P often compared himself in later days. (Photo: David Lindroth) never controlled it, like the Ex-President. (And of course he never lived to enjoy it.) Anyhow, others had been assassinated. No one else had a Resignation. No one else had the control. No one else had the tapes! Well, maybe Johnson did, but that didn't matter: Johnson, X-P felt, was Falstaff at best, while he (P and X-P) was Hamlet, Prospero, Richard III, united.

Next to the Ex-President's chair there is a table, with books on it. He does read now. He had included a reference to this change of image in his farewell speech, he remembers:

> As you know, I kind of like to read books. I'm not educated, but I do read books.

He reads, now, and *is* read. And after so many years as a practicing artist he now has the leisure, these last few years, to read theory. *The Tempest* has become his favorite play. He identifies with Prospero. He knows the feeling of being shut out and cheated of his rightful patrimony. More important, he fully understands the feelings, so bittersweet it is almost unbearable, of the political magician who has come to the point in his self-told story when he realizes the climax has come and he must give up control of his magistracy. He has often compared Prospero's farewell speech with his own. ("Now my charms are all o'erthrown/And what strength I have's mine own,/Which is most faint. . . . Now I want/Spirits to enforce, art to enchant;/And my ending is despair. . . . As you from crimes would pardoned be,/Let your indulgence set me free." Damn! he wishes he had known to quote it in his own speech!) He has read deeply in Renaissance political theory. Machiavelli, he thinks, was jejune, but Castiglione's *The Courtier* has become one of his favorite books. He was enthralled with the concept of *sprezzatura*!

Of course X-P reads the moderns, as well. Barbara Garson, Donald Barthelme—especially *Robert Kennedy Saved from Drowning.* "Something to it," he thinks, "Barthelme's no fool, he understands life as fiction." Mailer is on the list. *He* had the right idea, but he had such dull material to work with, X-P thinks. Certainly a peremptory life if there ever was one. A well-worn copy of Genet's *The Balcony* lies next to the chair as well. The Ex-President has read this several times and found it rough going. He has a feeling Genet knew more about this business than anyone else but the book is too slippery. Nevertheless, the whole idea of the "Nomenclature" as Genet described it: the overpowering importance of the record, the story as opposed to the reality, the close connection between politics and mythic fiction, the profound sexuality of power—these things haunt X-P. No one, he feels, has written about the phenomenon as well as Genet, at least from the *outside*. But P and X-P, they—he—have lived it.

Then there are sentimental favorites on the reading table, Samuel Beckett's *Krapp's Last Tape* chief among them. X-P is angry that this last had been so often alluded to by journalists during the time of the Resignation. They had cheapened this fine play. They didn't understand the emotional structure of it as the Ex-President did. A man sitting quietly with his bananas, listening to his tapes. It must have seemed comic to them, he supposes. But he knew the *Angst* of it all. He shares with Krapp the ecstatic knowledge that it is no longer necessary to live; it is only vital to *have* lived. He, X-P, knows the joy of having captured the present, made it prologue to the past (or does he have that backwards?). *He* knows the peace that comes with the recordings—having pinned one's life to the wall like an enormous restless butterfly (did Nabokov deal with these matters somewhere, he wondered?), having authored a life as well as acted it out.

But Krapp had writ small and he, X-P, had writ large. Not only author and hero, but what a hero! He had been: The President. He had authored: The Presidency. He was now: The Ex-President. The limitless power of it all thrills him once again as it has so many times in the past. His upper lip quivers—a remembered gesture. His arms rise, as he stands alone in the middle of the tape room, surrounded by the black-brown liquescent witness of the reels. His arms rise, they float depersonalized in front of him, mimicking the gestures—the ones he had painstakingly learned for his resurrection in the sixties—a finger rises in stern warning, the familiar V-sign jerks up, the other arm comes down in the graceful karate chop—the gesture with which Kennedy, so long ago, had outmaneuvered him (the one it had been most difficult for him to learn), then it raises itself high in the air in the stiff-armed salute he remembers from his favorite movie, *Patton.*

Of a sudden, his arms hug him tightly, he stands there swaying in the cool Pacific breeze. He swoons with it all, the glory, the power: The President, the Ex-President—no one had done it like this before! The Presidency! The Ex-Presidency!

A moment passes. With difficulty, he regains his composure. Had always been a problem, he thinks, but doesn't matter now. "I'm over. They can't see me anymore. I'm free." The last words of Krapp echo in his head:

> Here I end this reel. Box—[*pause*]—three, spool—[*pause*]—five. [*Pause.*] Perhaps my best years are gone. When there was a chance of happiness. But I wouldn't want them back. Not with the fire in me now. No, I wouldn't want them back.

The tape runs on in silence. The Ex-President is, once again, serene.

28. ROBERT KENNEDY SAVED FROM DROWNING
by Donald Barthelme

Fiction or reportage? Does it matter? This is Barthelme's own RFK.
The title alludes to Jean Renoir's 1932 film *Boudu sauvé des eaux.*

K. at His Desk

He is neither abrupt with nor excessively kind to associates. Or he
is both abrupt and kind.

The telephone is, for him, a whip, a lash, but also a conduit for
soothing words, a sink into which he can hurl gallons of syrup if it
comes to that.

He reads quickly, scratching brief comments ("Yes," "No") in
corners of the paper. He slouches in the leather chair, looking about
him with a slightly irritated air for new visitors, new difficulties. He
spends his time sending and receiving messengers.

"I spend my time sending and receiving messengers," he says. "Some
of these messages are important. Others are not."

Described by Secretaries

A: "Quite frankly I think he forgets a lot of things. But the things he
forgets are those which are inessential. I even think he might forget
deliberately, to leave his mind free. He has the ability to get rid of
unimportant details. And he does."

B: "Once when I was sick, I hadn't heard from him, and I thought
he had forgotten me. You know usually your boss will send flowers or
something like that. I was in the hospital, and I was mighty blue. I was
in a room with another girl, and *her* boss hadn't sent her anything
either. Then suddenly the door opened and there he was with the biggest bunch of yellow tulips I'd ever seen in my life. And the other girl's

boss was with him, and he had tulips too. They were standing there with all those tulips, smiling."

Behind the Bar

At a crowded party, he wanders behind the bar to make himself a Scotch and water. His hand is on the bottle of Scotch, his glass is waiting. The bartender, a small man in a beige uniform with gilt buttons, politely asks K. to return to the other side, the guests' side, of the bar. "You let one behind here, they all be behind here," the bartender says.

K. Reading the Newspaper

His reactions are impossible to catalogue. Often he will find a note that amuses him endlessly, some anecdote involving, say, a fireman who has propelled his apparatus at record-breaking speed to the wrong address. These small stories are clipped, carried about in a pocket, to be produced at appropriate moments for the pleasure of friends. Other manifestations please him less. An account of an earthquake in Chile, with its thousands of dead and homeless, may depress him for weeks. He memorizes the terrible statistics, quoting them everywhere and saying, with a grave look: "We must do something." Important actions often follow, sometimes within a matter of hours. (On the other hand, these two kinds of responses may be, on a given day, inexplicably reversed.)

The more trivial aspects of the daily itemization are skipped. While reading, he maintains a rapid drumming of his fingertips on the desktop. He receives twelve newspapers, but of these, only four are regarded as serious.

Attitude Toward His Work

"Sometimes I can't seem to do anything. The work is there, piled up, it seems to me an insurmountable obstacle, really out of reach. I sit and look at it, wondering where to begin, how to take hold of it. Perhaps I pick up a piece of paper, try to read it but my mind is elsewhere, I am thinking of something else, I can't seem to get the gist of it, it seems meaningless, devoid of interest, not having to do with human affairs, drained of life. Then, in an hour, or even a moment, everything changes suddenly: I realize I only have to *do* it, hurl myself into the midst of it, proceed mechanically, the first thing and then the second thing, that it is simply a matter of moving from one step to the next, plowing through it. I become interested, I become excited, I work very fast,

things fall into place, I am exhilarated, amazed that these things could
ever have seemed dead to me."

Sleeping on the Stones of Unknown Towns (Rimbaud)

K. is walking, with that familiar slight dip of the shoulders, through
the streets of a small city in France or Germany. The shop signs are in
a language which alters when inspected closely, MÖBEL becoming MEU-
BLES for example, and the citizens mutter to themselves with dark
virtuosity a mixture of languages. K. is very interested, looks closely
at everything, at the shops, the goods displayed, the clothing of the
people, the tempo of street life, the citizens themselves, wondering
about them. What are their water needs?
"In the West, wisdom is mostly gained at lunch. At lunch, people
tell you things."
The nervous eyes of the waiters.
The tall bald cook, white apron, white T-shirt, grinning through an
opening in the wall.
"Why is that cook looking at me?"

Urban Transportation

"The transportation problems of our cities and their rapidly expand-
ing suburbs are the most urgent and neglected transportation problems
confronting the country. In these heavily populated and industrialized
areas, people are dependent on a system of transportation that is at
once complex and inadequate. Obsolete facilities and growing demands
have created seemingly insoluble difficulties and present methods of
dealing with these difficulties offer little prospect of relief."

K. Penetrated with Sadness

He hears something playing on someone else's radio, in another part
of the building.
The music is wretchedly sad; now he can (barely) hear it, now it
fades into the wall.
He turns on his own radio. There it is, on his own radio, the same
music. The sound fills the room.

Karsh of Ottawa

"We sent a man to Karsh of Ottawa and told him that we admired
his work very much. Especially, I don't know, the Churchill thing and,
you know, the Hemingway thing, and all that. And we told him we

wanted to set up a sitting for K. sometime in June, if that would be convenient for him, and he said yes, that was okay, June was okay, and where did we want to have it shot, there or in New York or where. Well, that was a problem because we didn't know exactly what K.'s schedule would be for June, it was up in the air, so we tentatively said New York around the fifteenth. And he said, that was okay, he could do that. And he wanted to know how much time he could have, and we said, well, how much time do you need? And he said he didn't know, it varied from sitter to sitter. He said some people were very restless and that made it difficult to get just the right shot. He said there was one shot in each sitting that was, you know, the key shot, the right one. He said he'd have to see, when the time came."

Dress

He is neatly dressed in a manner that does not call attention to itself. The suits are soberly cut and in dark colors. He must at all times present an aspect of freshness difficult to sustain because of frequent movements from place to place under conditions which are not always the most favorable. Thus he changes clothes frequently, especially shirts. In the course of a day he changes his shirt many times. There are always extra shirts about, in boxes.

"Which of you has the shirts?"

A Friend Comments: K.'s Aloneness

"The thing you have to realize about K. is that essentially he's absolutely alone in the world. There's this terrible loneliness which prevents people from getting too close to him. Maybe it comes from something in his childhood, I don't know. But he's very hard to get to know, and a lot of people who think they know him rather well don't really know him at all. He says something or does something that surprises you, and you realize that all along you really didn't know him at all.

"He has surprising facets. I remember once we were out in a small boat. K. of course was the captain. Some rough weather came up and we began to head back in. I began worrying about picking up a landing and I said to him that I didn't think the anchor would hold, with the wind and all. He just looked at me. Then he said: 'Of course it will hold. That's what it's for.' "

K. on Crowds

"There are exhausted crowds and vivacious crowds.

"Sometimes, standing there, I can sense whether a particular crowd is one thing or the other. Sometimes the mood of the crowd is disguised, sometimes you only find out after a quarter of an hour what sort of crowd a particular crowd is.

"And you can't speak to them in the same way. The variations have to be taken into account. You have to say something to them that is meaningful to them *in that mood*."

Gallery-going

K. enters a large gallery on Fifty-seventh Street, in the Fuller Building. His entourage includes several ladies and gentlemen. Works by a geometricist are on show. K. looks at the immense, rather theoretical paintings.

"Well, at least we know he has a ruler."

The group dissolves in laughter. People repeat the remark to one another, laughing.

The artist, who has been standing behind a dealer, regards K. with hatred.

K. Puzzled by His Children

The children are crying. There are several children, one about four, a boy, then another boy, slightly older, and a little girl, very beautiful, wearing blue jeans, crying. There are various objects on the grass, an electric train, a picture book, a red ball, a plastic bucket, a plastic shovel.

K. frowns at the children whose distress issues from no source immediately available to the eye, which seems indeed uncaused, vacant, a general anguish. K. turns to the mother of these children who is standing nearby wearing hip-huggers which appear to be made of linked marshmallows studded with diamonds but then I am a notoriously poor observer.

"Play with them," he says.

This mother of ten quietly suggests that K. himself "play with them."

K. picks up the picture book and begins to read to the children. But the book has a German text. It has been left behind, perhaps, by some foreign visitor. Nevertheless K. perseveres.

"*A ist der Affe, er isst mit der Pfote.*" ("A is the Ape, he eats with his Paw.")

The crying of the children continues.

A Dream

Orange trees.

Overhead, a steady stream of strange aircraft which resemble kitchen implements, bread boards, cookies sheets, colanders.

The shiny aluminum instruments are on their way to complete the bombing of Sidi-Madani.

A farm in the hills.

Matters (from an Administrative Assistant)

"A lot of matters that had been pending came to a head right about that time, moved to the front burner, things we absolutely had to take care of. And we couldn't find K. Nobody knew where he was. We had looked everywhere. He had just withdrawn, made himself unavailable. There was this one matter that was probably more pressing than all the rest put together. Really crucial. We were all standing around wondering what to do. We were getting pretty nervous because this thing was really . . . Then K. walked in and disposed of it with a quick phone call. A quick phone call!"

Childhood of K. as Recalled by a Former Teacher

"He was a very alert boy, very bright, good at his studies, very thorough, very conscientious. But that's not unusual; that describes a good number of the boys who pass through here. It's not unusual, that is, to find these qualities which are after all the qualities that we look for and encourage in them. What *was* unusual about K. was his compassion, something very rare for a boy of that age—even if they have it, they're usually very careful not to display it for fear of seeming soft, girlish. I remember, though, that in K. this particular attribute was very marked. I would almost say that it was his strongest characteristic."

Speaking to No One but Waiters, He—

"The dandelion salad with bacon, I think."
"The *rysstafel.*"
"The poached duck."
"The black bean purée."
"The cod fritters."

K. Explains a Technique

"It's an expedient in terms of how not to destroy a situation which has been a long time gestating, or, again, how *to* break it up if it appears that the situation has changed, during the gestation period, into one whose implications are not quite what they were at the beginning. What I mean is that in this business things are constantly altering (usually for the worse) and usually you want to give the impression that you're not watching this particular situation particularly closely, that you're paying no special attention to it, until you're ready to make your move. That is, it's best to be sudden, if you can manage it. Of course you can't do that all the time. Sometimes you're just completely wiped out, cleaned out, totaled, and then the only thing to do is shrug and forget about it."

K. on His Own Role

"Sometimes it seems to me that it doesn't matter what I do, that it is enough to exist, to sit somewhere, in a garden for example, watching whatever is to be seen there, the small events. At other times, I'm aware that other people, possibly a great number of other people, could be affected by what I do or fail to do, that I have a responsibility, as we all have, to make the best possible use of whatever talents I've been given, for the common good. It is not enough to sit in that garden, however restful or pleasurable it might be. The world is full of unsolved problems, situations that demand careful, reasoned and intelligent action. In Latin America, for example."

As Entrepreneur

The original cost estimates for burying the North Sea pipeline have been exceeded by a considerable margin. Everyone wonders what he will say about this contretemps which does not fail to have its dangers for those responsible for the costly miscalculations, which are viewed in many minds as inexcusable.

He says only: "Exceptionally difficult rock conditions."

With Young People

K., walking the streets of unknown towns, finds himself among young people. Young people line these streets, narrow and curving, which are theirs, dedicated to them. They are everywhere, resting on the embankments, their guitars, small radios, long hair. They sit on the sidewalks, back to back, heads turned to stare. They stand implacably on street corners, in doorways, or lean on their elbows in windows, or squat in small groups at that place where the sidewalk meets the walls of buildings. The streets are filled with these young people who say nothing, reveal only a limited interest, refuse to declare themselves. Street after street contains them, a great number, more displayed as one turns a corner, rank upon rank stretching into the distance, drawn from the arcades, the plazas, staring.

He Discusses the French Writer, Poulet

"For Poulet, it is not enough to speak of *seizing the moment*. It is rather a question of, and I quote, 'recognizing in the instant which lives and dies, which surges out of nothingness and which ends in dream, an intensity and depth of significance which ordinarily attaches only to the whole of existence.'

"What Poulet is describing is neither an ethic nor a prescription but rather what he has discovered in the work of Marivaux. Poulet has taken up the Marivaudian canon and squeezed it with both hands to discover the essence of what may be called the Marivaudian being, what Poulet in fact calls the Marivaudian being.

"The Marivaudian being is, according to Poulet, a pastless futureless man, born anew at every instant. The instants are points which organize themselves into a line, but what is important is the instant, not the line. The Marivaudian being has in a sense no history. Nothing follows from what has gone before. He is constantly surprised. He cannot predict his own reaction to events. He is constantly being *overtaken* by events. A condition of breathlessness and dazzlement surrounds him. In consequence he exists in a certain freshness which seems, if I may say so, very desirable. This freshness Poulet, quoting Marivaux, describes very well."

K. Saved from Drowning

K. in the water. His flat black hat, his black cape, his sword are on the shore. He retains his mask. His hands beat the surface of the water which tears and rips about him. The white foam, the green depths. I throw a line, the coils leaping out over the surface of the water. He has missed it. No, it appears that he has it. His right hand (sword arm) grasps the line that I have thrown him. I am on the bank, the rope wound round my waist, braced against a rock. K. now has both hands on the line. I pull him out of the water. He stands now on the bank, gasping.

"Thank you."

29. HOW TO FIND YOUR MOST MAGNETIC SELF
by Mary McGeachy

Critics do it, novelists do it, football players do it, politicians do it, too. Now, you can do it. Mary McGeachy, who only recently learned herself, shows you how.

> The Lilyan Wilder Service is a service designed to aid Anchormen, Reporters, Sportscasters, and other personalities who appear before the camera in television to reach their maximum potential as communicators. . . . The performer is helped to be his most magnetic self.
>
> —From "The Prospectus" of the Lilyan Wilder Service

I arrived for my lesson a few minutes early. I had come for one session with Lilyan Wilder to get her judgment of my talent as a potential broadcasting drama critic. She normally doesn't take anyone for one session; but since I'd had some on-air experience and knew some of her students, she had agreed to take a look. I'd recently had a few unsuccessful auditions and wanted to know exactly where I was going wrong. Moments after I appeared at her Manhattan apartment she bustled into the living room, an energetic woman in her middle forties. Her first words were: "You're so pretty!" I liked her immediately.

But even at $50 per session, could she help me become my "most magnetic self"? Certainly she had helped dozens of others, from Kathleen Pepino, of Atlanta's WQXI-TV, to Cal Ramsey, who does "color" for the New York Knicks, to the entire staff of WCAU-TV in Philadelphia. More and more, would-be Walter Cronkites and Barbara Walterses are taking themselves—or being sent by their stations—to Lilyan Wilder. After looking over her impressive list of students, I thought maybe Wilder could explain why the Chauncey Howell you meet at a cocktail party—flamboyant, bouncy, funny, energetic—is not the same serious, reasoned Chauncey Howell, drama critic, you meet on WNBC-TV's *NewsCenter 4*, where the fizz seems to have gone out of him; why the Pat Collins you see at intermission in the theater—

personable, lively, real—is twice as interesting as the super-sincere Pat Collins who does reviewing on WCBS-TV; or finally, and ironically, why Rose Ann Scamardella (of the pronounced Brooklyn rasp) is exactly the same on WABC-TV as off.

Wilder led me down a hall to a small bedroom that was her studio and, without any preliminaries, said, "Let's get to work." For practice copy, I had written a review of the musical *Over Here* and a piece on comedian David Frye. I sat at a desk a few inches from a microphone and about two feet from her mini-camera. She stood by the tape machine about five feet away from me. I had heard that one of the best things about going to Wilder was being able to review yourself immediately on tape playback. She said encouragingly, "Well, read and let's see how you do." I read my copy to the camera as well as I could.

We watched the "instant replay" in silence. "What do you think?" she asked. I couldn't really pinpoint what was wrong, so I tried something like, "I sure look down a lot." Wilder turned off the machine, pulled up a chair a few feet in front of me and sat right next to the camera. In a sincere, imploring tone she said, "Now. Tell *me* about *Over Here*." I began to reread the review and she'd question or comment as if we were in conversation. Then she went back to the machine and said, "Do it again, just like you were talking to me a few minutes ago. As a viewer, I've got to know that you care about my reaction to your thoughts and you've got to give me time to react. The meaning of what you write is lost if you don't present it well. Now, let's try again."

The difference was startling when she played it back this time. I'd gone from a kind of glazed I'm-reading-this-review-to-you look into a normal human being trying to get the viewer interested in what I had to say. I would have hired me right then, only my head tipped to one side a little (she said it took away some of my authority). She placed a book on my head, as in the old modeling brochures. It was fun. I guess I seemed surprised at the immediate improvements and she said, "Television demands a definite technique. It's more creative than the single art of acting, writing, producing—it's the combination of those skills and it's very hard to do."

My hour was nearly finished. Wilder got down to specifics: Don't forget to emphasize strong verbs and nouns, know your copy, be very familiar with it. "Memorize it?" I asked (thinking that would be ideal). "Oh, no!" she said. "As a viewer I don't want to worry if you can't remember the next line—I *want* you to look down, otherwise I'm nervous for you. Know your first thought and the beginning of the second and then in the middle of the second thought look down and pick up the third." I tried it, and it worked. She said I should work on my "a"s and "l"s: "You're an intelligent-sounding person, so why let a harsh sound like your 'a' detract?" (I had a flat Midwestern "a.") " 'A' is softer if you keep your tongue down while forming the sound. And don't say 'mi-yun,' it's mi*ll*-ion."

Before I left, I read through my pieces a few more times. She complimented me again and seemed concerned that I didn't have a job in TV. *So* concerned, in fact, she gave me a name at Newsweek Broadcasting. Buoyed by her interest, I thanked her and said I'd be in touch. As I was leaving, she slipped a cassette into her videocorder to tape *The Pat Collins Show,* a daily WCBS-TV public affairs program in New York. Collins, a Wilder alumna, was interviewing one of her teacher's more recent students, Assemblyman Andrew Stein, about his role in the nursing home investigation. "I wish Pat wouldn't wear that glossy lipstick, and she has to watch that over-extending of her words," Wilder said. Both of us looked at Andrew Stein. She said she'd been working with him for several weeks and thinks he's smoother: "A lot of it has to do with the fact that he's matured through this nursing home thing—he's really grown up." I asked her who recommended that Stein work with her and she wouldn't say—like a psychiatrist, she didn't want to talk about her patients. She did mention that she had been at WNBC-TV's *NewsCenter 4* for consultation that morning, and talked with me about going on the road with CBS's *Game of the Week* sportscasters.

Five years ago, Lilyan Wilder was teaching voice and diction at the Lee Strasberg Institute in New York. A Method actress, with degrees in interpretation and theater from Northwestern University, she had taught public speaking at Brooklyn College and summer courses of "On-Air Delivery Techniques" at the Columbia University Graduate School of Journalism. (She's also done TV soaps, *The Defenders,* and understudied Faye Dunaway at the American Place Theatre.) WPVI-TV, the Philadelphia ABC affiliate, called the Strasberg Institute in search of a voice and diction coach for the New York Yankees ex-first baseman Bill White, then being groomed as a sportscaster. "Ex-athletes come from the physical world," explains Wilder. "It's a whole new world for them to use only their minds. The ex-jocks' dilemma is not being able to describe the game because they're too close to it. I have to teach them to think on their feet."

Bill White, now a Yankees announcer, didn't like the idea of lessons right away; he didn't want to lose his "black quality." "It took her about a month to win me over and then it all started making sense," he now recalls. "In the beginning there were certain phrases I wanted to hang on to—I guess they were clichés. Like I used to say, 'There ain't no way.' She convinced me they weren't professional sounding. She also helped me with diction and eye contact—making me believable." White is such a devotee of Miss Wilder's that he drives in from his home in Pennsylvania for coaching sessions, which undoubtedly helped him recently land a regular spot on the *Today* show.

(Last November, bolstered by Bill White's success, Wilder decided to go network with her sports coaching. She approached Bob Wexler, head of CBS Sports, after reading in *Variety* that Wexler wanted to bring "theatricality and excitement" to sports. She knew they'd had problems with Elgin Baylor last year so she offered her services to Oscar "Big O" Robertson and his basketball *Game of the Week* crew. CBS-TV hired her for intensive coaching wherever the games were being played. At out-of-town games she worked with the "Big O," converting any hotel room into a mini-studio.)

After the graying of Bill White in Philadelphia, Wilder's big break in TV news came in 1973 when producers of New York City newscasts were engaged in a ratings skirmish and brought in new, untried talent: Carl Stokes, ex-mayor of Cleveland and new anchorman in town, needed some emergency work over at WNBC-TV; Al Primo, then producer of WABC-TV's *Eyewitness News,* had a couple of amateurs on his hands, Rose Ann Scamardella and Jim Bouton; Ed Joyce, director of news at WCBS-TV, thought *all* of his reporters should go for at least one session with Wilder.

Would-be television stars make the pilgrimage to Wilder's studio for varying reasons. WCBS-TV's Trish Reilly wanted to lower her voice, simplify her writing and overcome her nervousness; Peter Bonventre, a sportswriter for *Newsweek,* wanted to loosen up in front of the camera for his Newsweek Broadcasting stints; Al Primo sent Bouton because his head kept bobbing up and down; veteran WPIX-TV anchorman, Joe Harper, was rusty; and Chauncey Howell, former feature writer/columnist for *Women's Wear Daily,* was sent because Earl Ubell, director of news at *NewsCenter 4,* thought him too animated for TV.

Ubell believes in voice coaching because he's been through the process himself. "A trained voice in television is as important as learning how to write," he says. A former baggy-pants journalist turned TV science reporter when the *Herald-Tribune* folded, he says he spent hours ridding himself of his Brooklyn accent, exchanged his baggy pants for TV tight ones and is proud of his transformation. He apparently sees no conflict in changing a reporter's appearance and speech patterns when, at the same time, he and Wilder insist they are striving to bring out the real person underneath.

Wilder and Ubell agree that the *Today* show's Jim Hartz is one of the best examples of a real person on television. The perfect broadcaster, Hartz is the same on camera as off. They marvel at his intimacy with the audience, his ability to convince his viewers *they* are the only thing that counts. "The off-camera persona is what I want to see on camera," insists Ubell. "The worst offense is to be something you're not." But what about Chauncey Howell? Wilder and Ubell have convinced him that his "off-camera persona" is a little too much for television. Howell agrees: "I mean, after watching Jim Hartz and those other people, I'd seem like a real ham to the viewer. At first I fought this because I thought it was boring, and that TV was filled with boring people. But, I realize now you can't be a ham on TV—we'd be monstrosities."

To tame such creatures, Wilder lets them indulge their taste for ham —in *her* studio. Howell, for example, renders passages from Dickens— so convincingly that Wilder sometimes cries. He also sings along with Paul Robeson records to deepen his voice. Scamardella sang along with

Ella Fitzgerald, but with less enthusiasm. "I sang 'April in Paris' in those sessions two times a week for four months, and I still sound like I come from Brooklyn." Bonventre crooned with Frank Sinatra. All this singing—there was poetry, too—scared Bouton off. "I didn't want to be slick or polished. I think I relate better and, besides, it's much easier to be myself. After a while your personality comes through anyway; you just have to know who you are."

Rose Ann Scamardella knew who she was—she was a personnel manager for a shipping company whisked away from her job to be made an *Eyewitness News* star. Wilder had a novice on her hands. She not only worked on Scamardella's voice, diction and projection, but tried to tidy her up, too. Managements encourage Wilder to discuss parts in your hair, make-up and clothing. Her sessions with Scamardella extended into Ohrbach's and Alexander's. "She wanted me to buy blouses with flowers," Scamardella recalls. "Everything I bought with her I haven't worn." Wilder suggested to Howell that he shop at an Italian import store, but he stuck with his prep-school-teacher look.

Sometimes a reporter's writing style won't do, either. Though TV news producers say they don't send people to Wilder to deal with "content," she says: "Through training with my students, I've learned an awful lot about writing and how to put a piece together. With what I call my 'twelve-year-old mentality' I'm not afraid to ask questions and in so doing I've simplified their writing." Print people slipping into TV find the transition difficult. When Trish Reilly, with six years of magazine writing behind her, arrived at WCBS-TV, one producer said: "You're a very good writer, and you're going to have to get over it." Reilly says Lilyan Wilder is great at spotting non-broadcast writing. She can point out a sentence that doesn't communicate because it is too tangled, or because it has a metaphor you can grasp when you read it on paper, but you can't when you hear it.

If a TV reporter doesn't untangle his metaphors and get rid of distractions—hair too short, old-fashioned glasses, shiny lipstick, tilted head, a squeaky voice—no one will listen, according to Wilder. She told Bonventre to get new glasses, a toupee, to trim his moustache and lose twenty pounds. "I think you're adorable," she told him, "but it just won't go over." Confused, Bonventre asked: "Well, if *you* think I'm adorable why won't other people think I'm adorable?" "It just won't do," she explained.

GOSSIP

30. WHY PEOPLE ARE TALKING ABOUT GOSSIP
by Alexander Cockburn

If you're not a work of art, other people are, and you want to read about them. There are lots of little resonances going on in this piece. Cockburn himself is a gossip par excellence. His weekly columns in *The Village Voice* are brimming with tidbits about the media world and politics. And, in fact, so is this analysis of the phenomenon which appeared, with justice, in *New York* magazine in the days of Clay Felker. *New York* was a prime leader in the gossip movement.

"Never lose your sense of the superficial" was the peremptory advice once given his editors by Lord Northcliffe, the founder of modern popular journalism. They've been following his advice in England, more or less, ever since. In the United States, on the other hand, where journalists have a higher view of their calling, it looked for a while as though seriousness and deep purpose were carrying all before them: reporters discarded the brashness of *The Front Page* for the solemnity of *All The President's Men.* But all is not lost. It's become evident over the last few months that more and more members of the Fourth Estate are recollecting the essential meaning of their trade, which is to discover the inconsequential and get it into print.

The spirit of triviality lurking in the bosom of the average newspaper reader will never be quenched, and is indeed now blazing up more fiercely than ever before. For a decade the dark clouds of the Vietnam war, of Watergate, of the recession, seemed to obscure the landscape. Now, with a "recovery," with the placid realities of structural unemployment and the prospect of a more or less steady run to the grave under either a Republican or a Democratic president, it is plain that what a large section of the literate citizenry is after is plenty of rousing chatter about other people. Gossip, in fact, has crawled out from under its stone and is now capering about in the full light of day.

There are, of course, problems with the word itself. In old thrillers the villain, advancing on the pinioned hero with whip and thumbscrew, used to say suavely, "Not *torture,* my friend. Shall we just call it . . .

persuasion?" Something of the same coyness now seems to envelop the notion of gossip.

Readers, hurrying home from the supermarket with copies of *People,* the *National Enquirer,* and the *Star,* tell you that they are just out for *entertainment*; reporters, bearing down on their victims, say they are after the *facts*; editors, with all due primness, tell you the public is now interested in *personalities,* and given half a chance will throw in a short lecture on the passing of the issue-oriented sixties. The truth of the matter is that they are all chasing after gossip, but like the old villain are too polite or are as yet unprepared to call the thing by its proper name.

"Gossip?" says Richard Stolley, managing editor of *People.* "We have expunged that word from our vocabulary. The term has held connotations of untruthfulness. If we're asked to describe what we are doing we prefer to call it 'personality journalism' or 'intimate reporting.' " That's awfully nice for Stolley, perched atop a circulation for *People* which is now reaching 1.8 million. I hope he sleeps the better for having the notion of "personality journalism" tucked under his pillow. Readers, scurrying out to buy last week's edition of his magazine, which has on its cover the words BARBRA STREISAND: FOR THE FIRST TIME, SHE TALKS ABOUT HER LOVER, HER POWER, HER FUTURE, presumably have a rather more zestful outlook on the situation.

Stolley is right, of course, in saying that the word "gossip" does have *louche* undertones. It is one stage nastier than "chatter," one stage seedier than "investigation." It's poised between rumor and the real, between the stab in the back and the handshake, between tastelessness and the libel lawyer's office. True gossip is only barely fit to print, is the rank underbelly of journalism. In the words of James Brady, vice-chairman of the *Star,* gossip is difficult if not impossible to confirm, but contains the elements of an accurate story. Gossip, in short, is nasty.

People magazine is right at the top of the ladder between decency and outrage. We find it near heaven along with the sedate chatter in *The New York Times'* "Notes on People" section. A little below, we find "People" in the *Washington Post* "Style" section. Then down we go, past Suzy, Maxine Cheshire, Liz Smith, Herb Caen, Sid Skolsky, Earl Wilson, *WWD* Interview, "The Ear" in the *Washington Post,* Sally Quinn, Ben Bradlee's memoirs, Rona Barrett, Cindy Adams, down, down into the caverns of the *Star* and the *National Enquirer* where spectral images of Jacqueline Onassis, Elizabeth Taylor, and Princess Margaret shriek for release from their eternal torment—a torment, incidentally, from which the entirely fictional French gossip sheet *France Dimanche* has just liberated Princess Margaret, since its headline recently announced LE SUICIDE DE LA PRINCESSE MARGARET.

In the pantheon of gossip it's becoming clear that a certain shift in personnel is occurring. Jostling in among film stars, royalty, and international refuse of every description have come "media stars" and, increasingly, politicians. A certain widening of gossip's focus is in fact taking place.

The most optimistic assessment of this new situation comes from a man who is in fact one of the true pioneers of a whole style of gossip— even though he resents the term. Lloyd Shearer started "Walter Scott's Personality Parade" in *Parade* magazine in 1958. About 20 million copies of *Parade* are presently inserted into 111 newspapers across the country, giving "Walter Scott" a readership of around 50 million people. And each week, addressed to "Walter Scott," come about 6,000 letters, mostly to get the facts straight about whatever piece of gossip happens to be on the writers' minds: "Is it true that Henry Kissinger is a secret massage-parlor freak?" "Who is the French blonde whose name has been linked with Prince Bernhard of the Netherlands?" Each week "Walter Scott" gives them the facts.

The pleasure of his column, so far as I'm concerned, is that you can eat your cake (the gossipy question) and have it too (the factual answer). I asked Shearer if he detected a new trend.

"I don't think gossip is on the increase at all," he retorted. "We don't traffic in gossip. Rumors and gossip originate somewhere else, and people write to us and ask if in fact something is true, and we spend a large amount of money and time checking it out among various sources. I think what has happened is that there has been a great growth of skepticism about people, which is understandable after the Kennedy, Johnson, and Nixon administrations. So there's mounting interest in politicians."

Over the years, Shearer says, *Parade* has received fewer and fewer letters about film stars, once the staple of the column. "What has happened is that motion pictures are no longer the mass medium in America. Motion picture stars were once the most colorful people in the world. Now that television has surpassed and supplanted motion pictures as the prime medium throughout the world, the stars of television are very circumspect, because the people who sponsor them won't put up with any nonsense. So you have in the mass-entertainment medium people who are not particularly colorful, not particularly maverick. I mean, what do you particularly want to know about Paul Newman? People know all about Barbra Streisand already, or they don't care anymore. As a matter of fact there's been a tremendous decline in the Walter Winchell type of gossip column. One of the reasons why the *Los Angeles Times* dropped Joyce Haber was there just wasn't enough material. She had to use names that were fairly esoteric in Peoria, Illinois. So, as you get a more educated electorate and because of circumstances, the readers are more interested in politicians and publishers. People are not so much interested in gossip as they are in truth."

This, you might say, is the up-side view of the whole gossip phenomenon. And, as if in testimony to such uplifting sentiments, the Sunday before last the cover of *Parade* presented Bob Woodward and Carl Bernstein to its 50 million readers. Now Woodward and Bernstein—

particularly in their recent investigative activities as displayed in *The Final Days*—have cast the whole matter of gossip in a particularly interesting light. Stimulated by Watergate, young people have been filling the nation's journalism schools, eager to learn the tricks of investigation and then hurry on out to expose evil men and possibly also to save the Constitution. Ecstatic with high purpose, they doubtless avoid undue consideration of the thought that Watergate, if it started with the Dahlberg check, seems to be ending with the news that Richard and Pat Nixon did not sleep together for twelve years.

Woodward and Bernstein have naturally defended all the allegations in their recent book on the grounds (a) that they are true and (b) that disclosure of these truthful allegations is essential to the understanding of the political personality of Richard Nixon. Maybe so, but the fallout is pure gossip—as is plainly revealed by the cover on the *Star* last week, which bears the headline PAT NIXON DRINK AND SEX CHARGES: FRIENDS TELL INSIDE STORY. The *Star,* at least, knows where the game is at. So indeed, in a more tasteful way, did *Newsweek* when it first presented excerpts from *The Final Days.* Gossip kept Watergate going and gossip seems to be seeing it into the grave: pain for Pat Nixon, pleasure for the people.

Some of the more seasoned practitioners, well aware that gossip can cause pain, emphasize that they try to keep clear of inflicting such damage. Suzy (Aileen Mehle), for example, now appears in eighty-nine newspapers going out to between 15 million and 20 million readers. Right at the start of her career she decided that the one thing she did not wish to confront for the rest of her working life was a roomful of people recoiling from her as at the sight of a viper. She also wished to keep her sources. "I knew about Princess Margaret and Roddy Llewellyn right from the start. Was I going to print it? No way!" So the nearest she'll get to conceding any aggressive edge to her project— which she defines as "sending it all up"—is to say that "I give them the needle, but in a way that they don't feel till three days later." Nor does she particularly feel that anything much new in the way of gossip is happening. "Gossip is the juice of life, but we've always had it." And, in a spirit of peace, off she plunges to her parties and her people.

Herb Caen similarly thinks that nothing new is going on. Caen, for those who have not sampled the unique pleasures of his column in the *San Francisco Chronicle,* is one of the best as well as longest-practicing gossips in the United States. "Gossip has never gone out. It's another media hype. I started writing gossip in high school in 1930 and it hasn't changed since then. That was forty-five years ago. I told who was holding hands with whom in the parking lot and everyone wanted to read it. It's still the same business. I don't see any change. I think there were better gossips in the old days than there are now. The *Los Angeles Times* is trying to get by without Joyce Haber, but people are screaming bloody murder. Even though she was one of the worst, and very heavy-handed, people still wanted to read it. People look for something light. They don't want to read the *Time* essay, they want to know what Princess Margaret was saying to Nureyev, which is why *People* was started."

But at least Caen is prepared to accept the nastier side of gossip. "There's gossip and chitchat. Chitchat is lighter in vein. Gossip should have some scandal to it. It's got to be a little nasty. A little bit of going for the jugular. Otherwise, what the hell's the point of it? I try to make it as nasty as possible, within the realms of good taste and the libel laws. There's a little bit of the cobra in all of us. *People* is just a bore, no knife edge to it at all."

And then Caen started talking about the British gossip columns. "They're marvelous," he shouted enthusiastically. "They're tougher . . . my idea of what a gossip column should be."

"Knife edge . . ." I wonder if people now gossiping about gossip, peering at Truman Capote fingering his stiletto on the cover of this month's *Esquire,* really know what might be in store for them. They could, of course, recall the manipulative savagery of Walter Winchell —blackmailing his subjects and touting stocks. But they might also peruse some of the British newspapers today, or—to be really thorough about the job—go back through the newspaper archives to the late 1950's when the art of the British gossip column was at its height.

In 1961 Penelope Gilliatt—the novelist, screenwriter, and *New Yorker* film critic—concluding a drive from London to Sussex in the company of the playwright John Osborne, climbed from the car to view their secret trysting place in the quiet village of Hellingly. Her pleasure was marred by the sight of a Fleet Street gossip columnist climbing out of the trunk of the same car, where he had—at great personal danger— secreted himself during the drive from London. The columnist forthwith proceeded to take photographs. From the hedgerows sprang other columnists also in pursuit of evidence of the Gilliatt/Osborne liaison. Osborne was married; so was Gilliatt, to Tony Armstrong-Jones' best man. The couple retired—for the duration of their stay—to the sanctuary of the cottage, later to be informed by the neighbors that these same neighbors had been offered large sums for news of "quarrels" and other domestic commotion.

Gilliatt had made the mistake of writing a fierce exposé of gossip columnists in *Queen* magazine in 1960. This was around the time that three journalists from the William Hickey column in the *Daily Express* had striven, in a couple of cunning ways, to enter a private party thrown by J. Paul Getty. One had disguised himself as a member of the band; the other two had hidden in the shrubbery and at an appropriate moment had emerged in full evening dress, clutching champagne glasses filled from a quarter-bottle brought along for the purpose.

It was also around the time—as related by Gilliatt—that the gossip writers had become angered by the refusal of the wife of one cabinet minister to reveal her private country address. A reporter telephoned her townhouse, pretending to be her child's godfather, told the housekeeper that he had a present that he wanted to get to the child, and on hearing that the nurse was going down to the country the next day and would take it, waited outside the house and followed her to earth.

Gilliatt discussed such practices; the elaborate stringer and payoff system maintained by the columnists; their innumerable cruelties, inaccuracies, and snobberies; above all, their insane hypocrisy as they detailed the socio-sexual activities of the upper classes. Her article provoked bellows of remorse and surprise from press lords such as Beaverbrook and Rothermere. Some of the columnists were sacked, others directed to mend their ways.

Shortly thereafter, amid the final spasm of the Profumo scandal, the art of British gossip-writing fell into a long decline. In its place came the jocular muckraking of *Private Eye,* the biweekly satirico-investigative sheet. Rather along the lines of Lloyd Shearer's present emphasis on people's lust for the truth as opposed to mere gossip, *Private Eye* detailed the activities of politicians, newspaper people, publishers, and the like. The order of the day was investigative journalism, or at least satirically investigative snippets.

At the start of the 1970's it became clear that the most readable stuff in *Private Eye* was, as signed by "Grovel," nothing other than our old friend Gossip in a fresh and somewhat tougher guise. "Grovel" was and is the work of Nigel Dempster, the man singlehandedly responsible for resurrecting British gossip-writing. At the age of thirty-four Dempster—who also writes a column in the *Daily Mail*—is flushed with triumph. He was, as he hastened to inform me the other day, the first person to reveal the full details of Princess Margaret's affair with Roddy Llewellyn. He gained much notoriety at the time Lady Antonia Fraser joined forces with Harold Pinter, by listing her alleged previous lovers. On December 15, 1975, he predicted to the day the moment when Harold Wilson would resign. Unscrupulous, devoid you might say of all decency, he best expresses what gossip-writing is all about.

"I think American gossip is tedious in the extreme. It's bad, it's boring, and it's about boring people. It's not revelatory. It's in no way intrusive. There's nothing there that causes any distress, that causes any harm and dissention—which is what we should be all about. We are here to write about things that are not welcomed by the subject of our inquiries. American columns are nothing but puff P.R. jobs."

Dempster, announcing that he had just been soundly thrashed by a member of the British equestrian team resentful of his activities, warmed to his theme. "Gossip must be nasty, because it is per se what you would not wish to be heard and spread abroad about your good self. The targets are surely those people who sell themselves to the public, those people who wish to parlay and trade with the public. I feel that the public has a right to find out any aspect whatsoever of these people's private lives. I go after privilege and I define privilege as existing for anyone with safeguards against the awful humdrum existence we are forced to lead, anyone who is elected to office, anyone who is in receipt of a title and uses it, anyone who uses the media to further his own ends, anyone who puts himself in the public eye for gain.

"My living doesn't depend on anyone I write about. I made a conscious decision many years ago that I didn't like a certain section of society, and as far as I'm concerned I've never had their society, their friendship, or their approbation and I've never sought it. That's why I can write about whom I want. This way you don't get those rather pathetic pleas to one's better nature—which I do not have.

"The one thing you've got to have in the gossip business is a target. In America there seems to be no taste, no instinct, no smell for it. There's no inquisitiveness there. Watergate got out through people gossiping. Gossip is the color of life, the fine, bold strokes. By which I mean that you and I—the purchasers of gossip—find out what color socks Nixon wears or whether he sleeps with his wife.

"Our sort of journalism is grudge journalism. You only get tip-offs from someone who has a grievance of some sort. It's all swordsmanship, in my view. I regularly get beaten up and things thrown at me. Two nights ago Harvey Smith (the horseman) hammered me into the ground. Last year I put myself up in a charity dance in front of all those idiots and they were able to throw pies at me. Ten pies at $50 each, and a dozen eggs at $20 each. I was in terrible shape for a while, but if you can't take it, then don't give it."

Dempster, reaching his finale, delivered what was to my mind a fairly accurate version of what a lot of journalism and all true gossip is all about. "I think human beings are unpleasant and they should be shown as such. In my view we live in a banana-peel society, where people who are having a rotten, miserable life—as 99.9 percent of the world is— can only gain enjoyment by seeing the decline and fall of others. They only enjoy people's sordidness, their divorces, whether their wives have relieved them of $5 million, how their children turned round and beat the crap out of them. Then they suddenly realize that everything is well in the state of Denmark, that everyone else is leading a miserable, filthy life which—but for me and other journalists around—they would not know about. They see that those who obtain riches or fame or high position are no happier than they are. It helps them get along, and frankly that is what I give them."

This sort of talk is, needless to say, a far cry from the encouraging noises made by purveyors of "personality journalism" such as Stolley. But Dempster—whose most recent coup has been to expose a Labor member of Parliament as a lesbian—talks of coming to the United States to run a syndicated gossip column. Perhaps he senses—as Truman Capote has sensed also—that the time is ripe here for true gossip. Dempster, a public-school boy in the twilight of Great Britain, is franker than many of his American counterparts about the realities of the trade: that almost all journalism in the end is gossip, and that the handmaidens of gossip are treachery, envy, and spite; that while many journalists may prattle on about the public's right to know, they are in their bones talking about their own need to tell.

Maybe it is premature to set such a parallel between the terminal spasms of the British way of life and actual and impending ailments on this side of the Atlantic. The British, after all, have long had an obsession with the realities and intricacies of class and with the presumed drama inherent in the sex lives of public figures. "Intimate reporting," as Richard Stolley termed it, need mean little more than a democratization of polite chatter, spreading out from Hollywood to encompass every profession in the country. As Stolley put it, "So-called superstars are now being produced in practically every field." This means in the end, I suppose, that the respectable reporters and researchers of *People* —constrained by large advertisers, good taste, self-esteem, and the libel lawyers—will ultimately be able to write "personality profiles" about everyone in the U.S.

It depends how far along the road we go. Yesterday's idols become today's chopping blocks. President Kennedy's sex life gets laid out in *Time* magazine. Joan Kennedy goes to a sanitorium for a cure for alcoholism and a couple of fellow patients sell the story to the *National Enquirer*. In a spirit of tranquil expectation the readers wait for more, read—maybe with outrage—but still read.

Perhaps, in answer to such expectation, American newspapers will rediscover the gross popular tradition lost to radio and now largely kept alive by British and Australian journalists on the *Enquirer* and the *Star*. Perhaps American journalists will slowly descend again into the mire from the pinnacles of high-minded respectability, of status-sodden intimacy with the likes of Henry Kissinger. Perhaps publishers, sensible of the importance of newsstand and supermarket sales, will push them in that direction anyway.

"Gossip?" said Gore Vidal. "Gossip is conversation about people. In the United States there has never been actual discussion of issues whenever a personality could take its place. We do that because we can never examine the sort of society we live in. Therefore candidates are rated according to their weight, color of eyes, sexual proclivities, and so forth. It avoids having to face, let us say, unemployment—which is a very embarrassing thing to have to talk about. Anything substantive is out. Otherwise somebody might say this is a very bad society and ought to be changed."

Defenders of gossip will doubtless controvert Vidal's gloomy assessment, point to crusading gossips in the tradition of Drew Pearson—who fulfilled the gossip's first function of simply daring to print the previously unprintable. The example of Pearson, the reporter-gossip, is a noble one and the sort of thing Lloyd Shearer evidently had in mind when he talked about people's desire for truth. But I'm not so sure it has much to do with the general trend of gossip, which has something to do with simple curiosity, much to do with snobbery, envy, cruelty, the fostering of antagonism, knowingness rather than knowledge, the creation of coteries and a perversely heightened sense of the trivial.

Who knows, though? Maybe *People* magazine will successfully domesticate gossip in the way that the American mass media have domesticated so much else, and the readers in search of thrills will come upon only sanitized fun, mere pap to trundle home from the supermarket.

31. THE REVITALIZATION OF CLAY FILTER: YET ANOTHER PASSAGE

by Nora Ephron

For a more thoughtful treatment of Clay Felker's trials and tribulations with the Australian Killer Bee, Rupert Murdoch, see Lucian Truscott's "Clay Felker: Requiem for a Winner" in the companion volume in this series, *Media Culture*. Ephron's fable is gossip, pure and simple, meant to be consumed like chocolates.

The Fractious Fifties

On the surface, Clay Filter would appear to have had everything he had ever wanted. (His name is fictitious.) The ginger-haired magazine editor might not have wanted the middle-aged spread that occasionally caused his shirt buttons to pop off, but otherwise he had achieved his life's dream. He had *gained his authenticity*. He had spent most of his Deadline Decade dreaming of running his own magazine, and finally he had come to do so. He lived in a beautiful apartment with a double-height living room which, had it faced south, which it did not, would have reflected the city he had built a magazine to. He had spent ten years off and on with the same woman, in a relationship I would call an *Off-and-On Relationship*; he had served as her Mentor (see pp. 14, 27, 51–2, 54, 76–7, 85, 109, 128, 131–2, 189–90, 280, 293; see also Career Women and Mentors, pp. 128, 132–5, 225, 226, 227), and he had only two complaints about her: he worried she would write about him someday and disguise him as thinly as she disguised everyone else she wrote about; and he occasionally became irritated at her uncanny ability to predict every adult crisis that was to befall him and then say, "I told you so," as soon as it did. Sometimes she went even further by insisting he had had a crisis when he thought he had merely had a bad cabdriver, but when he accused her of a priori reasoning, she simply reminded him that he was a classic wunderkind (see pp. 189–198) and that all wunderkinder tend to deny they have mid-life crises. He dozed off as she rattled on about patterns of wunderkinder: "They were afraid to admit they were not all-knowing. Afraid to let anyone come too close. Afraid to stop filling their time with external challenges they could probably surmount, for fear of glimpsing that vast and treacherous interior which seems insurmountable. Afraid that the moment they let down their guard, someone might ridicule them, expose them, move in on their weaknesses and reduce them again to the powerlessness of a little boy. It is not their wives they are afraid of. It is themselves. That part of themselves I have called the Inner Custodian, which is derivative of parents and other figures from childhood." She paused. "Do you understand what I'm saying, darling?"

Clay Filter snapped awake and nodded comprehendingly. The truth, though, was that he could never figure out what she was talking about when she went on in this way. He knew it sold magazines, and books, and that someone must understand it, but he knew he didn't, and he wasn't sure what he could do about it if he did. He had pushed himself through the Trying Twenties and the Catch Thirties and the Switch Forties. He had fought the fight between his Merger Self and his Seeker Self, giving in to his Merger Self on only two or three occasions, if you counted living arrangements. He had survived the Seesaw Years and the Pulling Up Roots Years, and now here he was, and part of the problem was that he wasn't sure just where he was at. Years before, he had altered his birth date in *Who's Who*, and he now no longer knew for certain how old he was. Freud would call this *self-deception*, and Jung would call this *silliness*, and Erikson would call this *ridiculous vanity*, but I call it *The Refusal To Deal with the Age-Forty Crucible*. The catch was that he no longer knew whether he was at the tail end of the Switch Forties or on the verge of the Fractious Fifties, and while he didn't much care one way or the other about it, the woman he had been with for ten years in the *Off-and-On Relationship* cared deeply.

"The crisis will emerge . . . around fifty," she said. "And although its wallop will be greater, the jolt may be just what is needed to prod the resigned middle-ager toward seeking revitalization."

"I'm sick of all this talk about my crisis!" Clay Filter shouted. "I'm too old to have a crisis!"

"It's never too late to have a crisis," she said. "Anyway, darling, don't think of it as a crisis. Think of it as a *passage*. Does that help?"

"No, it doesn't help!" he shouted. "Crisis is a perfectly good word. Why coin another?"

At moments like this, she wondered whether he might not turn out to be an exception to all her theories. He had an explosive temper. Perhaps he would spend his crisis in little bursts, piggyback one mini-crisis atop another and avoid the big bang. Just the other night, unaccountably, he had blown up at her for using piggyback as a verb. Then, when she defended herself, he threatened to rip the italic bar from her typewriter. Outbursts like that were becoming more frequent. She realized it was more important than ever for her to be supportive in order to help him find his way up the developmental ladder.

"Each one of us has our own *step-style*," she said one day as he stared, preoccupied, at the rug, "the characteristic manner in which we attack the tasks of development and react to the efforts we make. Some of us take a series of cautious steps forward, then one or two back, then a long skip up to a higher level. There are those of us who thrive on setting up sink-or-swim situations. . . . Others, when face-to-face with each task, sidestep it for a time in a flurry of extraneous activity."

"Do you think I should buy *The Village Voice?*" he asked, looking up.

"This could be your step up to a higher level," she replied.

"I don't know anything about money," he said.

"On the other hand," she said, "this could be your flurry of extraneous activity."

"This isn't my flurry of extraneous activity," he said. "That comes later, when I recklessly fly off to the Bahamas."

"Then perhaps it's your sink-or-swim activity."

"I think I'll let Felix make the deal," said Clay Filter.

She made a note for a new syndrome. She would call it *You Can Turn Over the Closing to the Broker, But YOU Pay the Mortgage.* She would tell him about it at some point, but now he had fallen asleep.

Some months later, when he awoke, he discovered that Felix had gotten things backward. In the course of buying *The Village Voice* for Clay Filter's magazine, Felix had accidentally sold Filter's magazine to *The Village Voice.* This was an extremely confusing turn of events. Confusing turns of events often precipitate crises. Just as often, they do not. It is possible that had Clay Filter realized either of these points, he might have been able to avert what was to happen. Instead, he started a new magazine and began flying back and forth across the country each week. He was spreading himself too thin, except for the aforementioned part of him that was simply spreading itself. One morning, after he stepped off the Red Eye from Los Angeles, he was forced to stand for two hours in the freezing cold at Kennedy Airport, and when he finally got a taxi, the driver was surly and unpleasant and a reader of *Cue.* This so infuriated Filter that he marched into a board of directors meeting and demanded a raise, two houses and a limousine. The board of directors, already upset about the profit picture, turned Filter down in an extremely acrimonious session and then went off to plot ways to sell their stock.

"I think I'm having a crisis," he said to her that night.

"Don't be silly, darling," she replied. "You merely had a bad cabdriver."

When the crisis finally began, he recklessly flew off to the Bahamas. When he returned, he lost his temper and alienated the principal stockholder, who decided to sell out to an Australian. In the end, Clay Filter got one and a half million dollars and the love and devotion of several dozen employees who had previously been ambivalent toward him. But he lost his magazine, and his magazine was his life. He had offers, and he had ideas, and he would return, but there was a nagging part of himself—the part of himself physiologists call *The Brain*—that suspected that all of this could have been avoided. He suggested this to her.

"Wrong, darling, wrong," she said. "All of it was necessary. And more than that, it was thrilling. It was so *predictable*. The wallop. The jolt. Just what is needed to prod the resigned middle-ager toward seeking revitalization." She smiled. "Oh, darling," she said. "I'm so happy for you."

32. *PEOPLE'S* BIG IN PEORIA
AND HEAD PERSON DICK STOLLEY
IS ONE REASON WHY,
AND ANOTHER IS CHER,
AND THAT'S NOT ALL, EITHER
by Lew Grossberger

Lew Grossberger put together this sharp parody for *The Village Voice* in the spring of 1977.

Nearly three years ago, a new product popped up amid the freeze-dried coffee and powdered soup lining America's supermarket shelves. Market tested, glossy packaged for maximum impulse-buying pull, tasty and whipped smooth but not overly spicy, it carried the *People* label, and soon it became the hottest brand to jangle through the checkouts since presugared cornflakes, even though if you poured milk and sliced bananas on top of it, you'd wind up with a soggy wad of indigestible pulp.

Okay so far, but by the second graph we've gotta get right down to the gist of the thing, i.e.: Top honcho of this retailing bonanza is 48-year-old white male American managing editor Richard ("Dick") Stolley, a native Illini and veteran Life-Timer. Observes Stolley, 48: "I think I know what plays in Peoria, since that's where I grew up," he quipped. (Actually, it was in nearby Pekin, Illinois, since we like our gossip factual around here. Time Inc. ain't *Confidential,* ya know.)

The low-key Stolley holds sway on the 29th floor of Time's Sixth Avenue tower, amiably reigning over *People*'s small, young editorial staff of 25 full-timers (total age: 867). "I try to be enormously accessible to people on this magazine," notes Stolley, who may have turned 49 by now. He works hard and stays late. "He's the best editor I've ever worked for," observed one admiring staffer, 29. "That's right," added another, 33.

Thorough, maybe even compulsive (get quote from expert shrink), Stolley personally sifts each syllable that passes through *People*'s gullet ("I may edit very lightly or sometimes I'll totally rewrite") and orders a word count every issue to make sure those short articles aren't creeping upwards on him.

Noted J. Pierce Hubbard, a Peoria sales executive: "I never met him personally, but I hear he's a nice guy."

Stolley lives with his wife of 22 years, Anne, 45, a former newspaper reporter. They have four daughters: Lisa, 21, a Zoli model and NYU student; Hope, 18, a student at Denison University in Ohio; Melinda, 16; and Martha, 13. They live in a large, uninsulated, Victorian-style three-story wooden house, 75, in Old Greenwich, Connecticut, about 100 yards from Long Island Sound. "Jesus, it's cold," exclaimed Stolley. Their pet cat died recently after a long illness.

Home is a key element in *People*'s modus operandi. "One of the things we insist on," Stolley said, "we want to go home with them, we want to see how their homes are decorated and how their children act and how they deal with wives and husbands, roommates or whatever."

(Sure, that's fine for him, but you expect me to schlepp up to Connecticut and freeze my ass off just to look at somebody's wife? Oops, wait a minute, fate is on my side . . . Oldest daughter arrives at office during interview . . . Gods of Journalism intervene again . . . let's just eavesdrop here and see how they get along.)

"I'll just pop out and say hello. My daughter just came in, I'll say hello to her. [*Walks to outer office.*] Hi, Lisa."

"Hi, Dad."

"How are you? How are you feeling?"

[*Response garbled.*] Coughs.

"I'm getting interviewed."

"You're getting interviewed?"

"Yes."

"By who?"

"*Village Voice.*"

[*Laughter.*]

"Is that all you've got on, for God's sake? You've got a cold." [*Or possibly coat.*]

"I don't have a coat." [*Or possibly cold.*]

(Delete all above, totally unusable, what the hell you think this is, Andy Warhol's *Interview* magazine?)

Note: The interview, basic tool of journalism, is believed to have been invented in the Pleistocene epoch, about 86,000 years ago (check clips) when personkind discovered the interrogative grunt. However, the first known Qs went unAed for it was to be another 30,000 years before anyone thought to invent the reply. Most of these early replies were crude models comprised of exaggerations or preposterous lies. But the trail had been blazed. Ahead lay wonders the likes of which Neanderthal Being had never dreamed of: the wire-bound notebook, the tape recorder, the talk show, the slick weekly, and the Oriana Falacci, 44 (check age). Who can say what new marvels await our ever-diminishing attention spans?

(No digressions, please.) Stolley grew up a twin (brother Jim, also 48, is a vice-president of the Hammermill Paper Company in Erie, Pennsylvania) surrounded by facts and dates, which we'll give you a few of but nothing to slow down the pace. Father managed a yeast factory and Mom was an English teacher.

But back to the present; no time for a lotta growing-up stuff. Stolley's stalwart efforts spew out a product eagerly lapped up by 1.8 million shoppers a week, exactly the kind of people any advertiser of people-oriented products wants to talk to, the kind who brought *People* from 43rd to 14th in PIB ad pages in the first half, whatever the hell that means. (I read it in a full-page ad in *The New York Times.* Sounded impressive.)

But, ask the consumer-conscious, how much nourishment does it contain? Isn't there too much sugar and carbohydrate? What about protein and vitamins? Certainly not enough roughage to keep you reading regularly . . . Christ, this metaphor's gone out of control, they're not supposed to keep running on this long, are they? Copy Desk!!!

Whew, that was close. Uh, something about the cover. Right, the cover sells the magazine. "You've got to be at the right place at the checkout counter, which is eye level," noted Stolley, who has not aged perceptibly in three consecutive paragraphs. With 85 per cent of its readers newsstand buyers, *People* needs a coverperson everyone knows—and more important—wants to know better. Liv Ullmann (a cipher in Peoria) and Mary Tyler Moore (too easily deciphered) blew their covers, couldn't move the goods. But the mighty Cher has fronted *People* FOUR hot-selling numbers—her last *People*'s all-time best seller, when she appeared with new husband Gregg, ex-baby Chastity, and new baby whoever.

Estimated one aberrant though prescient rummy, 35: "By the fall of 1993, everyone in country will have gotten picture in *People* at least once. This will mean end of gossip as we now know it, and dawn of new era in which everyone will be declared famous by statute and forced to reveal all innermost secrets to magazine of choice. Yet scandal of all kind will soon become so boring and predictable, revelations will become obsolete, and public will begin reading law reviews for excitement."

(Rewrite this graph. Cut quote down. See, what we want here is a more brisk and chipper flow, you know, the thing rolls in, gets the job done and cuts out, no hot-dogging, no self-indulgence.)

Gossip, in the traditional sense of juicily malicious rumor spreading, actually has nothing to do with Stolley's *People.* Fact is, it's all factual. But Stolley fumes when critics call his baby bland. (That's better.) "I think people who criticize us for being bland are criticizing us for something we don't intend to be."

Wait a minute. I think I got an even better bland quote further down the tape. Yeah, here it is: "When we began, there was a lot of feeling about what the magazine would be like that bore no relationship to what I had planned for this magazine, and a lot of criticism against Time Inc. that they would bring out an uptown movie magazine or a magazine of triviality or gossip. It seems to me that nothing was more important in our first year or so than establishing credibility, that what we were publishing was the truth. If that means sometimes leaving out fascinating, scurrilous, unprovable material that you could probably get away with—I mean even if the stuff turned out not to be true, it's not the sort of thing you'd get your ass sued off on—my decision was that we don't do that. . . . If that resulted in a certain blandness, then it was quite calculated on my part." (Much too long. Go with first one.)

The style is not far from Basic Newspaper Featurestory, slightly slicked and with elements of *Time*style occasionally creeping in. Lotsa pix, but not as good as *Life*'s used to be. "We do not do stories on people if we are simply going to dismantle them," he noted. "I don't think they fit into the formula of this magazine."

Formula, that's it, not blandness, really, but sameness, that's the rap. That formula—personality first—homogenizes, reduces. Everyone starts sounding, looking the same, just folks . . .

For Adolf and Eva, It's a Quiet Sunday in the Mountains After a Tough Week of Blitzkrieging Poland . . .

Dr. Guillotin Sticks Out His Neck on a Sharp New Gadget . . .

One awaits with quivering anticipation the Gary Gilmore cover. "We will never do a story that concentrates entirely on the dark side of someone's life," observed Stolley. It will be a challenge. Oh, quit editorializing and finish the damn thing. I've caught you reading it at the checkout counter yourself and anyway, you're out of space. Nothing goes over 2000 words, not even Cher. Or, as one veteran *People*-watcher, 17, noted: "They don't worry about transitions much and they always end with a quote."

33. CONFESSION FEVER: TALES OF BETRAYAL AND HEARTBREAK

by Ron Rosenbaum

Like most other celebrity phenomena, gossip has turned in upon itself. The self is not only a work of art; the self is money in the bank. If most of us will eventually retire to the basement television room to plug all five senses into the fiction machine, it's worth considering that some of us will remain outside, transmitting. Here are the current candidates. Rosenbaum's *MORE* piece was greeted by much literary protestation. Karen Durbin insisted vociferously that she *was* alone on the beach—as if it really mattered.

Isn't it obvious by now that the public act most characteristic of the seventies is the Pious Snitch? The Confession, as the people who do it prefer to call it. I'm not talking about gossip. Gossip is about other people, the guilty pleasure of outsiders. Confession is the self-righteous revelation of an insider betraying not only himself but his partners in crime or in bed. For all the newsmagazine cover stories, there's nothing new about gossip these days but quantity. But something different is happening with the confession. It's become the new national obsession.

Look back over the history of the decade so far. Start with Dan Ellsberg (I used to be a war criminal but snitching on these other war criminals will absolve me), and don't forget poor Sid Zion maligned for snitching on Ellsberg because he beat Ellsberg out of his chance to confess first. Then take all leaders of the sixties like Tim Leary and Eldridge Cleaver who now confess they were false prophets— and Jerry Rubin who confessed the Chicago Seven *were* guilty all along.

Add in all the women suddenly confessing to illicit affairs with past presidents all the way back to FDR. Most recently Dwight D. Eisenhower's wartime chauffeur Kate Summersby not only confessed an affair with Ike, she quoted the Supreme Allied Commander blaming his impotence on poor Mamie. Judith Exner in her confession revealed something far more embarrassing than that about JFK— she claimed he played the soundtrack album of *Camelot* on the White House stereo for her as a preliminary to confessing his undying romantic love. Doris Kearns reports LBJ crawled into her bed, although she claims she crawled out to take notes and nothing untoward happened. Then there is the shameless White House physician who listened to Pat Nixon confess her unhappy sexual relationship with Dick Nixon and promptly snitched to Woodward and Bernstein about it.

Count in the confessions of Jimmy Carter (lust in my heart) and Elizabeth Ray (Wayne in my bed). Consider the public fascination for super-snitches Serpico and Deep Throat. Don't forget Watergate penitents Charles Colson (born again) and Jeb Magruder (born yesterday). And of course John Dean, born to be a journalist.

John Dean, journalist. This perfectly appropriate career choice can be perfectly maddening to certain reporters for its symbolic implications about the nature of the profession. The other day I listened to an exceptionally sophisticated Washington journalist rant at the effrontery of Dean—"a snitch, a self-serving snitch"—for taking the name journalist in vain.

We may as well face up to the fact that all journalism, particularly investigative reporting (but not exempting essays such as this one) involves snitching on other people.

But until recently, journalists were content to snitch on strangers. Joan Didion's celebrated warning—never trust a journalist, he'll betray you every time—applied mainly to those situations in which you spend time with people you meet in the course of doing a story, have some drinks, some good times, a meal or two at their home, play with their children, pay them with sympathy until they loosen up enough to confess something worth betraying in print. Up until recently it was only novelists who exercised the freedom to betray lovers, family and close friends with impunity, and then only by changing their names and, usually, some descriptive details.

But now journalists do it without even changing the names, or making the slightest effort to disguise the identity of an unnamed subject. It's called confessional journalism and people get hurt by it, but it's all done in the name of truth. Husbands write about their wives, wives husbands, parents children, brothers sisters. You could look upon it as a replication in the private relationships of media people of the big public snitch—every couple harboring a potential John Dean taking notes. In any case, confession fever, the itch to snitch, has become a media epidemic, a disease spread by intimate contact—not unlike the case of crabs whose spread from writer to writer Nora Ephron artfully detailed in an *Esquire* story that worked both as a paradigm and a clever satire of the whole genre.

Certain novelists, too, have come under fire recently for works that are not so much invasions of privacy as wholesale expropriations inadequately masked by the fig leaf of a changed name. And some apparently are suffering a backlash. A former wife of a Nobel prize-winning novelist is reportedly distressed at the treatment "her character" has received in his work. Lois Gould recently complained in the Guest

Word column of *The New York Times Book Review* that vulgar
Philistines in the media swamp were annoying her with knowing
remarks about who the characters in her novel were "in real life."

"I don't do confessional work," says Lois Gould flatly, with the
distaste of Chandler's private eye when he says, "I don't do divorce
work."

But an increasing number of works of confessional journalism,
and novels too, are just that—"divorce work" or "failure of relationships" work, and nobody seems to know what's fair and what isn't,
what constitutes betrayal and what's fair game. What follows are
stories that explore the netherworld of pain, heartbreak and guilt
that are the consequences of this confusion.

All Flesh Is Grist

Back in 1974 Susan Braudy published a satirical fantasy which
perfectly defines the difficult questions faced by people who make
their living writing about "relationships." She began a fantasized
conversation with her tax accountant by telling him she wants to
write off all sorts of expenses she incurred in the process of divorcing
her husband (among them a bottle of good bourbon to ease the pain),
since, after all, she was writing a book about the divorce.

When the accountant objects she carries the logic a step further
and tells him, "I am sometimes in the business of writing about my
life, as are many feminist journalists. Thus all the expenses that I
incur in the living of my life, and then write about—well, they can
be written off." In fact, she tells the accountant, "I've just decided
this morning to write a book about my next marriage," and just to
make sure she can write the whole thing off she intends to be the
one to propose to whatever partner she ultimately chooses.

Were one to take Braudy at face value, this announcement might
be a kind warning to any man that might wander into her life that
anything he says or does is "on the record" since he's a potential
partner and her book is going to be about choosing partners. In fact,
he's almost certain to be written on in order to be written off.

The fantasy may have been a jest at the time, but the reality was
no joke to her husband. Just a few months after her write-off story
appeared, he came back from a vacation and found a copy of the
manuscript of her book on their divorce (*Between Marriage and
Divorce: A Woman's Diary*) on his doorstep. Along with it was a
request from Susan that he sign a release waiving his right to sue
for invasion of privacy or libel. The book was a project he had
encouraged at the beginning of their separation. But after a first
installment appeared as a magazine article he had begun to have
doubts; after he read the entire manuscript he called a lawyer. Hurt
and angry over matters of fact and interpretation, over what he
considered a mean-spirited characterization of his new wife in the

book and an overall subcurrent of revenge-seeking, he refused to sign the release until his lawyer had extracted from her lawyer some changes in the manuscript.

Among them: his first name was changed, first to "Seymour," then to the more neutral "Paul." Susan also agreed to a number of detail changes that would disguise somewhat his professional identity. Much of the agreement reflects hard bargaining over seemingly trivial details which nevertheless seem to have been charged with all the emotional tension between them. For instance: "Author agrees to change the name of their cat to Frank." And "Author agrees to eliminate remarks about a handshake" between her husband and one of her lovers. "In return," the husband "agrees to withdraw his request that that author eliminate her remark about his new wife's ex-husband's passive attitude at parties."

Despite this experimental property settlement, both parties remained hurt and angry in the aftermath of the book. He feels that a distorted image of himself was locked into cold type and frozen for all time. She feels too upset about the unpleasant aftermath to want to speak about it. Two people who might have survived a divorce with some kind of mutual regard after ten years of marriage no longer speak. Words spoken in anger during a divorce may fade with time, but books written in anger don't. After her book came out he vented his anger by writing an acid parody of it, focusing on her contention that her exposure of their intimate life together was justified by the selfless pursuit of journalistic truth. His title: *All Flesh Is Grist*. He hasn't decided yet whether he wants to publish it.

Dead Baby in a Desk Drawer

It sounded like a great idea at first. Here are these two writers, a man and a woman. They meet, they're attracted to each other. They get to talking about marriages, affairs, "relationships." About why so many go wrong these days. About all the confessional post-mortems being published by men and women about their affairs and what went wrong with them. And about what went wrong with that whole genre—why are those autobiographical novels, nonfiction confessions, novelistic diaries, what have you, inevitably end up sounding self-serving and self-righteous, less than honest and useless as a guide to behavior.

The problem, they decided, was Final Cut, as they say in the picture business. As long as just one of the two people in a relationship is writing about the end of the affair for an audience of millions of strangers and a few close friends—or even if both parties to an affair are writing about it for separate publishers, a phenomenon increasingly evident as inbreeding among media people increases—the power of that Final Cut is corrupting.

That's when they came up with the idea that sounded so great at first. The two of them decided to have an affair and collaborate on a book about it while they were having it. Or maybe they began to have an affair and *then* decided to collaborate on a book about it.

"I can't tell you which came first," he says. "The seductions were both literary and upfront."

The advance was $10,000. An equal amount would be handed over to them upon delivery of the completed manuscript in twelve months.

One year later, the two of them walked into their publisher's office with a completed 50,000-word manuscript ready for submission. Their editor had their second check all filled out on his desk, ready to hand to them. Just as the exchange was about to be made, the woman spoke up.

No book, she said. She just couldn't go through with it. She would not allow it to be published. Ever.

We'll change the names, we'll disguise your identity, whatever you want, said the editor and co-author. Never in any form, said the woman; nothing will change my mind.

Nothing did. That was a year ago. When I first got word of the story a couple of months ago and called the man involved, he told me the book was dead and he hadn't been able to look at it in the nine months since that awful day. The affair was just as dead, he told me. The woman was living with another man somewhere in the Orient, and he personally was still devastated by the whole experience and could speak about it only in a voice filled with pain.

"Oh God, how did you hear about it? It's very difficult to talk about . . . A year of my life."

When I agreed to keep his and her name out of the story, he agreed to tell me something about the collaboration and what went wrong. His version anyway.

"In the beginning she was very enthusiastic," he said. "We'd get together for four or five days and just write and split up and write about it." They'd agreed to do the book in his-and-her-chapters, on each event in their relationship, vowing to hold nothing back about what they felt. There is obviously much potential for hurting and getting hurt in such a situation, particularly if there is an imbalance of feelings on one side or another. No final cut, but the power to cut each other up one chapter at a time right in the middle of the relationship. And hanging over it all was the question apparently unresolved at the beginning of the enterprise: was it a media romance that would end when the deadline was met, or was there something they wanted to preserve for themselves once the manuscript had been dispatched?

According to him, she began to feel wounded first. "It was a strange adventure neither one of us had bargained for. Gradually she began to realize we were playing with something that was very powerful. I think she sensed it earlier. She began to get very nervous . . . We were rushing a deadline and it began to terrify me."

I asked him what "it" was that terrified him.

"It was the thing itself, the idea of forcing yourself to say everything you think. We were tampering with things we both had doubts about. Eventually toward the end there was a crisis that culminated in an explosion."

Aha, I'll confess I thought to myself. Here comes the juicy stuff. "What, ah, led to the explosion exactly?" I asked.

"Look, I feel pretty vulnerable on this," he said. "I can't in any good conscience say I can't answer you, being a writer who's always probing other people myself, but talking about it would be a violation of something I had dealt myself out of. Talking about why would be almost like I'm doing some sort of secondary violation."

I felt it would be cruel to try to extort further intimate details. Instead I asked him why didn't he revive the project by turning it into a novel? Change the names, a few physical details, to veil her identity. That's what everyone did with their affairs these days.

"People say that, but I couldn't do it. I can't even bear the idea of looking at the manuscript. It's like having a dead baby in my desk drawer."

Dr. Jong Meets Dr. Wing

Erica Jong is pissed off. She can't stand the way people repeatedly make up stories about her which confuse her private life with the fictional life of Isadora Wing, the heroine of *Fear of Flying*.

Like the story I was checking with her, for instance. According to what I'd heard, Erica's ex-husband, Dr. Jong, the Oriental child psychiatrist, was raising legal objections to Erica's as yet unpublished new novel, because passages in the novel about Isadora's Oriental child psychiatrist husband Dr. Wing might cause Dr. Jong embarrassment in his profession. (The current standard applied in libel law holds that an individual can win a judgment against a novelist if one of the novelist's characters is "readily identifiable" as the plaintiff and the behavior of that character libels the individual by association.) The story I'd heard went on to say that Erica's plans to continue writing about her husband had contributed to the break-up of her marriage, not long after the publication of *Fear of Flying*.

As I said, this kind of thing pisses her off.

"There are all sorts of vicious rumors that circulate when you become a public person," she told me on the phone. "That lawsuit thing is completely untrue and most likely the product of fears of people who are nervous about writing their own book and are looking for excuses, and are saying 'I could be successful as she but if I did my husband would sue me.' This is more in the area of a psychoanalytic problem for the people who say such things," she says, warming to the subject. "I've heard so much of this—the marriage break-up. Nobody's marriage breaks up because of a book.

It's just people saying, 'I could do it, too, and I could be famous like her, only my husband would leave me.' "

In fact, says Erica, her real-life ex-husband has done very well because of *Fear of Flying*. "He read every word of it before it was published. He heartily approved and never said a word against it, not as long as I was married to him. Whatever people say later after a marriage comes to grief is something else, but at the time he was very proud of it, both as my husband and as a psychoanalyst who's with a person who's making a breakthrough. I think he's gained a lot of honor. A lot of people regarded him as a sort of guru. I know when we broke up a lot of people wanted to go out with him, they saw him as the godfather who helped develop my talent. It gave him an awful lot of status which he used and which a lot of women found attractive." (I was unable to confirm with Dr. Jong whether he indeed enjoyed this state of post-marital bliss. He did not return phone messages.)

Erica denied flatly that her ex-husband—she left him about a year after the success of *Fear of Flying*—had taken any legal measures in regard to his portrayal in her second novel, although she conceded the manuscript had been "read and reread by many, many lawyers."

She returns to the subject of the insensitivity of the public to the distinction between author and persona in her work. "Take Henry Miller," she says. "He uses his own name, yet he's nothing like the Henry Miller of the book. On a couple of occasions Jonathan [Erica's current lover and companion] and I have grilled him—did he ever really stick the carrot in anybody's vagina, did he ever do some of those outrageous things; and he'd say, 'Oh God no! Everybody makes these things up.' People were always asking Philip Roth stupid questions like, 'Do your parents speak to you?' People in novels like these become mythic figures. My husband has a place in literary history because of it."

By way of illustrating the purely esthetic anti-biographical thrust of her argument she cites Tolstoy's discovery of a "real" Anna Karenina—a coarse, vulgar woman from a nearby village who happened to get herself run over by a train in Tolstoy's presence. "She was supposed to be ugly, short and squat, a scheming adulteress, but in writing about this chapter Tolstoy fell in love with her, and transformed her," Erica said. "That's what fiction is about."

I was fairly satisfied with this elevated explanation of Erica's literary ambitions until I ran into a woman who had just finished reading the galleys of Erica's second novel. This is a sophisticated woman writer who respects Erica's work and is perfectly capable of distinguishing between author and persona, but nevertheless seemed shocked and bemused by what she'd just read.

"Remember the husband, the guy with the hairless balls? Well, she was careful about his image in *Fear of Flying*—remember he was always such a good lover, never impotent, all that. Well in this new one she's continuing the story after *Fear of Flying*—only now

Isadora is leaving the guy after writing a best seller and now she says he really wasn't that good at all, she just had to say it because she was still married to him when she wrote the first novel. But now that it's over she can really say how rotten he was in every respect and how great her new lover is—how he's got this great cock and he's more sensitive. But I'll tell you, you know who I think must be in a worse position psychologically than the ex-husband at this very moment?"

"Who?"

"The new lover. Don't you think he must be worrying what happens when it's his turn next? It must put a lot of pressure on him."

Intrigued by this description, I tried to get advance galleys of the second novel. It wasn't easy. In fact, the publicity people at Erica's publishing house denied any had been sent out. Publication date is not until March, galleys won't go out until January and everything's top secret until then, they told me. When I told them I had spoken to someone who had just been sent galleys, they suggested I "confront" that person and tell whomever it was they must be mistaken or pulling my leg.

Well, come on, publicity people. It took me a day to find a source inside your own conglomerate who provided me with a red-bound copy of *How To Save Your Own Life*, and because you fibbed about it I'm going to break the release date and give away a little of the plot.

How To Save Your Own Life brings us the further adventures of Isadora Wing, some three years after her return, at the close of her *Fear of Flying* fling, to the home of her husband "Bennett Wing," the Oriental child psychiatrist. In the interim we learn Isadora has written a best-selling sexy autobiographical confessional novel (called *Candida Confesses*), and amidst media stardom, lesbian affairs, Hollywood hustlers, an orgy and a serious new male lover, decides the time has finally come to divorce Dr. Wing.

The failures of Dr. Wing as husband and human being are pitilessly detailed—he is "cold and reptilian," pathetically dependent on his own analyst. Worse, she reveals, with enormous outrage for someone who published a book about her own infidelities, he's unfaithful and a hypocrite about it: he *failed* to confess his affair to her when she confessed her *Fear of Flying* affair to him. He fiendishly allowed her to go ahead and write her novel feeling more guilty than she needed to about her infidelity. She decides she will make up for it in the next novel.

But Dr. Wing's most serious transgression—the one that's at the core of the confessional dilemma the novel tries to explore and the one that hints at a legal struggle or threats of it behind the scenes—is the good doctor's attempt to prevent Isadora from writing about *his* extra-marital affair in her next novel. Apparently he threatens to leave her (she hasn't yet decided whether to leave him) if she goes ahead. This inspires Isadora to the following apostrophized address to him:

"Now you have told her [about the affair]—but you have also told her that if she ever writes about *this*, if she ever dares to expose the fact that you have sexual fantasies too, you will surely leave her. It is one thing to demythicize women to expose oneself— but it is quite another to demythicize men to expose one's husband . . . the most momentous event in my recent life has been declared off-limits to me. Jealousy is what I want to write about. Jealousy is the subject of my new novel. But I have been told I cannot write it. He points out to me frequently that he and I have the same name and that my writing might be an 'embarrassment' to him in his professional career."

Isadora chooses the novel over the marriage and breaks it up herself. It's an affirmation of something like a Heisenberg's Uncertainty principle of autobiographical writing: she can't write about the relationship objectively while she's part of it without changing it fundamentally. It's a kind of objectivity she doesn't bring to bear on her relationship with her new lover, because she's still within it as she writes it and obviously wants to preserve it beyond publication date.

She envelops her new lover with a dreamy, idealizing romanticism in the novel. Flattering as this may be, the new lover is aware of the pitfalls ahead for a character having a relationship with a confessional novelist. At one point "Josh" taunts Isadora by saying he's "looking forward to your next book so I can see how I rated on your scorecard. . . . I love you but what the hell good is it going to do me?" he exclaims. "I don't want to wind up in a book . . ."

That the plaintive cry of her new true love in a moment of greatest vulnerability—"I don't want to wind up in a book"—should, in fact, wind up in the book, is probably the best paradigm of the cannibalistic compulsiveness of the confessional impulse. The irony of that passage is undoubtedly intentional—one of the undeniable achievements of the novel is the way in which it exploits tensions engendered by the flirtation between autobiography and fiction. And it's a brave book (the cowardly attack on the Oriental child psychiatrist aside). Because for all the talk of Anna Karenina, by putting that watchcry "I don't want to wind up in a book" in a book, she risks the possibility she'll never meet a man, a woman, anyone, who will trust her with any feeling or confidence they can't trust to a book. The practitioners of the confessional literature may ultimately be more victimized by confession fever than the people they write about.

The Decline of the Male Confession

A feminist with whom I was discussing the confessional question suggested in a challenging way that the majority of the confession stories I was writing about were by women. Part of that can be explained by the increase in the number of women breaking into print. But it did set me to thinking that something had happened to the male confessional.

Take a look at the change in subject matter, first of all. Men used to confess to promiscuity and infidelity, abandoning children. Women do that now. Over the past decade the subject of male confessional has gone from masturbation to homosexuality to impotence, and most recently unrequited lust and even virginity (Charles Reich, *Greening of America* author, confessed in his new book that he was a virgin till age forty-three). A regression from sins of commission to sins of mere emission and finally omission. A landmark in this decline—and probably the single most unappealing confessional vignette in recent literature—was an attempt several years ago by an ambitious writer for *New York* magazine to leap with one article into the footsteps of Podhoretz and Roth by compressing into one unforgettable image the themes of competition, ambition, masturbation, Jewishness and—his own contribution—fat.

He pictures for us a scene from his fat-tormented adolescence in a poor Jewish neighborhood, torment brought on by the competitive drive to make it (the Podhoretz part). He's standing in the bathroom of his parents' tenement trying to masturbate (the Roth part) but finding it tragically difficult to pry his penis out from under the folds of fat that envelop it (his part). It's actually not a bad metaphor for the diminished state of the contemporary confession genre —fruitlessly trying to extract some nugget of justification from within all the blubbering.

Nevertheless there was something genuinely courageous about committing that image to print. There's no way in which it can be found charming on any level. And the desire to charm, the desire to have people read one's confessional and say, "Oh what a devilish rogue and reckless sinner he is," the tendency to turn the so-called confession into a sly boast, is the fatal flaw in almost every male confessional.

The Acid Test

In fact, the Looking Good problem sabotages the integrity of most confessionals, male and female. I can offer a crude but useful acid test for confessional works. If you like the person after you've finished reading his confession, don't trust it; if you feel the person has genuinely embarrassed himself and risked universal contempt, it's a rare and striking confessional achievement. Of course, if you then admire the person for that achievement, you're in a Catch-22 situation: if he looks bad it's good, but if it's good he doesn't really look bad, does he? Perhaps the rule is better stated this way:

for a confession to succeed on a generic level, the author must risk appearing contemptible on a human level.

Unfortunately, most of what passes for confessional today is contemptible on a generic level, asking not for forgiveness but for approbation. Typical is the glut of "goodbye to all that, hello maturity" genre.

Some middle-class former youth who's spent one summer in Berkeley, or maybe on a commune or in a sublet on the Lower East Side in the sixties will "confess" how naive the romanticism and idealism of his generation or the Movement or the sexual revolution of the sixties was, and how many hard-won, complex truths about life and work and traditional values he's learned, all the while leeching authenticity from a movement he never was part of in order to betray it. Op-ed pages and fortyish editors of monthly magazines have an insatiable appetite for such penitent ass-kissing works by people in their late twenties because it helps reassure them that they really didn't miss out on the sixties by not being young. In the same way, legitimate feminists are being plagued these days by self-proclaimed feminists who confess that the women's movement has failed them, or that they still like romantic love or the Rolling Stones. Then there's an oily specimen of male who's fond of confessing how he *used* to be just a male chauvinist, real macho, treated women like sex objects, plenty of 'em, too. In most cases this sounds suspiciously like a sneaky excuse to do some old-fashioned sexual boasting. Then there's a whole other species of confession you can spot as fraudulent from the first five words. Those are the ones that begin, "I know it's not fashionable . . ." evoking images of the furies of opposition their confessions will arouse. Rest assured they've calculated that whatever they "confess" to *is* fashionable with the people they want to impress.

Do any confessional works pass the test? Mailer's *Advertisements for Myself*, godfather of the contemporary genre, in some respects. Not for the Dionysian elements, the sex, drugs, the lust for greatness, but in the mean, petty, careerist things he forces himself to confess to—the humiliation of having to try to wheedle a book jacket blurb for *Deer Park* from his idol/rival Hemingway. That took courage. Writing *Making It* was a courageous thing for Norman Podhoretz to do because not only was he daring to confess to a belief in his own virtue, he was confessing to the least attractive of virtues, those of the straight-A student, a truly reckless act more brave than his landmark confession of his "Negro problem." Podhoretz paid the full price for rare honest confessional extracts: reviewers heaped contempt on him for totally wrong-headed reasons. Instead of applauding his honesty, they ridiculed the values he was honest about.

The response Podhoretz received was so severe it may have had a chilling effect on the entire genre. Since then people only confess to groovy sins, and exceptions are rare. Jill Johnston for a time made some breakthroughs, Mailer when not fatally undermined by his desire to charm, the now notorious Barney Collier whose horrible yet brilliant book *Hope and Fear in Washington* is the confession of a self-hating journalist doing to the top journalists in the Washington press corps all the rotten, cruel, distorting and hurtful things journalists do to people.

Fortunately I have a solution that will reverse the decline in the male confessional genre. It's very simple. All those men who are now being written about by women should start taking notes. Write about what it's like being written about and what the other side of the story is. Wouldn't almost everyone who read *Fear of Flying* love to read *The Confessions of Erica Jong's Husband*? Maybe that's why she's so careful with her new lover: he's a writer, too. There's already one fairly trashy precedent, *My Life with Xaviera*, by Larry "The Silver Fox," one of her lovers. Women diarists have always provided a corrective down-to-earth view of famous male authors. There are fascinating stories waiting to be written from the inside about what happens to the dynamics of a relationship that is confessionalized. The two tales of confession fever that follow suggest the possibilities, both funny and sad, of the counter-confession.

A Media Soap Opera for Those in the Know

They were a media couple, both young writers with lots of media friends. Then things started to go awry between them and she began to write about it. In fact it's not too much of an exaggeration to say she pyramided an entire career as essayist and journalist upon the ruins of their relationship. First a big article on sexual jealousy which made much use of melodramatic fights between them, including what she described as a sleeping pill suicide threat on her part. The article described the unhappy consequence of attempting to carry on an "open" relationship—and confessed her belief in the legitimate old-fashioned jealousy as against the "fashionable" new theories that it was regressive. The saleability of this demonstration of the New Maturity was quickly evident. It was just the attitude a magazine for young ladies wanted for its Sex Advice column, and soon leftover anecdotes from The Big Relationship were warmed over to pep up the advice. In one article she recounted a seduction attempt (repulsed, naturally) by a mutual friend who may not have been aware he was making his play on a public stage. And there she is again in the pages of *Harper's* Wraparound "reeling" through the streets of lower Manhattan confessing to a friend that the on-again off-again relationship had suffered another relapse.

She never used his name, of course, but since so many media people knew them both she was in a sense conducting the relationship like a private soap opera for those in the know.

Someone once asked him what would happen to her literary

career if they ever finally broke up for good: what would she have to write about? "That's when I start writing about her," he's reported to have said with a laugh.

The other day I asked him if he'd be interested in writing about what it's like being written about (they seemed to have broken up for good).

"I don't know," he said. "The thought has crossed my mind. The funny thing, looking back on it, is that she asked me to help edit that first story and I did."

"You helped edit it?"

"Maybe it was naive of me," he says with a kind of amused detachment. "Maybe she just wanted me to be part of the process so she wouldn't feel guilty or I wouldn't feel betrayed. I guess I didn't know what I was letting myself in for."

Does he feel betrayed?

"No, not really. I feel sort of flattered in some ways. And now that the relationship is over, I can read about it with a kind of detached interest in each story, since it's no longer interpretable as a weapon or a maneuver in the relationship between her and me." He confesses he did consent to the use of some dramatic license in the original story. He wasn't really sure there were enough pills around to make for a serious suicide attempt, for instance. However, he doesn't think it's worth bothering to write his side of the story because by now the relationship has been over for some time, he's attained a certain distance from the whole thing and she hasn't made use of its increasingly ancient history in any of her more recent essays.

Just one week later, though, there she was back in print with a big essay on women and loneliness. And there he was in the opening section—or there *they* were together again, breaking apart, a trauma which, she writes, set her on the long road to the discovery of the values and perils of living alone.

I called him. "Have you seen it? She's struck again."

"Oh, no, what is it this time?"

"It's an essay about how difficult it is adjusting to being alone after the big break-up with you."

"That's weird," he said. "She's had a very strong relationship with this one guy for eight months now."

"Maybe the piece has been on overset for a while," I suggest.

"Could be. Well, how much is there about me in it?"

"Just a few paragraphs about the agonizing break-up in the beginning. There is another suicide attempt at the end, though. Well, it's not actually a suicide attempt, it's a near drowning. She's talking about how she became so happy being alone she began to carry it to extremes—spending days all by herself in some beach house, going swimming alone. And how one day she goes out into the ocean too far and—it gets very metaphorical here—feels herself drawn into the lonely darkness of the ocean floor and nearly going under until a couple happens by and rescues her."

"Oh, I remember that one," he says. "I was out there with her that day."

"You were? Because she says she stumbles back into the empty beach house after her rescue groping desperately for some connection back to life, touching the furniture for contact."

"Well that's true," he says, "only there was a person sitting on the furniture."

The Fall of the Father Confessor

You could call him the Father Confessor. There are those who credit—or blame—him for engendering a whole species of early-seventies sexual confessionals. And then at the peak of his career, a couple of things started to backfire on him.

It started innocently enough. At forty, the man had risen to an editorial position of some power at a certain periodical about the same time his marriage was breaking up and he was deep into psychoanalysis.

Naturally enough, many of his talks with the women writers who frequented his office would turn to such subjects of common interest as "relationships," feminism, psychoanalysis, jealousy. He was an extremely intelligent and sympathetic listener, gently paternal in manner but not condescending, quick to share confidences about his own personal life, confessions of pain and bewilderment and vulnerability. Women responded by opening to him their secret feelings about their own relationships. He had a comfortable way with feminist catchwords and concerns which gave him an ability to ask what otherwise might seem like intrusive questions about sexuality with dignity. All day long he would ply women with confessions and they would reply with theirs. From many of these sessions of oral confessional intercourse, articles were conceived, nurtured and brought to term. Some of the most celebrated confessionals of a confession-filled season.

Enter the American Express card. The publication gave him a company card; expense account lunches began to supplant the austere office conferences. Dinners followed. The atmosphere and the wine encouraged thoughts of more than confession-swapping intimacy. Fantasies were more accessible. And of course in the spirit of frankness previously established, they were talked about. Occasionally they were acted upon. But not as often, it turned out, as some were led to believe. Meanwhile the cross-pollination of confessions went forward at an even more fevered pace as he buzzed from one frank and intimate conversation to another, often sweetening the next with some provocative material from the last, spicing that with one from the day before and voilà: a "trend in relationships" is discovered and a confessional article is commissioned.

But then, trouble: the poem in *Screw*. One of the women whose poetry he had been printing broke off her relationship with him and published a poem about it in *Screw* which readily identified him in obscene and comic fashion.

Well, people began to talk. Questions were raised about other women whose work he'd published, and, often quite unfairly, the phrase "casting couch" was brought to bear. In the midst of all this, a woman reporter began investigating his private life, asking people all around him, including the women themselves. A few confessed to entertaining fantasy-talk about affairs with him, but nothing more.

Now it happened that the woman doing the investigating was in a good position to know about this sort of thing, since she herself had been the subject of his fantasies. She even told some people she interviewed about the father-confessor's fantasies about her and described the letters he would write her envisioning romantic liaisons.

For his part, the father confessor decided he'd handle the situation by confessing even more. He'd already confessed a lot to that woman reporter about his marriage (what he didn't know was that she'd managed to have a long talk with his wife, who confessed even more), so he might as well confess the whole truth to her about his affairs: they'd been much fewer and farther between than anyone suspected, for some embarrassing reasons which he also confessed to her. For some reason, he believed that if he entrusted her with this sort of intimate confession she'd have to be fair to him, put it all in perspective.

She wasn't and she didn't. She took the tangled threads of confessions, twined them together and hanged him with it. The only thing she left out was the part she played in his life. Even his critics were appalled, although it might be said that confessional karma had caught up with him.

In the shocked aftermath of this betrayal, the career of the father confessor underwent a curious change. He ceased generating confessional stories by others and began to write a few himself. The usual things: feminism, psychoanalysis, "relationships," all written from a carefully sensitive, heavily psychoanalyzed male point of view. It's possible to think, of this development: how pathetic; the poor guy never learned a lesson from the quicksand of confessionals he created last time. But there's another interpretation: he may be building up to writing about that woman. He has a lot to say. It's one confessional I'm looking forward to.

The Surgeon General Solution

When I first set out to explore the confessional morass I thought it might come down to a question of manners. If a confessional etiquette that made sense could be agreed on, fewer people would be left feeling betrayed by writers and fewer writers would have to feel they're engaged in something sneaky, snitchy. There would be rules, and people would know when they're broken. An etiquette of "fair warning," for instance, that would answer the question: at what point in a relationship does a writer about relationships let the person with whom he or she is relating know that their mutual experiences may end up in a book or a magazine piece? First date? First base? First anniversary? First draft?

One problem with this is that often people who end up most hurt by confessionals are those who are not taken by surprise. Indeed, they're complicitous, encouraging, editing, confessing more and still more, thinking they're engaged in a common truth-seeking enterprise. Until final cut and they discover it's not *their* book, it's *his* book or *her* book, and it's too late.

The other objection to an etiquette is that writers believe that bad manners are a sign of good art, and if they've got something juicy they'll find all sorts of artistic and philosophic justifications for sweeping aside convention to allow their genius to spill unchecked onto the page.

Giving up on an etiquette, much less a morality, I began to wonder if there wasn't yet something feverishly pernicious about the whole confessional genre, that like some breeder reactor overtopping critical mass it was creating self-destructive chain reactions all over the place and desperately needed a cooling-off period. I toyed with the idea, a modest proposal, of suggesting a one-year moratorium. For twelve months writers would forego writing about their "relationships"—and themselves—and try learning to write about, dare I suggest it, other people. A year of off-the-record relationships might mean a chance to discover the simple pleasures of living an emotional life for its own sake rather than for the quality of the "material" it supplies.

Well I backed off that idea fast, I'll confess, when I realized I couldn't trust myself to hold to that standard. No writers are trustworthy. And that's when I came up with what I'll call the Surgeon General Solution. Don't ban writers because they're dangerous, instead, protect the innocent public by making them bear warnings, sewn into their clothes or tattooed on the palms of the hand. I think the wording dictated by the Supreme Court in its Miranda ruling against confessions obtained without warning from suspects would serve. You remember it:

You have the right to remain silent.
Anything you say may be held against you.

YOU'RE GOING OUT A YOUNGSTER, A YOUNGSTER, BUT YOU'VE GOT TO COME BACK A STAR!

34. OYA LIFE THESE DAYS
by Garrison Keillor

"It may be true that the Oya have much to teach us, but, unless we
are mistaken, they have not done so up to the present." If the self
is a mirror rather than a work of art, you see, none of this stuff
matters: not celebrity, not persona, not gossip, not fiction, not
Patty, not even Farrah.

Let's move on out. But remember, take plenty of money to pay
for doughnuts.

The Oya people is the bunch that lives in the Oya Valley, as the neighbors will quickly tell you if you go looking for Oya in the hills. "We
are not Oya!" the neighbors shout through locked screen doors. "We
are decent, hardworking people, who hardly deserve this."

By "this" they mean the Oya custom of going visiting and remaining
behind after their ride has left. Apparently, Oya, whose name means
"The Us," do not distinguish between themselves and others, and anyone they meet is assumed to be one of them, or one of "The Us," and
therefore interested in their comfort and anxious to see that they have
enough to eat. But if that person fails to show interest, Oya don't become angry. They wait. Soon enough, they believe, they'll be asked to
stay.

To the visiting scholar with a keen interest in Oya ways* and plenty
of money to pay for doughnuts, this facet of Oya life seems harmless
and even gentle, but to the neighbors, who have their own row to hoe,

---

* Despite their keen interest, scholars have learned practically nothing about the
Oya (pronounced *O-yah*), because of the Oya's equally keen interest in them.
Whenever a research team arrives in the valley, normal activity (if there is such a
thing) ceases as the Oya gather around and watch intently. If the scholars ask,
"But what do you *do*?," the answer is "What would *you* like to do?," or "It's all
right, we can always do that later." Occasionally, the scholars amuse their audience
with a short talk, which seems to be much appreciated. But the Oya never seem
to get around to just being themselves. Some Oya, apparently anxious to please
the visitors, may sit on a stump engrossed in thought, but only a few, and never
for longer than a few hours.

it is known as "the Oya problem." This refers to the difficulty of conversing with Oya.

An Oya converses by means of questions, if at all. His opening remark might be "That's quite the deal, isn't it?" if his host is busy, or "Not too busy today, huh?" if the host is relaxing. Next, he might well ask, "What do you have in your hand there? A sharp stick?," for by this time the host has realized that he is in for a long afternoon unless he takes stern measures. He must at all costs drive the Oya off before he is asked, "What is the matter? Why don't you like me?"

It's impossible to answer that last question in a way that will satisfy an Oya. Because he doesn't dislike himself, hostility only makes him curious; he wants to know what he can do to make the host feel better, such as putting an arm around him. Right here is where most personal Oya injuries occur—here and, back home, falling out of bed.

Why are Oya disliked so intensely by their neighbors? The neighbors, who are godly persons, have tried to find the answer to this one themselves. Prayer meetings are held frequently to discover the Lord's will in regard to the Oya problem. It is a hard matter. Clearly, the guiding principle should be "Love thy Oya as thyself," but how can one do that, many ask, when Oya behave as if they *are* thyself?

And such, it seems, is the case. An Oya is quite capable of showing up on Tuesday morning and staying until Sunday night, sitting in your chair, walking beside you through the garden, eating at your table, and not saying anything you'd be able to recall a few minutes later. It is said that the Oya believes that since you and he are both of "The Us," it is the same as if you were alone. And some neighbors say that during an Oya visit they have come to believe this, too—that they are talking to themselves.

It is hard to say definitely what Oya believe, however. One can only make suppositions, based on statements of our own that no Oya has seen fit to contradict (e.g., "You don't seem to be in a big rush to leave"). Many younger people in the neighborhood have come to believe that Oya have reexamined the concept of individuality and found it wanting, that Oya has attained loss of self. No Oya has disagreed with this.

It may be true that the Oya have much to teach us, but, unless we are mistaken, they have not done so up to the present. They seem to feel it is all the same to them one way or the other. After a visit to an Oya home, one comes away with the feeling they may be right.

The Oya personality has been described in conflicting terms. One aspect of it is bliss. Oya seem to have a knack for being "knocked out" by ordinary phenomena, such as a faucet dripping, motes of dust in a beam of light, or the sound of their own throats clearing. It is enough for them if an afternoon brings a light breeze to stir the leaves. This attribute may help to explain their inability to socialize. When spoken to by another, an Oya is fascinated by the speaker's lips.

The other essential Oya characteristic is "politeness." An unspoken

Oya rule is "Let's wait and see what everyone wants to do." The result is that Oya spend hours waiting, lose track of time, and fall asleep early, missing their favorite programs.

Sleep is an ever-present danger, for a strange facet of Oya life is the high number of strenuous sleepers. All Oya thrash about to some extent (some have been known to rise from their beds and strip wallpaper), but many must actually be tied down, lest they get up in their sleep and walk away. The sleeper's family is reluctant to restrain him, or uses only a very light string, and the resulting departures account for the diminishing Oya population in the valley. Someday, it seems, there will be no Oya left here. This prospect neither saddens nor pleases them. It seems that they cannot conceive of a place with no Oya, and they have made no plans to assure that anybody stays around.

READING ABOUT CELEBRITY

Very little of value has been written about the phenomenon of celebrity. Any serious investigation should begin with RICHARD SCHICKEL's *His Picture in the Papers: A Speculation on Celebrity in America Based on the Life of Douglas Fairbanks, Sr.* (New York: Charterhouse, 1973) and DAVID THOMSON's invaluable survey of star personas, *A Biographical Dictionary of Film* (New York: William Morrow and Co., 1976).

MAILER has thought hardest about the job, but his evidence is spread throughout a number of works since *Advertisements for Myself*. See his exegesis of *Last Tango in Paris,* "A Transit to Narcissus," *New York Review of Books,* May 17, 1973. ROLAND BARTHES' *Mythologies* (New York: Hill & Wang, 1972) and *Roland Barthes* (New York: Farrar, Straus & Giroux, 1976) are of interest.

THOMAS CARLYLE's *On Heroes, Hero-Worship, and the Heroic in History* provides the nineteenth-century background. It is available in a paperback edition from Doubleday.

Also of interest: EDGAR MORIN, *Les Stars* (Paris: Editions du Seuil, 1957); ALEXANDER WALKER, *Stardom* (New York: Stein & Day, 1970); DANIEL J. BOORSTIN, *The Image: Or What Happened to the American Dream* (New York: Atheneum, 1962); and C. WRIGHT MILLS, *The Power Elite* (New York: Oxford University Press, 1956).

My own *How to Read a Film: The Art, Technology, Language, History, and Theory of Film and Media* (New York: Oxford University Press, 1977) includes some material on the development of star personas and the history of celebrity. See especially Chapter 4.

NOTES ON CONTRIBUTORS

DONALD BARTHELME is the author of several books, both fiction and non-fiction, including, most recently, *Amateurs, The Dead Father,* and *Guilty Pleasures.* He lives and works in New York and contributes frequently to *The New Yorker.*

ROLAND BARTHES, a leading French critic, is the author of, among other works, *The Pleasures of the Text, S/Z, Roland Barthes, Writing Degree Zero/Elements of Semiology,* and *Mythologies.*

REES BEHRENDT, a former associate editor at *Esquire,* is currently a copywriter for a major advertising agency in New York.

INGMAR BERGMAN is working with Liv Ullman again after a lapse of several years. His most recent film is *The Serpent's Egg.* He no longer lives in Sweden.

ROY BLOUNT, JR., is a columnist for *Esquire* and the author of *About Three Bricks Shy of a Load.* He was born and raised in Decatur, Georgia and is currently at work on a book about the South, tentatively titled *Trash No More.*

SAUL BRAUN lives and works in Stockbridge, Massachusetts, where he is involved in group dynamics and is currently preparing a catalogue on sexual consciousness.

ALEXANDER COCKBURN is a columnist for The Village Voice.

BILL DAVIDSON, a veteran magazine writer based in Los Angeles, is a contributing editor of *TV Guide* and the author of *Collura: Actor With a Gun,* about an undercover police detective.

JOAN DIDION, essayist and novelist, is the author of *Slouching Towards Bethlehem* and, most recently, *A Book of Common Prayer.*

NORA EPHRON is a contributing editor at *Esquire* and the author of several books of essays, including *Crazy Salad* and, more recently, *Scribble, Scribble.*

LOIS GOULD, novelist and essayist, is the author of *A Sea Change* and *Such Good Friends,* among other books. Her columns for *The New York Times* (including the one reprinted here) were recently published in *Not Responsible for Personal Articles.*

LEW GROSSBERGER is a free-lance writer who lives in Manhattan. He was formerly a reporter for *Newsday* and *The New York Post.*

GARRISON KEILLOR writes for *The New Yorker.*

MAUREEN LAMBRAY is a photographer working in New York. Her most recent book is *American Film Directors.*

JOHN LEONARD, novelist, essayist, and editor, is cultural correspondent for *The New York Times.* His most recent book—a collection of his columns of the same name—is *Private Lives.*

DAVID LINDROTH, a native New Yorker, is a book designer and illustrator with a special interest in the media.

KLAUS LUCKA is a photographer who specializes in beauty and national advertising. He was born in Germany and currently lives in New York.

MARY MCGEACHY, a free-lance broadcast entertainment critic currently living and working in San Francisco, was formerly a movie critic for NBC radio.

NORMAN MAILER, perhaps the most well-known living American novelist, is the author of numerous books, many of which blur the fine line between fiction and nonfiction.

JAMES MONACO is the author, most recently, of *Media Culture* and *Alain Resnais.* He lives in New York.

SYLVIA PLACHY is staff photographer for *The Village Voice* and specializes in portraits and photojournalism.

RON ROSENBAUM has written articles for numerous magazines and is the former managing editor of *MORE.* A collection of his magazine pieces will be published soon.

CHARLOTTE ROSENBERG is a photographer and former editor who lives and works in New York.

ROGER ROSENBLATT is literary editor of *The New Republic.* He also writes a column for *The Washington Post.*

MORLEY SAFER is a correspondent for CBS News and currently appears on *60 Minutes.*

RICHARD SCHICKEL is the author of numerous books on film. He has devised, written, and hosted several series for PBS, and he writes film reviews for *Time* magazine.

PETER SCHRAG is a writer based in San Francisco. His most recent book is *Mind Control*.

WILFRID SHEED is the author of many books of fiction and nonfiction. His novels are often set in the New York media world.

DAVID THOMSON is an English film critic currently teaching at Dartmouth. He is the author of *A Biographical Dictionary of Film* and *America in the Dark*.

HASKELL WEXLER is an Academy award-winning cinematographer. He has directed several documentary films in addition to *Medium Cool*.

INDEX

A Page Reference in Italics Indicates a Photograph